Logic Pro
Professional Music Production

David Nahmani

Apple Pro Training Series

Apple
Certified

Logic Pro – Apple Pro Training Series: Professional Music Production
David Nahmani
Copyright © 2025 by David Nahmani. All Rights Reserved.

Peachpit Press
www.peachpit.com
Peachpit Press is an imprint of Pearson Education, Inc.
To report errors, please send a note to errata@peachpit.com.

Apple Series Editor: Laura Norman
Development Editor: Robyn G. Thomas
Senior Production Editor: Tracey Croom
Technical Editor: John Moores
Copy Editor: Robyn G. Thomas
Compositor: Cody Gates, Happenstance Type-O-Rama
Proofreader: Scout Festa
Indexer: Rachel Kuhn
Cover Illustration: Von Glitschka
Cover Production: Chuti Prasertsith

Acknowledgments I would like to express my thanks to my wife, Nathalie, and to my sons, Liam and Dylan, for their support and encouragement; to Bill Burgess, for believing in me and encouraging me when I first started; and to my editors, Robyn Thomas, John Moores, and Laura Norman, for being by my side and enabling me to write the best book I could write.

My deepest gratitude to the artists and producers who agreed to provide their media, songs, and Logic projects for this book: Distant Cousins, for their song "Lights On"; Darude, for his song "Moments"; and Jon Mattox, for providing drum samples.

Contents at a Glance

Table of Contents

Getting Started

Welcome to the official Apple Pro Training Series course for Logic Pro 11. This book is a comprehensive introduction to professional music production with Logic Pro 11. It uses real-world music and hands-on exercises to teach you how to record, edit, create, arrange, produce, mix, and master music in a professional workflow. So let's get started!

The Methodology

This book takes a hands-on approach to learning the software, so you'll be working through the project files and media you download from *www.peachpit.com*. It's divided into lessons that introduce the interface elements and ways of working with them, building progressively until you comfortably grasp the entire application and its standard workflows. (See the "Access the Lesson Files" section for more information on accessing the project files and media.)

Each lesson in this book is designed to support the concepts learned in the preceding lesson, and first-time readers should go through the book from start to finish. However, each lesson is self-contained, so when you need to review a topic, you can quickly jump to any lesson.

The book is organized as 13 lessons that are designed to guide you through the music production process as it teaches Logic Pro.

Lesson 1 establishes a solid foundation of key skills: navigation and zooming. You'll become familiar with the interface and the various ways to navigate a project.

Lesson 2 walks you through creating a project from the ground up, using Apple Loops and editing regions in the Tracks area to create an arrangement.

In **Lesson 3**, you'll explore effect and instrument plug-ins, use the Library to load patches and presets; and save your own plug-in settings.

Lesson 4 dives deeper into typical situations that you may encounter when recording audio sources, such as microphones, guitars, and MIDI keyboards.

Lessons 5 through **8** explore the new Session Players to create virtual drum, bass, and keyboard tracks. You'll then create your own custom chord progressions in the Chord track to make them play in harmony.

Lesson 9 sets you up to create content by programming MIDI in the Piano Roll, creating drum beats and step automation in Logic's new Step Sequencer, editing Audio regions; and adding fades and turntable start and stop effects.

In **Lesson 10**, after separating instruments from a fully mixed audio file, you'll sample vocals and drums from the separated tracks and import them into Quick Sampler and Sample Alchemy to create a variety of sampler instruments. You'll play with Beat Breaker to reshuffle and manipulate slices from a guitar arpeggio.

Lesson 11 explores various ways to edit the pitch and timing of your recordings, using Smart Tempo to ensure that all your audio files play at the same tempo; creating custom tempo curves; using groove tracks and Varispeed; time-stretching audio; and tuning vocals.

In **Lessons 12** and **13**, you'll study the end processes of music production: mixing, and automating using track stacks and EQ, compressor, limiter, delay, and reverb plug-ins. You'll export your final mix as a stereo audio file after optimizing it with Mastering Assistant.

Appendix A, which is online, offers a series of Q&A's to test your newly acquired knowledge, while **Appendix B**, which is also online, lists all the keyboard shortcuts used in the book to streamline your workflow.

System Requirements

Before jumping into *Logic Pro—Apple Pro Training Series: Professional Music Production,* you should have a working knowledge of your Mac and the macOS operating system. Make sure that you know how to use the mouse or trackpad and standard menus and commands, and how to open, save, and close files. If you need to review these techniques, refer to the printed or online documentation included with your system.

Logic Pro 11 and the lessons in this book require the following system resources:

▶ macOS Ventura 13.5 or later

▶ 72 GB (minimum) of storage space for full Sound Library installation

▶ High-speed internet connection for installation

▶ MIDI keyboard (optional but recommended to play and record software instruments) connected via USB or via a compatible MIDI interface

> **NOTE** ▶ ChromaGlow and Stem Splitter are available only on Macs with Apple Silicon processors (M1, M2, M3, M4, and so on). Some projects in this book use ChromaGlow, so if you open these projects on an Intel-based Mac, you'll receive a message indicating that ChromaGlow is unavailable. Click OK and proceed with the exercises as usual. While the project may not sound exactly as intended, you'll still be able to complete the exercises.

Prepare Your Logic Pro Workstation

The exercises in this book require that you install Logic Pro 11 along with the full Apple Sound Library (not including the Legacy and Compatibility content). If you have not yet installed Logic Pro, you may purchase it from the App Store. When your purchase is completed, Logic Pro 11 will automatically be installed on your hard drive, and you'll be prompted to perform various tasks:

1   When prompted, download and install Essential Sounds. You must enter your password to complete the installation.

2   When prompted to download more sounds, continue to download and install all the sounds.

3   When prompted to download the instruments and loops for Session Players, click **Download 3 Packages**.

4   To make sure the complete Apple Sound Library is installed on your Mac, choose **Logic Pro** > **Sound Library** > **Open Sound Library Manager**. Resize the window as needed to see all the packages listed and make sure everything (except for Legacy and Compatibility) is installed.

Some of the instructions and descriptions in this book may vary slightly, depending on the sounds you have installed.

NOTE ▶ If you choose not to download the entire Logic Sound Library, you may be unable to find some of the media needed in the exercises. Missing media will appear dimmed with a down arrow icon. Click the down arrow icon to download that media.

Access the Online Appendix A, Appendix B, and Lesson Files

Use the following instructions to claim the full benefits of your guide purchase.

If you purchased an eBook from a different vendor or bought a print book, you must register your purchase on *Peachpit.com* to access the online content:

1 Go to *peachpit.com/logicpro11*.

2 Sign in or create a new account.

3 Access the online Appendix A, Appendix B, and lesson files through the **Registered Products** tab on your Account page. Click the *Access Bonus Content* link below the title of your product to proceed to the download page. Click the link to the lesson files or the online appendices to download them to your computer.

4   Unzip the file(s) you downloaded to access a folder titled **Logic Book Projects**, which you should save to your Mac desktop or to a folder of your choice. Each lesson explains which files to open for that lesson's exercises.

> **NOTE ▶** If you've enabled the Desktop and your Document folder to sync to iCloud, you are strongly advised not to copy your lesson files to your Desktop. Choose another location, such as the Logic folder within your Music folder.

Use Default Settings

All the instructions and descriptions in this book assume that you are using the default Logic Pro settings (unless instructed to change them).

If you have changed some of your Logic Pro 11 settings, you may not see the same results as described in the exercises. To make sure that you can follow along with this book, it's best to delete the Logic Pro PLIST file before you start the lessons. Keep in mind, however, that when you delete the PLIST file, you lose your custom settings and key commands, and later you may want to reset your favorite settings manually.

> **NOTE ▶** To locate your Logic Pro PLIST file, it's essential that you follow the following instructions for accessing your user Library folder. If you go to *Macintosh HD/Library/Preferences/* instead, you won't find it.

1   Quit Logic Pro.

2   In the Finder in the menu bar at the top of the screen, click **Go**.

The Go menu opens.

3   Hold down **Option**.

The hidden Library folder appears in the Go menu.

4   Inside the **Go** menu, click **Library**.

5   Inside the **Library** folder, open the **Preferences** folder.

6   Inside the **Preferences** folder, locate **com.apple.logic10.plist** and move that file to your desktop.

7   Open Logic Pro.

8 If a dialog prompts you to download more sounds, click **Download Later**.

9 If a window titled **What's New in Logic Pro** opens, click **Continue**.

10 If a window titled **Session Player Instruments** opens, click the **X** at the top left of the window to close it.

Enable Complete Features

This book assumes that you have enabled the complete features. Choose **Logic Pro > Settings > Advanced** and make sure that **Enable Complete Features** is selected.

Use the U.S. Key Command Preset

This book assumes that you are using the default key command preset for a U.S. keyboard. If you have customized your key commands, you may find that some of the key commands in your Logic Pro installation do not function as they are described in this book.

If at any point you find that the key commands don't respond as described in this book, make sure the U.S. key command preset is selected on your Mac by choosing **Logic Pro > Key Commands > Presets > U.S.**

Screen Resolution

Depending on your display resolution, some of the project files may appear different on your screen than they do in the book. When you open a project, make sure you resize the project window as needed to see the entire project.

When using a small display, you may need to zoom or scroll more often than instructed in the book when performing some of the exercise steps. In some cases, you may need to temporarily resize or close an area of the main window to complete an action in another area.

About the Apple Pro Training Series

Logic Pro—Apple Pro Training Series: Professional Music Production is a self-paced learning tool developed by experts in the field.

For a complete list of Apple Pro Training Series books, visit *www.peachpit.com/apple*. For more on certification, visit *training.apple.com.*

Resources

Logic Pro—Apple Pro Training Series: Professional Music Production is not intended as a comprehensive reference manual, nor does it replace the documentation that comes with the application. For comprehensive information about program features, refer to the following resources:

▶ Logic Pro Help, accessed through the Logic Pro Help menu, contains a description of most features. Other documents available in the Help menu can also be valuable resources.

▶ The Apple websites *www.apple.com/logic-pro/* and *www.apple.com/support/logicpro/*.

▶ The official Logic Pro release notes: *https://support.apple.com/en-us/HT203718/*.

▶ The Logic Pro Help website, an online community of Logic users moderated by the author of this book, David Nahmani: *www.logicprohelp.com/forums*.

▶ For additional help with accessing the lesson files, you may send email queries to *ask@peachpit.com*.

1

Lesson Files	Logic Book Projects > 01 Project One
Time	This lesson takes approximately 75 minutes to complete.
Goals	Navigate the project
	Continuously repeat a section
	Zoom in to and out of the workspace
	Explore the Logic Pro main window interface

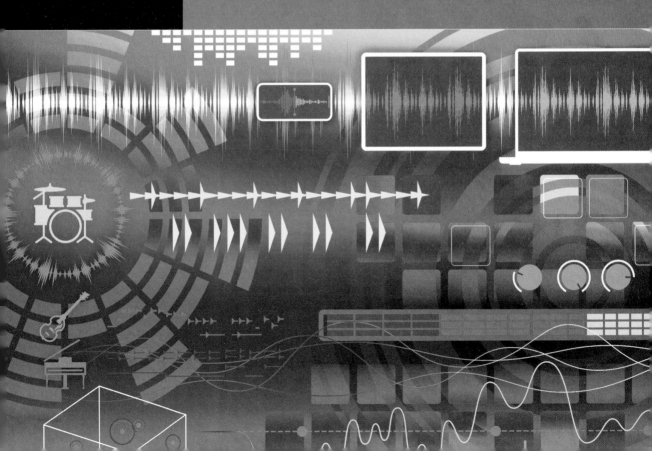

Lesson **1**

Master Essential Navigation Skills

When you're producing music, time is of the essence. Many production tasks are repetitive, and you may find yourself starting and stopping playback, jumping to a different part of the song, and zooming in and out every few seconds.

If you're not familiar with the basic techniques to navigate your project, you can be sidetracked by the technical aspects of getting Logic Pro to do what you want, and as a result waste a lot of valuable time.

To work efficiently, you'll need to become proficient with key concepts such as positioning the playhead, creating a cycle area to loop over a section, and zooming on specific areas. In this lesson, you'll get an overview of the editor panes that you can open in the main window and how to switch between them. Navigating a project will soon become second nature so you can focus on the creative aspect of music production.

Navigate the Project

Logic offers many ways to navigate your project. In the following two exercises, you'll use the transport buttons and their key commands to start and stop playback, move the playhead, quickly go back to the beginning, and continuously repeat a section of the project.

Use Transport Buttons and Key Commands

To control playback, it may seem easier at first to click transport buttons with your mouse. However, moving a mouse with your hand while tracking the pointer on the screen is time-consuming. Using key commands to control playback can significantly improve your workflow efficiency.

Let's open the example project you'll be working on and use the transport buttons and their corresponding key commands to play the song.

1   Open Logic Book Projects > **01 Project One**.

   NOTE ▸ If an alert pops up saying "ChromaGlow is not available. It requires the unique architecture of the Apple M1 chip or later," click OK and continue. For more details, see the Getting Started section of this book on page x.

2   At the top of the main window, in the control bar, click the **Play** button (or press the Space bar).

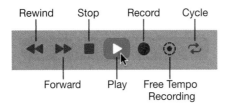

In the Tracks view, playback begins, the playhead starts moving, and you can hear the project.

At the beginning, the drums introduce a funky groove for two measures. A guitar lick leads into the main groove, which begins on bar 3 with an intoxicating, gnarly bass line. Strings join in a few bars later to provide a lush harmonic backdrop. At bar 11, an echoing guitar *stab* (short note) piques your interest while a reversed cymbal builds up, leading into the final section, where the strings stop to make way for a bluesy slide guitar riff.

3   In the control bar, click the **Stop** button (or press the Space bar).

The playhead stops moving, and the Stop button is replaced with a Go to Beginning button.

4   In the control bar, click the **Go to Beginning** button (or press Return).

The playhead returns to the beginning of the project.

5   Click the **Forward** button, or press . (period on the keyboard) a few times.

The playhead jumps one bar forward each time.

6   Click the **Rewind** button, or press , (comma on the keyboard) a few times.

The playhead jumps one bar backward each time.

TIP To fast-forward eight bars at a time, press Shift-. (period); to fast-rewind eight bars at a time, press Shift-, (comma).

You can also position the playhead precisely by clicking the ruler.

7   In the lower half of the ruler, click bar 11 to move the playhead to that location.

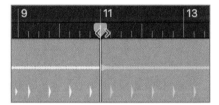

TIP To start or stop playback at a specific location, double-click the lower half of the ruler.

You can also Shift-click an empty space in the workspace to position the playhead.

8   **Shift**-click in the background of the workspace.

The playhead moves to where you clicked.

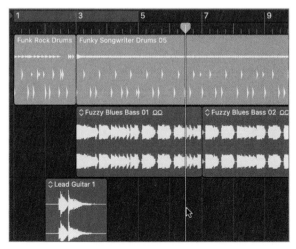

Now, you know the basic navigation techniques for positioning the playhead using the ruler or key commands, starting and stopping playback, and returning the playhead to the beginning of the project. Let's continue navigating the song.

Continuously Repeat a Section

When working on a specific part of your project, you may want to repeat a section multiple times without stopping playback. As you're working, the beat keeps going, and you can focus on the task at hand without having to worry about navigation.

Let's see how you can use the Cycle mode to loop over the desired section of your arrangement.

1   In the control bar, click the **Cycle** button (or press C).

In the ruler, the cycle area turns yellow, indicating that Cycle mode is enabled.

2   Press the **Space** bar.

Playback starts. When the playhead reaches bar 5, it jumps back to bar 1 and continues playback.

3   Press the **Space** bar to stop playback.

The cycle area shows the section of the song that repeats during playback. The start and end position of the cycle are called *left* and *right locators*.

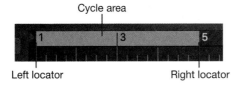

To continuously repeat the section with the guitar stabs that starts at bar 11, you'll move the cycle area in the ruler.

4   Position the pointer over the cycle area so that it shows a hand tool, and then drag it to bar 11.

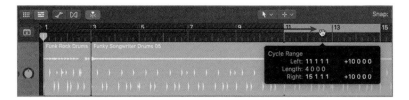

5   Press the **Space** bar to start playback.

Playback starts at bar 11, and when the playhead reaches bar 15, it jumps back to bar 11. To focus on the transition from that guitar stab section into the slide guitar section that's right after, you can adjust the positions of the left and right locators.

6   Press the **Space** bar to stop playback.

7   Drag the right edge of the cycle area to bar 16.

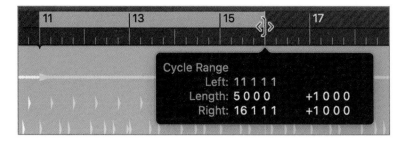

As you drag the right locator, the Help Tag shows information about the cycle range:

▶   Left: 11 1 1 1 —The position of the left locator

▶   Length: 5 0 0 0 —The length of the cycle area

▶   +1 0 0 0 —The amount by which the cycle area is extended

▶   Right: 16 1 1 1 —The position of the right locator

▶   +1 0 0 0 —The amount by which the right locator is moved

The Help Tag displays positions and lengths with four values: bars, beats, divisions, and ticks. In Logic Pro, you refer to a position or a length with those four numbers.

▶   The bar (or measure) is the main number displayed in the ruler. It consists of several beats (four beats in the 4/4-time signature here).

▶ The beat is the denominator in the time signature (quarter note here).

▶ The division determines how the grid is subdivided in the ruler when zoomed in horizontally (sixteenth note here).

▶ A clock tick is 1/960 of a quarter note. A sixteenth note contains 240 ticks.

It's a crucial skill to ensure that you position locators, regions, or notes precisely. To make sure the groove keeps going without skipping a beat, you generally need locators or regions placed exactly on a bar. Use the Help Tag to check that the three trailing values of the position are *1 1 1*. For example, to make sure the right locator is exactly on bar 16, the Help Tag should display *Right: 16 1 1 1*.

To make sure a cycle area (or a region) length has an exact number of bars, check that the three trailing values are *0 0 0*. In this example, to make sure the cycle area is exactly 5 measures long, the Help Tag should display *Length: 5 0 0 0*.

8   Drag the left edge of the cycle area to bar 14.

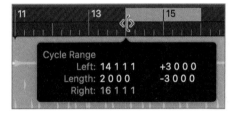

9   Press the **Space** bar to start playback.

The playhead continuously repeats over the section from bar 14 to bar 16, which allows you to focus on the transition between the two sections of your song.

10 Press the **Space** bar to stop playback.

An easy way to position the cycle area over a region or a group of regions is to select the region(s) and use a key command to make the cycle area match the selection.

11 On track 7, at bar 15, click the **Delta Mud Slide Guitar** region to select it.

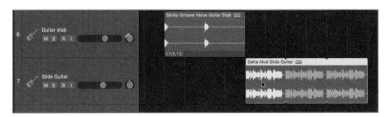

12 Choose **Navigate > Set Rounded Locators by Selection and Enable Cycle** (or press U).

> TIP ▶ When choosing a command in a menu, the corresponding key command is usually displayed to the right.

The cycle area starts at bar 15 and ends on bar 21, matching the selection.

13 Press the **Space** bar to listen to the slide guitar section of your song.

14 Press the **Space** bar to stop playback.

15 Click the **Cycle** button (or press C) to turn off Cycle mode.

Setting locators to adjust the cycle area is a technique you'll use often to focus on part of a project—for example, to adjust an edit or when mixing an instrument. If you work with other musicians in your studio, they'll love you for not interrupting the playback (and ruining their creative flow) every few bars!

Zoom In and Out

When a task requires precision, zooming in gives you a closer look at the areas you want to see. You can work with more confidence and complete the job faster.

Zooming horizontally makes it easier to fine-tune the position of a region or an edit because the ruler provides a finer resolution. Zooming vertically gives you a more detailed display of the waveform in an audio region, making it easier to distinguish its content.

In the following exercises, you'll learn three zooming techniques to control exactly what part of the project is visible on your screen.

Zoom Incrementally

One of the most obvious methods for zooming is to incrementally increase or decrease the zoom level using zoom sliders or their corresponding key commands. If you don't know exactly how close you need to zoom, this allows you to get closer and closer until you reach the desired zoom level.

To get a closer look at the waveform, let's zoom in on the attack of one of the notes in the bass track.

1 Press **Return** to make sure the playhead is at the beginning of the project.

2   Click the **Drums** track header (track 1) to select that track.

3   At the upper right of the Tracks area, drag the **Horizontal Zoom** slider to the right (or press Command-Right Arrow a few times).

The playhead stays at the same position on your screen while the regions and the grid expand on the right.

It can be challenging to get the desired zoom level with the zoom sliders. Using key commands gives you more precision—each keypress adjusts the zoom slider by one increment.

4   Drag the **Horizontal Zoom** slider back to the left (or press Command-Left Arrow).

TIP ▶ On a trackpad, use a pinch motion to zoom horizontally.

5   Drag the **Vertical Zoom** slider to the right (or press Command-Down Arrow).

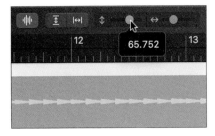

The workspace is zoomed in vertically.

6 Drag the **Vertical Zoom** slider back to the left (or press Command-Up Arrow).

Now let's practice by zooming in on the attack of the bass note at bar 5. To anchor the workspace, you need to deselect all regions and position the playhead.

7 Click the background of the workspace.

All regions are deselected.

8 Click the lower half of the ruler at bar 5 to position the playhead.

9 Press **Command-Right Arrow** a few times.

The playhead stays at the same position in the workspace as you're zooming in horizontally.

NOTE ▶ When regions are selected, the left edge of the selection stays anchored when zooming (unless the playhead is within the borders of the first selected region, in which case the playhead stays anchored).

As you're zooming in, the ruler shows more subdivisions. After pressing Command-Right Arrow a few times, you can see each individual division of the first beat (*5 1 2, 5 1 3,* and *5 1 4*). Note that the fourth time value (tick) is omitted until you zoom in closer. The division is a sixteenth note, and at that zoom level you can see that the bass note you want to see is on *5 1 3*, which is 2 sixteenth notes (or 1 eight note) after the downbeat.

To zoom in closer, let's anchor the workspace closer to the attack of the bass note.

10 Position the playhead on *5 1 3*.

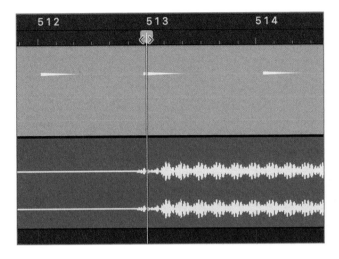

11 Press **Command-Right Arrow** a few times.

Now you'll zoom vertically to better see the waveform. When zooming vertically, the selected track determines where the workspace is anchored, so let's make sure you anchor the bass track.

12 Click the **Bass** track header (track 2) to select it.

13 Press **Command-Down Arrow** a few times.

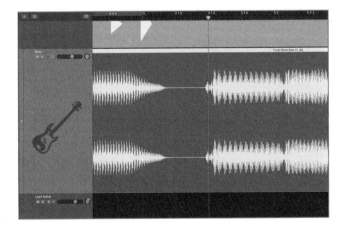

The top edge of the Bass track stays at the same position on the screen as you're zooming in vertically.

Continue using the Command and arrow keys to practice your zooming chops, and after you're finished, zoom back out so you can see your entire project and get ready for the next exercise.

Take some time to practice your zooming skills, making sure you've anchored the track and position you want before zooming in. Even if you've used another zooming technique to get into the ballpark of the area you want to see, you can use the Command and arrow keys to fine-tune the zoom level.

Use the Zoom Tool

The Zoom tool lets you zoom in on a specific area in a single operation and will probably become your go-to method for zooming. It requires a little more dexterity, but it's well worth the time it takes to master it.

Don't be afraid to make mistakes. If you zoom in too close or over the wrong area, you can easily go back to your previous zoom level and try again.

1   Hold down **Control** and **Option**.

> The cursor turns into a Zoom tool. To zoom in on an area, draw a blue highlight rectangle over that area with the Zoom tool. The smaller the rectangle that you draw, the closer you'll zoom in.

2   **Control-Option**-drag to draw a blue rectangle around a few regions.

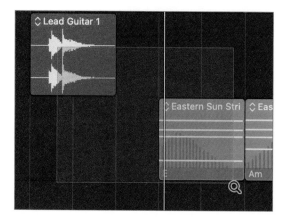

The area you highlighted expands to fill the workspace. The ruler has more resolution, and you can see more details on the waveforms inside the audio regions.

Let's zoom out.

3   **Control-Option**-click anywhere in the workspace.

The workspace returns to its previous zoom level.

Now you'll zoom in multiple times to see more detail on the waveform of a region.

4   **Control-Option**-drag to draw a blue rectangle around the Lead Guitar 1 region on track 3.

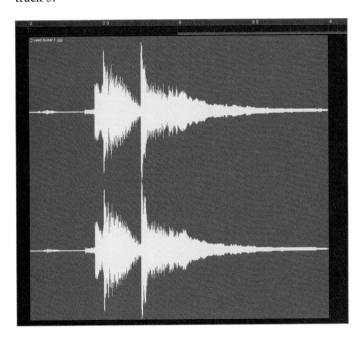

At the beginning of the region (in the first beat of bar 2), you see a section where the waveform has a small amplitude that could not be seen at the previous zoom level. Let's listen.

5   Click the **Lead Guitar 1** region to select it.

6   Choose **Navigate > Set Rounded Locators by Selection and Enable Cycle** (or press **U**).

7   Press the **Space** bar.

If you listen carefully to the first beat of bar 2, you can hear a faint howling guitar note. Let's zoom closer.

8   Press the **Space** bar to stop playback.

9   **Control-Option**-drag to draw a blue rectangle around the attack of a guitar note.

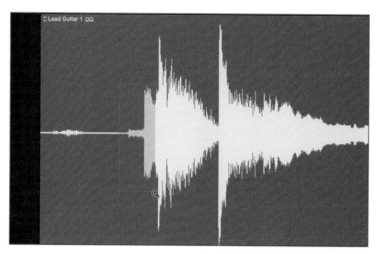

Continue using the Zoom tool a few more times to get closer to one of the two wave-forms of this stereo audio region. You can see a line that goes above and below a central horizontal axis. Remember to draw small rectangles to zoom in closer.

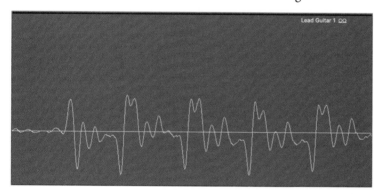

NOTE ▶ An audio waveform is a graphical representation of the electrical audio signal. When converted by a speaker into sound waves, the waveform illustrates the displacement of the speaker membrane around its central resting position.

Now let's zoom all the way out.

10   **Control-Option**-click anywhere in the workspace.

Continue clicking the workspace with the Zoom tool to go through all your previous zoom levels until you're back to the original zoom level, where you can see your entire project.

11 Click the **Cycle** button (or press C) to turn off Cycle mode.

The Zoom tool is available in many editors other than the Tracks area. Before you know it, you'll use the Zoom tool so often that it will become second nature.

Zoom to Fit the Selection or the Entire Project

In this exercise, you'll use the key command Toggle Zoom to fit Selection or All Content (the Z key) to achieve two goals. When regions are selected, pressing Z makes the selected regions fit the screen. When no regions are selected, pressing Z shows you all the regions present in your workspace, so you can see your entire project.

1   Click the **Reverse Cymbal Riser 03** region to select it.

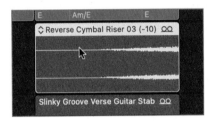

2   Press **Z**.

The region fills the workspace.

3   Press **Z** again.

The workspace goes back to its previous zoom level.

You can also use the Z key to zoom in on multiple regions.

4   Drag the pointer to draw a blue rectangle over the four audio regions on tracks 6, 7 and 8.

The four regions are selected.

5   Press **Z**.

The four regions fill the workspace.

Feel free to practice your chops with all the zooming techniques you've learned: the zoom sliders and their corresponding key commands, the Zoom tool, and the Z key.

No matter which zooming techniques you've used and how many times you've zoomed in, you can always go back to seeing all the regions in your workspace.

6   Click the background of the workspace.

All regions are deselected.

7   Press **Z**.

The workspace sets the zoom level necessary to display all the regions.

As you become comfortable with the various zooming techniques you've learned, you'll find that you may want to combine different techniques to adjust the area you're seeing on your screen. For example, you can use the Zoom tool to zoom in approximately on an area, then fine-tune the view incrementally using the Command and arrow keys.

Explore the Panes of the Main Window

While producing music, you spend most of your time in the main window, where you can toggle various editing areas depending on the task you're working on. You'll now explore the different panes of the main window to familiarize yourself with the tools that Logic Pro has to offer. By developing your ability to access the tools you need quickly and effortlessly, you'll be able to clear your mind and focus on your music.

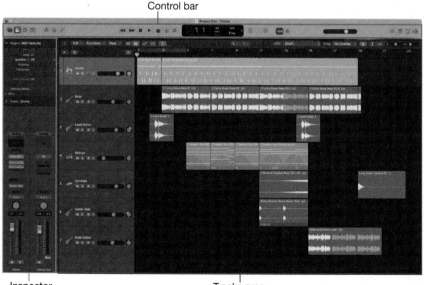

Control bar

Inspector   Tracks area

In its default configuration, the main window has three areas:

▶ **Control bar**—The control bar contains buttons to toggle areas on and off; transport buttons to control playback operations (such as play, stop, rewind, and forward); an LCD display to indicate the playhead position, project tempo, time, and key signatures; and mode buttons such as Count-in and Metronome.

▶ **Inspector**—The inspector provides access to a contextual set of parameters. The specific parameters displayed depend on the selected track or region, or the area in key focus.

▶ **Tracks area**—In the Tracks area, you build your song by arranging regions on tracks on a timeline. You can toggle the Tracks view to display the Live Loops grid, where you trigger individual loops or scenes that automatically sync to the beat in real time.

To access more tools, you can open additional panes to the left, bottom, and right of the Tracks area.

Some panes are contextual—the tools they display depend on the type of track or region selected. In this project, regions and tracks have the default color code:

▶ Yellow regions = Session Player

▶ Blue regions = Audio regions

▶ Green regions = MIDI regions

▶ Blue tracks = Audio tracks

▶ Green or yellow tracks = Software Instrument tracks

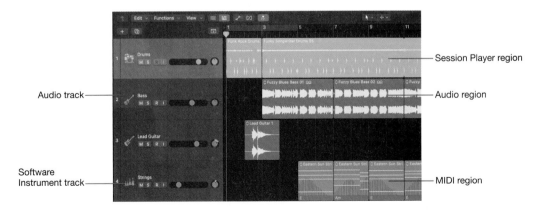

The Left-Side Panes

To the left of the Tracks area, you can open two panes: the Library and the inspector. You can open both the Library and the inspector at the same time.

1   In the control bar, click the **Library** button (or press Y).

The Library opens to the left of the inspector. It displays patches that you can load onto the selected track.

The Library is contextual—the type of patches displayed depends on the type of track selected.

2   In the Tracks area, click the **Bass** track header (track 2).

The Library shows patches that can be loaded onto an audio track.

3   In the Tracks area, click the **Strings** track header (track 4).

The Library shows patches that can be loaded onto a software instrument track.

4   In the control bar, click the **Library** button (or press Y).

The Library closes.

Let's look at the inspector, which is also contextual.

5   Click the **Lead Guitar 1** region (track 3).

The region is selected, and its parameters are displayed in the Region inspector.

6   Click the **Strings** track header (track 4).

Below the Region inspector is the Track inspector, which is named after the selected track. (You can click the > disclosure triangle to see the track parameters.)

At the bottom of the inspector, the left channel strip, Strings, controls the sound of the selected track. The right channel strip, Stereo Out, controls the sound of the mix of all tracks.

NOTE ▶ When multiple regions are selected, the Region inspector shows the number of selected regions, and you can change parameters on all selected regions simultaneously.

7 On the left channel strip (Strings), drag the **volume fader** up.

In the Tracks area, on the Strings track header, the horizontal volume fader moves accordingly.

8 In the control bar, click the **Inspector** button (or press I).

The inspector closes. Closing the inspector is useful when you need to see more of your Tracks area.

9 In the control bar, click the **Inspector** button (or press I).

The inspector reopens.

10 In the control bar, click the **Quick Help** button (or press Shift-/).

At the top of the inspector, Quick Help opens.

11 Position your pointer over various elements of the main window.

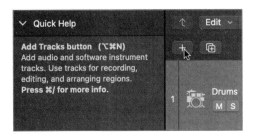

Quick Help displays the name of the interface element, its associated key command, and a brief description.

12 In the control bar, click the **Quick Help** button (or press Shift-/).

Quick Help closes.

The Bottom Panes

At the bottom of the Tracks area, you can open the Smart Controls, the Editors area, or the Mixer. Only one of the three areas can be opened at a time.

1   In the control bar, click the **Smart Controls** button (or press B).

The Smart Controls pane opens below the Tracks area. It gives you quick access to the main parameters of the patch loaded onto the selected track without having to open individual plug-ins.

2   Click the **Mixer** button (or press X).

The Mixer opens.

3   Click the **Editors** button (or press E on your keyboard).

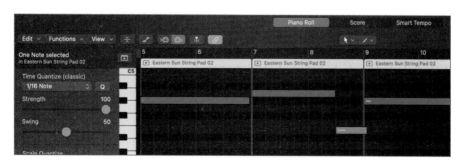

The Editors pane opens, and the Piano Roll shows the content of the four selected MIDI regions.

4   In the Tracks area, click the **Lead Guitar 1** region on track 3.

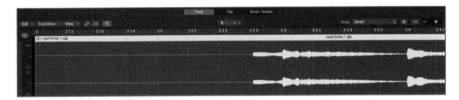

The Audio Track Editor opens, showing the waveform of the selected audio region.

5   In the Tracks area, click the **Funk Rock Drums 01** region on track 1.

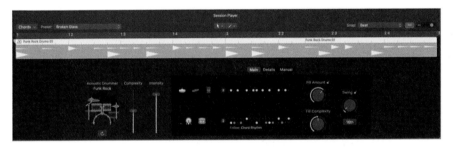

The Session Player Editor opens, showing controls for editing the performance in the selected Drummer region.

6   Click the **Editors** button (or press E).

The Editors pane closes.

The key concept of the main window is that you broadly organize regions in the Tracks area, and then do detailed editing of the contents of those regions in the editors you open at the bottom.

The Right-Side Panes

To the right of the Tracks area, you can open various list editors and browsers.

1 In the control bar, click the **List Editors** button (or press D).

The List Editor pane opens. At the top, four tabs let you switch between different list editors, allowing you to see lists of MIDI events, markers, tempo changes, or time and key signature changes.

Let's look at the contents of a MIDI region.

2 In the Tracks area, click the first green MIDI region on track 4.

L M	Position		Status	Ch	Num	Val	Length/Info	
	5 1 1	1	♩	2	G#4	1	1 3 3 106	
	5 1 1	1	♩	3	B3	1	1 3 3 106	
	5 1 1	1	♩	4	E3	1	1 3 3 106	
	5 1 1	1	♩	5	E1	1	1 3 3 106	
	5 1 1 33		⊥	1	1	58	Modulation	⬍
	5 1 1 110		⊥	1	1	55	Modulation	⬍

The Event list shows four notes representing the chord performed in the region. The series of modulation events control the dynamic and vibrato of the performance. This amount of detail is useful for troubleshooting or for high-precision edits; however, you'll generally edit notes and controllers in the Piano Roll, where they're displayed in a more user-friendly graphical format.

3   Click the **Note Pads** button (or press Control-Shift-P).

The Note Pad opens. You can take global notes in the Project tab, and individual track notes for the selected track in the Track tab.

TIP ▶ You can drag and drop images in the Note Pad, which is useful to recall external gear settings. Make sure you click the Edit button before you type text or drag images.

4   Click the **Loop Browser** button (or press O).

The Loop Browser opens. It allows you to browse the Apple Loops from the Apple Sound Library.

5   Click the **Browsers** button (or press F).

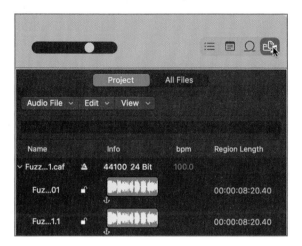

The Project Browser opens. It lists the audio files used in the current project. The All Files tab gives you access to all the media files that Logic Pro can use.

6   Click the **Browsers** button (or press F) again to close the Browsers pane.

You now have a set of tools to help you navigate and zoom in on what you need. You'll continue to use them in upcoming lessons, sharpening your skills as you go. This firm grasp of the interface lets you efficiently open only the panes you need and close the ones you don't to make room for what you need to see.

Key Commands

Keyboard Shortcuts	Description
Transport	
Space bar	Starts or stops playback
Return	Returns to beginning of project
. (period)	Forwards one bar
, (comma)	Rewinds one bar
Shift-. (period)	Forwards eight bars
Shift-, (comma)	Rewinds eight bars
C	Toggles Cycle mode
U	Sets rounded locators by selection and enables Cycle mode
Zooming	
Control-Option-drag	Expands the dragged area to fill the workspace
Command-Right Arrow	Zooms in horizontally
Command-Left Arrow	Zooms out horizontally
Command-Down Arrow	Zooms in vertically
Command-Up Arrow	Zooms out vertically
Z	Zooms to fit selection or all content

Keyboard Shortcuts	Description
Panes	
Y	Toggles Library
I	Toggles inspector
Shift-/	Toggles Quick Help
B	Toggles Smart Controls
X	Toggles Mixer
E	Toggles Editors
D	Toggles List Editors
Control-Shift-P	Toggles Note Pad
O	Toggles Loop Browser
F	Toggles File Browsers

2

Lesson Files	None
Time	This lesson takes approximately 75 minutes to complete.
Goals	Create and save a new empty project
	Preview Apple Loops and add them to your project
	Move and copy regions
	Loop and repeat regions
	Split and resize regions
	Edit with the Marquee tool
	Transpose regions and change their playback speed
	Choose icons, names, and colors
	Create a rough mix

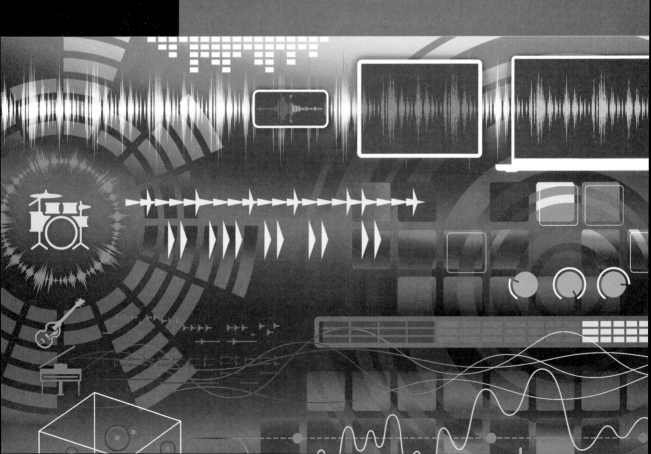

Edit and Arrange Regions

Creating an arrangement is a little like playing with building blocks—
you move, loop, copy, resize, or repeat regions as needed to determine
at which points specific instruments start and stop playing.

In this lesson, you'll start from scratch and build the song you used in Lesson 1.
You'll import Apple Loops and arrange them on a grid in the Tracks view. You'll
edit the regions and apply fades. After choosing custom names, colors, and
icons for your regions and tracks, you'll open the Mixer and adjust the volume
and pan positions of your instruments to mix the song.

Add Apple Loops

You'll now start previewing and combining *Apple Loops*, which are prerecorded music snippets that automatically match the tempo and key of your
project and are designed to be repeated seamlessly.

Professional music producers use Apple Loops all the time as the basis for
a song, to create video soundtracks, to add texture to a beat, to create unex-
pected effects, and so on. Several major hit songs were produced using some of
the loops included with Logic Pro. The Apple Loops included with Logic Pro
are royalty free, so you can use them in professional projects without worrying
about licensing rights.

Create and Save a New Empty Project

It's good practice to save your project before you begin working on it. When
saving the project for the first time, you can choose to organize it as a package
or a folder, and which assets you want to copy into your project. These settings
are critical to ensure that you won't lose any audio files and the project will
find all the assets needed when you reopen it.

1   Choose **File** > **New** (or press Command-Shift-N).

    The Create New Track dialog opens.

2   Click the **MIDI** button and make sure **Software Instrument** is selected.

You'll be adding Apple Loops to the track later. Apple Loops automatically load their own instrument, so let's make sure no instrument is loaded now.

3   Click the disclosure triangle (>) to expand the Details area.

4   In the Details area, click the **Instrument** pop-up menu and choose **Empty Channel Strip**.

5   Deselect **Open Library**.

6   Click **Create** (or press Return).

The Software Instrument track (Inst 1) is created, and in the inspector, the Inst 1 channel strip is empty.

NOTE ▶ When you change the settings for a track type in the New Track Dialog and create a new track, the settings are retained, and will be reapplied the next time you create a new track of the same type. For example, if you choose Track > New Software Instrument Track (or press Option-Command-S), your new settings will be applied.

Let's save your project right away.

7 Choose **File** > **Save** (or press Command-S).

You're saving this project for the first time, so a Save dialog appears. The first time you save a file, you must provide:

▶ A filename

▶ A location on the hard drive where you want to save the file

8 In the **Save As** field, type your project name, *Lesson 2 Song*.

9 In the sidebar, select **Desktop** (or press Command-D).

10 Select **Organize my project as a Folder**.

Organizing your project as a folder makes it easy to look inside the folder and check that all necessary assets are saved along with the project.

11 Make sure **Audio files** is selected.

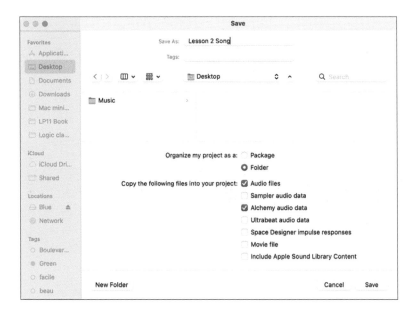

It's highly recommended to consistently save audio files in your project folder to avoid the dreaded "*audio file not found*" errors when reopening your project.

On your desktop, a *Lesson 2 Song* folder is created. That project folder contains an Audio Files folder, which is where the audio files used or recorded in the project will be copied or created, along with the *Lesson 2 Song* project file.

As you build the project, remember to repeatedly save it to ensure you don't lose any of your work.

12 Click **Save** (or press Return).

> **NOTE** ▶ Logic Pro automatically saves your project while you're working on it. If the application unexpectedly quits, the next time you reopen the project, a dialog prompts you to reopen the most recent manually saved version or the most recent autosaved version.

You've saved your new project, organized it as a folder, and made sure audio files will be saved inside that folder. With a blank canvas ready, you can start being creative. In the next exercise, you will select Apple Loops for your drum track.

Browse and Add Apple Loops

To start building your song, you'll preview loops and choose which ones to use. The Loop Browser is the perfect tool for this job. It allows you to browse loops by instrument, genre, mood, and other attributes.

1 In the control bar, click the **Loop Browser** button (or press O).

The Loop Browser opens.

2 In the Loop Browser, click the **Instrument** button.

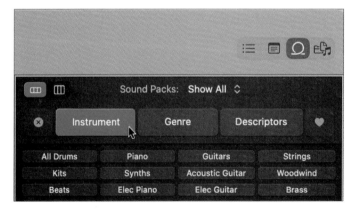

3   Drag down the divider at the bottom of the keyword area to see more keyword buttons.

Feel free to adjust the size of the keyword area as needed.

4   Click the **Kits** keyword button.

The number of items in the search results is listed at the bottom right of the Loop Browser. Let's narrow the search.

5   Click the **Genre** button.

6   Click the **Rock/Blues** keyword button.

You can also specify the region types you want to search for.

7   At the top left of the search results, click the **Loop Types** button.

Loop Types button

8   Click **Session Player Loops**.

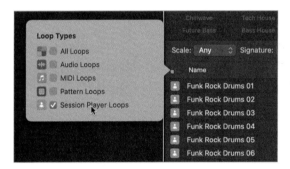

All other loop types are deselected, and the search results lists only Session Player loops.

9   At the top of the search results, select **Funk Rock Drums 01**.

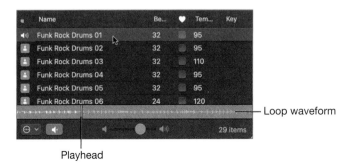

Loop waveform

Playhead

The loop is selected, its icon turns into a speaker, and the loop plays. The loop's waveform is displayed at the bottom of the Loop Browser. To preview different sections of the loop, you can click anywhere on the waveform to move the playhead.

10 Drag the loop to track 1 at bar 1. Before you release the mouse button, make sure that the position in the Help Tag shows *1 1 1 1*.

The eight-bar Session Player loop is added to the track. It's the first loop that you're adding to your project, so the project tempo is set to the tempo of the loop (95 bpm) in the LCD display at the top of the main window.

11 Choose **File** > **Save** (or press Command-S) to save your project.

Let's add one more drum loop of a different genre.

12 Under the Genre button, click the **Rock/Blues** keyword button to deselect it.

13 Click the **Other Genre** keyword button.

14 Scroll down to see the Funky Songwriter Drums loops.

15 Drag **Funky Songwriter Drums 05** to track 1 at bar 11.

You've used the Loop Browser to search for a couple of drum loops, narrowing your search by instrument and genre keywords as well as loop type. After previewing your loops, you added them to a track in your project, ready to be arranged.

Preview Loops While the Project Plays

You'll now add a couple of bass loops to create a bass track to go along with your drums. To determine which bass loops work best with your drums, you'll use Cycle mode to continuously repeat a drum loop as you preview bass loops in the Loop Browser.

1   At the top left of the Loop Browser, click the **X** button to reset all keyword buttons.

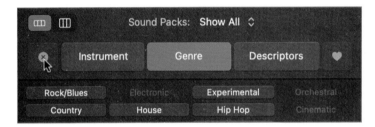

Let's also reset the Loop Types selection.

2   Click the **Loop Types** button and click **Session Player Loops**.

All loop types checkboxes are selected again.

3   Click the **Instrument** button, and then click the **Bass** keyword button.

4   Click the **Genre** button, and then click the **Rock/Blues** keyword button.

Time-stretching algorithms that are used to make Apple Loops match the project tempo can create artifacts when the tempos are very different. For optimal sounding results, it's ideal to find a loop that has a tempo that is close to the project tempo.

5   At the top of the search results, click the **Tempo** column label (Tem…).

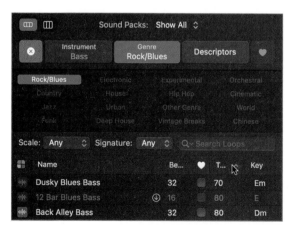

In the search results, the loops are now sorted by ascending tempo.

6   Scroll down to find loops that have a tempo of around 95 bpm.

To hear your drums while previewing bass loops, let's loop the playback around the second drum loop in the drum track.

7   In the Tracks area, click the **Funky Songwriter Drums 05** region at bar 11.

The region is selected.

8   Choose **Navigate > Set Rounded Locators by Selection and Enable Cycle** (or press U).

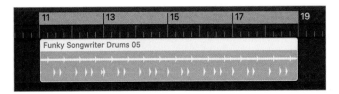

Cycle mode is enabled, and the cycle area matches the selected region.

9   Press the **Space** bar.

The cycle area starts playing, and you can hear your drums.

10   In the Loop Browser, click a bass loop.

You hear the bass loop play along with the drums.

At any time, you can click another loop to preview it, or click the currently playing loop to stop playback. You can also press the Up Arrow or Down Arrow keys to play the previous or next loop in the list.

11   Press the **Down Arrow** key.

You hear the next loop in the search results. Feel free to preview a few bass loops to see how well they groove with the drums in your project.

12   Drag **Fuzzy Blues Bass 01** to the workspace below the drum loop at bar 11.

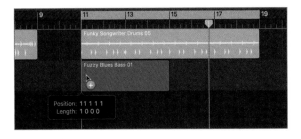

A new track is created for the new Fuzzy Blues Bass 01 region. That region is only four bars long, so it's shorter than the drum loop. You'll take care of this later.

13 Listen to the drums and bass in the cycle area.

The loops work well together, but the bass loop sounds low. The loop automatically plays at the project key (C Major); however, in the Loops Browser search results, you see that the Fuzzy Blues Bass loop's original key is E.

Let's change the key signature of the project.

14 In the LCD display, click the **Cmaj** key signature and in the key signature pop-up menu, choose **E Major**.

Now the bass loop sounds as its producer intended, and less pitch shifting is going on, reducing the chances of hearing artifacts.

15 Click the cycle area or the **Cycle** button (or press C) to disable Cycle mode.

You're starting to become a real navigation ninja, using key commands to loop the playback over your drums while you preview other loops to add to your project! Not having to worry about the technical aspects of running a production session lets you keep your creative flow uninterrupted.

Edit Regions

You'll now edit the drum and bass regions to create a drum and bass arrangement that will provide the backbone for your song.

It's a good time to put your navigation and zooming skills to use. While arranging your song and editing regions, you'll often want to hear the result of your actions. Feel free to listen to the section of the song you've just edited before moving on to the next step.

Resize, Move, Loop and Repeat Regions

In this exercise, you'll shorten the first drum loop to create a short intro, then move, loop, and repeat the other drum and bass loops to establish the main groove after the intro.

To achieve a professional sounding result, it's crucial to edit regions with the utmost precision, so use the Help Tag to check the exact values for the position of your edits. Fear not, as editing regions in the Tracks area is nondestructive. Should you make a mistake, you can always undo to retrace your steps and try again.

1   On track 1, bring the pointer over the lower-right corner of the Funk Rock Drums 01 region.

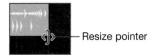 — Resize pointer

A Resize pointer appears.

2   Drag the **Resize** pointer to the left to shorten the region so its length is *2 0 0 0*.

When you resize a Session Player region, the performance inside the region is refreshed to correspond to the new size. Here, a fill is added at the end of bar 2, ready to lead into the next section that will start at bar 3.

Now let's move the drum and bass regions that form the main groove to right after the intro.

3   Drag a rectangle to select the drum and bass regions at bar 11.

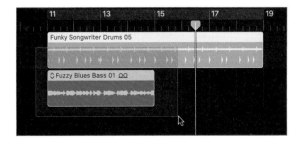

Both regions are selected.

4   Drag the selected regions to bar 3.

5   Click the background (or press Shift-D) to deselect all regions.

Let's loop the drums to extend the groove.

6   Move the pointer to the upper-right corner of the Funky Songwriter Drum 05 region.

 Loop pointer

A Loop pointer appears.

7   Drag the Loop pointer to the right until the Loop Stop in the Help Tag shows *19 1 1 1*, and you get two repetitions of the region.

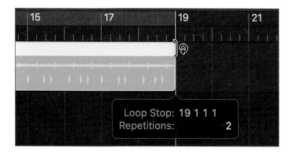

TIP ▶ When the last repetition is shorter than the original region, the Help Tag displays a + sign after the number of repetitions. If you're not seeing a + sign, you know that all the repetitions have the same length.

8   Click the **Fuzzy Blues Bass 01** region to select it.

9   Choose **Edit** > **Repeat** > **Once** (or press Command-R).

A copy of the region is created to the right of the original region.

10 Press **Command-R** two more times.

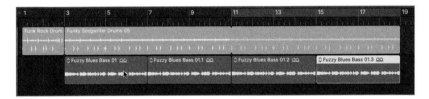

Two more copies are created, and the bass track has the same length as the looped
Funky Songwriter Drum 05 region on track 1.

11 Listen to your song.

The two bars of drums introduce the main groove, which lasts for 17 bars. At bar 19,
the music ends quite abruptly... but you're not finished yet!

> **TIP** You can also choose Edit > Repeat > Multiple, and then enter the number of
> copies you want in the Repeat Regions/Cells/Events dialog. However, it's often quicker
> to press Command-R a few times until you have enough regions to fill the desired area.

Your drum and bass groove is complete. The bass track needs further editing so that it
plays one last note on the downbeat at the end of the song. Let's jump right into it.

Select with the Marquee Tool

To end the bass track, you'll copy the first note of a bass region to bar 19 so that it plays
on the downbeat. Until now, you've used the Pointer tool to select entire regions. To select
only a portion of a region, you'll use the Marquee tool.

At the top of the Tracks view, look at the tool menus.

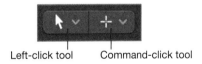

Left-click tool   Command-click tool

The left-click tool is assigned to the Pointer tool (arrow icon) and the Command-click
tool is assigned to the Marquee tool (crosshair icon). If you're curious, feel free to click
one of the tool menus to see what's available, and then click it again to close it.

> **TIP** For a faster workflow, avoid switching the assignments in the tool menus
> whenever possible. The default tools, combined with modifier keys, can achieve most
> of the functionality offered by other tools.

1   Press **Command-Down Arrow** a few times to zoom in vertically.

2   Hold down the **Command** key.

The pointer turns into a crosshair, symbolizing the Marquee tool.

3   On the Bass track (track 2) at bar 15, Command-drag from *15 1 1 1* to *15 4 1 1* .

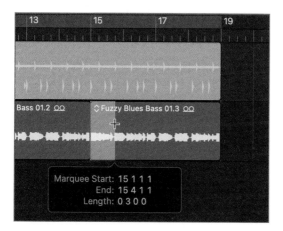

The area you dragged with the Marquee tool is highlighted to indicate that it is selected.

TIP ▶ Command-Shift-drag the edge of a marquee selection to adjust the selection.

If you're not happy with your marquee selection, click outside the selection to clear it and try again.

4   **Option**-drag the selection after the last region on the Bass track (bar 19).

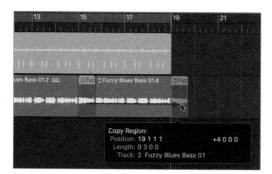

When Option-dragging to copy regions, always make sure you release the mouse button before you release the Option key. If you try to release both at the same time, you may sometimes release the Option key slightly before the mouse button, and the region is moved instead of copied.

TIP ▶ To reverse an action, choose Edit > Undo [name-of-last-action], or press Command-Z.

When you Option-drag a marquee selection, Logic Pro creates a new region where you drag that corresponds to the selection to be copied. When you release the mouse button, the original region should remain intact.

If you've copied your marquee selection successfully, your workspace should look like this:

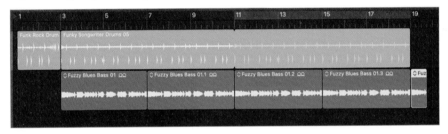

Let's zoom in on the selected region you just copied to the end of the Bass track.

5   Press **Z**.

The selected region fills the workspace. Now that you see more detail on the waveform, you can see that your region contains more than one note. Let's listen.

6   Choose **Navigate > Set Locators by Selection and Enable Cycle** (or press Command-U).

TIP ▶ When a region fills the screen and its length isn't a whole number, it's important not to set *rounded* locators so that the cycle area is exactly the same length as the selected region. This ensures the playhead doesn't run off to the right of the region, and the workspace stays put.

7   Listen to the bass.

You can hear five bass notes.

8   Resize the region so it contains only the first note.

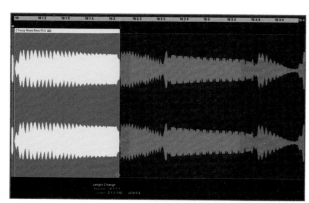

TIP ▸ To temporarily disable snapping, start dragging and hold down Control, or Control-Shift for even greater precision.

The region should end a little after the *19 2* grid line in the ruler. Don't worry about being very precise for now, as you'll add a fade later.

9   Listen to the bass again.

Make sure you hear only one note. You might hear a click at the end of the region. The fade-out you're going to add in the next exercise will take care of this issue.

With the Marquee tool, you've selected a portion of a region to copy somewhere else in the arrangement. Whenever you need to perform an edit without being tied to region boundaries, use the Marquee tool.

Apply a Fade to an Audio Region

To smooth out the end of the bass region you edited in the previous exercise and remove the click noise you heard, you'll apply a fade-out at the end of the region.

To apply a fade, hold down both Control and Shift while you drag the pointer over the edge of the region. Always start dragging from inside the region toward the outside.

1   **Control-Shift**-drag from left to right over the right edge of the bass region to draw a rectangle around the region border.

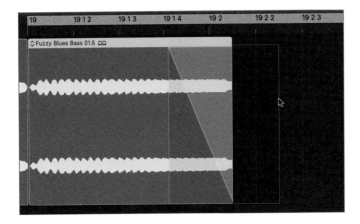

A fade-out is applied to the end of the region.

2   Listen to your fade.

You no longer hear a click at the end of the region. Job done! You can fine-tune the length and the curve of your fade to control exactly how the bass fades out.

3   Place the pointer in the middle of the fade and **Control-Shift**-drag horizontally to adjust its curve.

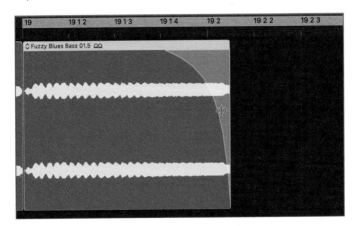

Make sure you listen closely. Sometimes Logic Pro may take a moment after you adjust an edit to update the playback, so it's best to stop and restart playback to make sure you're hearing what you're seeing.

4   Place the pointer on the left side of the fade, and **Control**-**Shift**-drag to adjust its length.

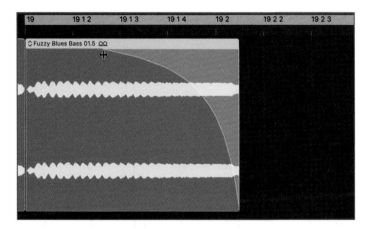

Let's turn off Cycle mode and zoom out.

NOTE ▶ If there's no region adjacent to the left of a region, to apply a fade-in, Control-Shift-drag from inside the region toward the left. When two regions are adjacent, Control-Shift-drag over their intersection to apply a crossfade.

5   Click the **Cycle** button (or press C) to turn off Cycle mode.

6   Click the background of the workspace (or press Shift -D) to deselect all regions.

7   Press **Z**.

The workspace is zoomed out to show all regions. Because you have only a few regions on two tracks, the regions are still huge!

8   Press **Command**-**Up Arrow** a few times to zoom out vertically.

9   Press **Command**-**Left Arrow** once to zoom out horizontally.

Let's unsolo the bass.

10   In the Bass track header, click the **S** (Solo) button.

You've applied a fade-out to the end of a region to remove the click sound caused by a previous edit. As you edit regions, always be on the lookout for undesirable noises that may result from your edits, and use fades to produce smooth transitions.

Switch to Different Loops in the Same Family

Some Apple Loops belong to a family of loops that offer variations around a similar theme and are meant to work together. To introduce variety, you'll substitute two of the bass regions with another loop in the same family.

1   Listen to the song.

On the Bass track, the same four-bar loop repeats four times.

2   On the second bass region at bar 7, click the up and down arrows to the left of the region name.

A pop-up menu lists all the loops in the same family.

3   In the pop-up menu, choose **Fuzzy Blues Bass 02**.

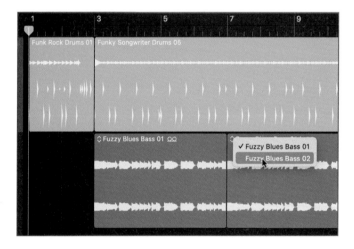

4   Replace the fourth bass region at bar 15 with Fuzzy Blues Bass 02 as well.

5   Listen to the song.

The bass guitar no longer plays the downbeat at the beginning of the second and fourth regions (at bar 7 and bar 15), which helps the groove move along.

When you're repeating the same loop multiple times, switching some of the regions to different loops in the same family is an efficient way to prevent monotony.

Add More Loops

You'll now add all the remaining loops needed to complete your song. To speed up the process, use the search field in the Loop Browser. Often, typing only one or two of the words in a loop's name is enough to find your loop.

1   At the upper left in the Loop Browser, click the **X** button to reset all keyword buttons.

2   In the search field, type **delta lead**.

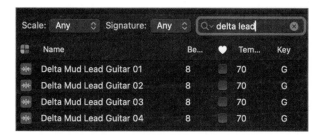

Only four loops are displayed.

3   Drag **Delta Mud Lead Guitar 01** below the bass track at bar 2.

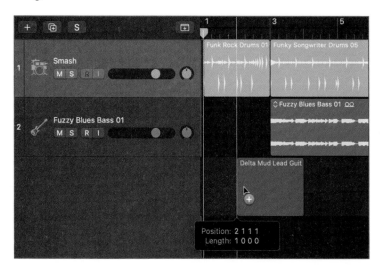

The guitar lick helps lead into the main drum and bass groove.

4   In the Loop Browser search field, enter **east pad** and drag **Eastern Sun String Pad 01** below the guitar track at bar 7.

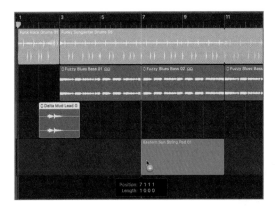

NOTE ▸ Some Apple Loops contain chord progressions, and after adding them to the workspace, their chord progression is displayed in the ruler. You'll learn how to use chords and the Chord track in Lesson 8.

5   Search for **Reverse Cymbal Riser 03** and drag it below the string pad track at bar 11.

6   Search for **Long Crash Cymbal 03** and drag it to the same track as the previous cymbal at bar 19.

7   Search for **Slinky Groove Verse Guitar Stab** and drag it below the cymbal track at bar 11.

8   Search for **Delta Mud Slide Guitar** and drag it below the previous track to bar 15.

9   Click the **Loop Browser** button (or press O) to close the Loop Browser.

Your workspace should look like this:

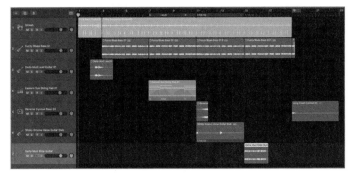

You have imported all the loops you need to build your song, and you're now ready to start editing the regions to build your arrangement.

Rename Tracks and Regions

Before going further, you'll rename the tracks and one of the regions to give them shorter names that will be easier to see and that better describe the instruments on each track.

1   On the track 1 header, double-click the track name (Smash).

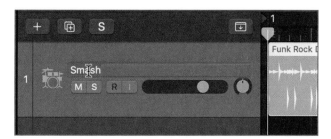

A text field opens.

2   Type **Drums** and press **Tab**.

Track 1 is renamed Drums, and the text field opens on track 2.

3   Type **Bass** and press **Tab**.

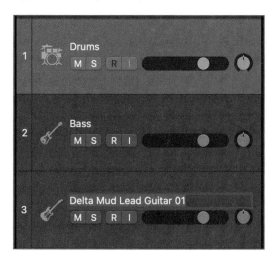

4   Continue this process to rename the remaining tracks, and then press **Return** after
entering the name of track 7.

▶   Track 3 = **Lead Guitar**

▶   Track 4 = **Strings**

▶   Track 5 = **Cymbals**

▶   Track 6 = **Guitar Stab**

▶   Track 7 = **Slide Guitar**

Now let's rename a region.

5   Click the **Delta Mud Lead Guitar 01** region on track 3.

The region is selected.

6   Press **Shift-N**.

A text field opens.

7   Type **Lead Guitar** and press **Return**.

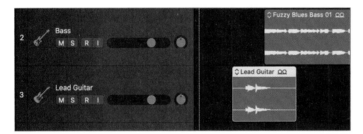

The region is renamed Lead Guitar.

Using straightforward names makes it easier to identify tracks. Since the track names are
reflected on the corresponding channel strips, it will also help you identify them later
when you adjust the volume of your instruments in the Mixer.

Split Regions and Adjust Playback Speed and Transposition

To finish arranging your song, you'll continue editing the loops you've added to complement the Drum and Bass tracks.

1 On the Lead Guitar track (track 3), **Option**-drag the Lead Guitar region to copy it to bar 18.

2 On the Strings track (track 4), click the **Eastern Sun String Pad 01** region to select it.

3 Press **Command-R** to repeat the region once.

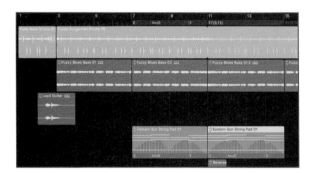

4 On the first Eastern Sun String Pad 01 region at bar 7, click the up/down arrow symbol and choose **Eastern Sun String Pad 02**.

You'll now split that first string region in two equal halves. To split a region, you can double-click with the Marquee tool. But first, let's zoom in.

5 Click the **Eastern Sun String Pad 02** region (at bar 7) to select it.

6 Press **Z** to zoom in.

7 Place your pointer below the bar 9 grid line, and **Command**-double-click the region.

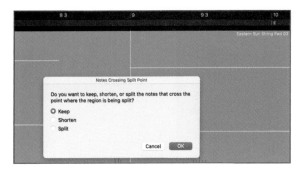

Since some notes overlap the split point, the Notes Crossing Split Point dialog opens. The dialog asks what you want to do to the overlapping notes:

▶ Keep—The notes keep their original length.

▶ Shorten—The notes are shortened so they end at the split point.

▶ Split—The notes are split in two at the split point.

8 Make sure **Keep** is selected and click **OK** (or press Return).

The region is split at bar 9. Let's zoom out.

9 Click the background (or press Shift-D) to deselect all the regions.

10 Press **Z**.

You can see all your regions. Let's complete the string arrangement.

11 On the Strings track, **Option**-drag the second **Eastern Sun String Pad 02** region (at bar 9) to bar 5.

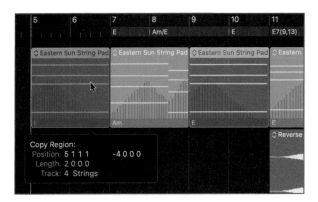

Now let's work on the Reverse Cymbal Riser 03 loop. You'll lower the playback speed of the loop so the riser lasts longer.

12 On the Cymbals track (track 5), select the **Reverse Cymbal Riser 03** region at bar 11.

13 At the lower left in the Region inspector, click the > disclosure triangle to display more parameters.

The Speed parameter is set to 2x, meaning the loop plays at twice the speed.

14 Click the value (2x) of the Speed parameter, and in the pop-up menu, choose **1/2x**.

The riser is now four bars long. Its high pitch makes it sound a little brittle and aggressive. To transpose it, you need to drag the value of the Transpose parameter in the Region inspector. Since that value is currently *0*, it is currently hidden, but you can click-hold immediately to the right of the word Transpose, where the value normally appears, and drag down to change it.

15 In the Region inspector, place your pointer immediately to the right of the word Transpose.

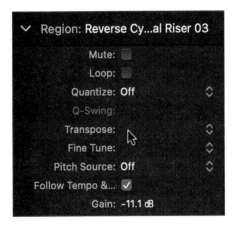

16 Drag downward to set the Transpose parameter to *-10*.

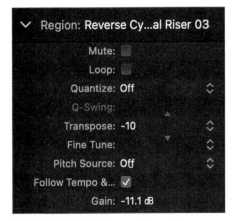

On the region in the Tracks area, the transposition value (-10) and the speed (1/2x) are displayed next to the region name.

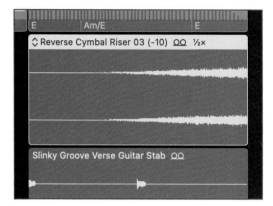

The riser creates a much slower build-up effect with a lower, less aggressive tone, which is a very efficient way to transition into the lead slide guitar section at the end of the song.

17 Place the pointer at the upper right of the Loop Mud Slide Guitar and drag the Loop pointer to bar 21 to get three repetitions.

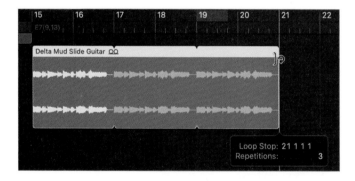

The song is now fully arranged! Make sure you listen to your arrangement and verify that everything sounds good. The volumes of the instruments are all over the place, and you may have noticed that some of them are too soft or too loud. In the next exercise, you'll do a rough mix to balance the levels and spread the instruments around in the stereo field.

Mix the Song

To create a rough mix of your song, you'll balance the levels of the instruments and spread them around so they take up the full width of the stereo field and don't compete against each other.

Choose Custom Colors and Icons

It's a good idea to color the tracks and their regions using your own color code (yellow for drums, orange for bass, and so on). Later when you open the Mixer, this will help you see the relationship between the regions you've edited up until now and the channel strips that control their sound.

Let's first choose colors for the regions in the workspace. You'll give each track the same color as its regions.

1   Click the **Bass** track header.

All the regions on the Bass track are selected.

> **TIP** ▶ To select a track without selecting its regions, Option-click the track header.

2   Choose **View** > **Show Colors** (or press Option-C).

The Color Palette opens. In the palette, a white frame indicates the color of the selected regions.

3   In the Color Palette, click an orange square.

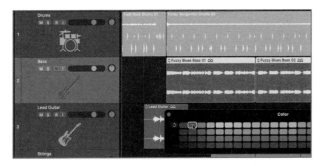

All the bass regions are orange.

4   Click the **Cymbals** track header.

5   In the Color Palette, click a purple square.

The two cymbal regions are purple.

6   In the control bar, click the **Mixer** button (or press X).

The Mixer opens. The color bar at the bottom of the channel strips still shows the original track colors. You'll give the tracks and channel strips the same colors as their regions in the workspace.

Let's make sure you can still see all your tracks now that the Mixer is open.

7   At the top right of the Tracks area, click the **Vertical Auto Zoom** button.

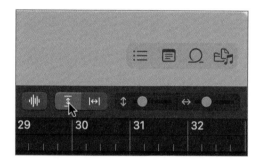

If the tracks are now too thin, you can resize the Mixer to make room for a taller Tracks area.

8   Position the pointer between the Tracks area and the Mixer, and drag the divider down.

As you reduce the height of the Mixer, the Tracks area expands, and the vertical zoom level of the tracks increases.

9   In the Tracks area, **Control**-click a track header, and choose **Configure Track Header** (or press Option-T).

10 In the Track Header Components popover, select **Color Bars**.

Colored bars appear to the left the track headers.

11 Click outside the Track Header Components popover to close it.

12 In the Tracks area menu bar, choose **Select** > **All** (or press Command-A).

> **TIP** ▸ To use a keyboard shortcut when multiple panes are open, make sure the desired area has key focus, indicated by a blue frame around the area. To move the key focus to different panes, press Tab or click the background of the desired area.

All the regions are selected.

13 In the Tracks area menu bar, choose **Functions** > **Color Track by Region/Cell Color** (or press Option-Shift-Command-C).

To the left of the track headers and, in the Mixer, at the bottom of the channel strips, the color bars have the same color as the regions.

14 Choose **View** > **Hide Colors** (or press Option-C) to close the Color Palette.

15 On the Cymbals track, **Control**-click the track icon, click **Drums**, and choose a cymbal icon.

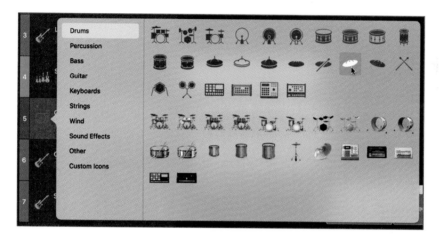

16 Choose **File** > **Save** (or press Command-S) to save your project.

Now that you've picked your own custom colors for regions, tracks, and channel strips, it's easier to see the relationship between the regions in your Tracks area and the channel strips in the Mixer.

Adjust Volume and Pan Position

With your own custom colors, names, and icons assigned, your Mixer is ready. You'll now adjust some of the instruments' volume levels with the volume faders, and their positions in the stereo field with the pan knobs. When adjusting instrument volume levels, it's recommended to avoid turning volume faders up to avoid overloading the mix. Instead, determine which instruments you want to stay loud in the mix, and lower the others to your taste. In this song, you'll keep the drums and bass loud and clear, as they form the foundation of the groove, and you'll lower the guitars, strings, and cymbals so they just flesh out the drums and bass backbone.

1 Listen to the song.

At the end of the intro, the guitar lick comes in a little loud.

2 In the Mixer, on the Lead Guitar channel strip, lower the fader to *-4.3 dB*.

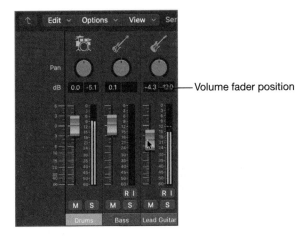

— Volume fader position

At bar 5, the strings are coming in way too loud, and really need to be reined in so they blend into the background.

3 On the Strings channel strip, lower the fader to *-20.0*.

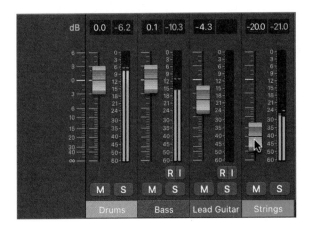

TIP The Mixer has its own undo history. To undo your last action, in the Mixer menu bar, choose Edit > Mixer Undo [*name of last action*].

The Cymbals track contains two regions, and changing the volume fader in the Mixer would affect both. To lower the volume of only the first cymbal region, you'll change the gain in the region parameters.

4 In the Tracks area, click the **Reverse Cymbal Riser 03** region at bar 11.

5 In the Region inspector, drag the value of the **Gain** parameter down to *-20.5*.

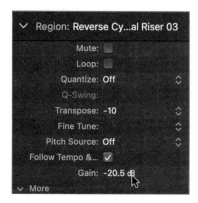

Let's adjust the volume of the remaining guitars in the Mixer.

6 On the Guitar Stab channel strip, lower the fader to *-7.2*.

7 On the Slide Guitar channel strip, lower the fader to *-4.8*.

Now you'll use the pan knobs to spread the instruments across the stereo field. Drag the pan knob up to turn it to the right, and drag it down to turn it to the left.

8   On the Lead Guitar channel strip, drag the pan knob up to *+27*.

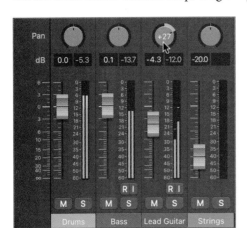

9   On the Strings channel strip, drag the pan knob up to *+9*.

10   On the Guitar Stab channel strip, drag the pan knob down to *-33*.

11   On the Slide Guitar channel strip, drag the pan knob down to *-6*.

Now the instruments sound balanced in level and are nicely spread out in the stereo field so that they don't step over each other and add width to the mix.

You've built a project from a selection of Apple Loops that you've edited and arranged to make up a song. In the process, you've learned foundational editing techniques, and you dialed in a rough mix of your song. Later in Lesson 12, you'll work with this logic project again to add color to the mix with distortion plug-ins.

Key Commands

Keyboard Shortcuts	Description
Global	
Command-Shift-N	Opens new empty project
Command-S	Saves the project
Command-Z	Reverses the last action
Command-A	Selects all
Shift-D	Deselects all
Tracks area	
Option-Command-S	Creates new software instrument track
Command-U	Sets locators by selection and enables cycle
Command-R	Repeats selection once
Shift-N	Renames the selected region(s)
Option-T	Opens track header configuration popover
Option-C	Toggles the color palette
Option-Shift-Command-C	Colors track by region color
macOS	
Command-D	Selects Desktop in Save dialog

3

Lesson Files   Logic Book Projects > 03 Fast Jam

Time   This lesson takes approximately 60 minutes to complete.

Goals   Insert effect and instrument plug-ins on channel strips

       Select plug-in settings and patches from the Library

       Edit a patch with Smart Controls

       Use bus sends to route to an auxiliary channel strip

       Pack tracks in a summing stack to create a layered synth patch

       Enable patch merging to load only part of a patch

       Reorder and copy plug-ins

       Save user plug-in settings and patches

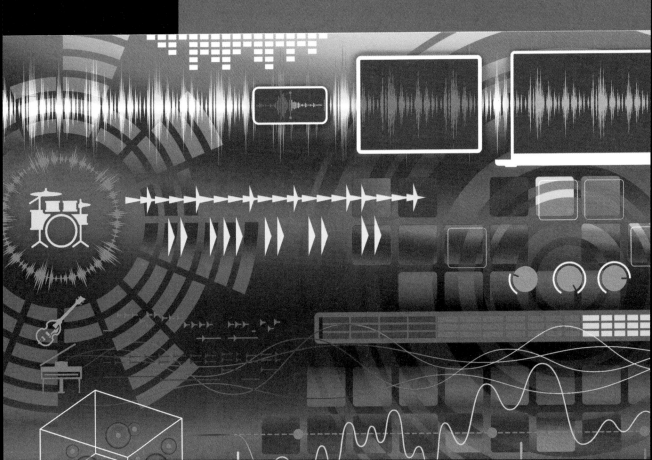

Use Effect and Instrument Plug-ins

Logic comes with a massive collection of plug-ins that you can insert on your channel strips. Software instrument plug-ins can reproduce a vast range of instruments, from realistic models of acoustic instruments (drums, guitars, strings, horns, and so on) to the most complex synthesizer and sampler sounds you can imagine. Audio effect plug-ins, such as compressor, EQ, distortion, or reverb, process the audio signal produced by a software instrument or an audio track to manipulate the sound and add color.

In this lesson, you'll work with a fast-tempo rock song that was built by arranging a few Apple Loops. You'll browse and choose patches from the library, insert individual effect and instrument plug-ins directly into channel strips, move and copy plug-ins in the Mixer, and save your own user settings and patches in the Library.

Insert Plug-ins

During playback, the data on a track is routed to the top of the track's channel strip, which is displayed on the left in the inspector. On audio tracks, the audio signal from the audio regions goes directly into the Audio FX area, where you can process it using audio effect plug-ins. On software instrument tracks, the notes inside MIDI regions are routed through a MIDI FX area, and then to a software instrument plug-in that produces an audio signal. That audio signal is then routed to the Audio FX area. You'll first insert audio effect plug-ins on audio tracks, and then later insert MIDI effect and instrument plug-ins on software instrument tracks.

Preview Regions in Solo Mode

Sometimes you may have to complete work on a Logic Pro project that you weren't involved in putting together from the beginning. For example, an artist wants you to add new tracks to a song they started, or a producer has completed a song and they want you to mix it. In those situations, you can solo regions to identify the instruments they play and become familiar with their sound.

1   Open Logic Book Projects > **03 Fast Jam**.

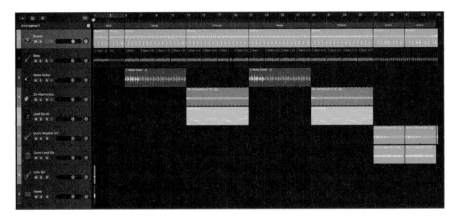

2   Listen to the song.

The song structure works, but some of the instruments sound bland. To bring them to life, you'll later add effect plug-ins and patches to their channel strips. For now, let's get to know the different tracks.

3   In the control bar, click the **Solo** button.

The Solo button is turned on, and the LCD display and playhead are yellow. In the workspace, all the regions are dimmed to indicate they're not playing. When the Solo button is on, only selected regions play back.

4   Click the **Drums** track header (track 1).

All the drummer regions on the track are selected and soloed.

5   Listen to the Drums track.

The drums play a straightforward rock beat. Let's listen to the bass guitar along with the drums.

6   **Shift**-click the **Bass** track header (track 2) to add all the Bass regions to the selection.

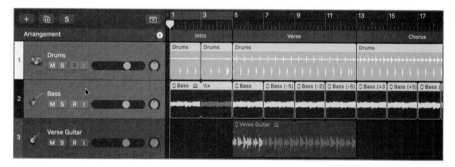

You can now hear only the bass and drums. The Bass track sounds good the way it is, and you won't add any plug-ins on that track.

7   Click the **Verse Guitar** track header (track 3).

The regions on track 3 are selected and soloed. On that track, there are regions only during the verses. If your playhead is currently in another section, you are out of luck and won't hear anything. That's when the Play From Selection key command (Shift-Space bar) comes in handy.

8   Press **Shift-Space** bar.

The playhead jumps to the beginning of the selection (bar 5) and playback continues. This guitar is a dobro, and you can hear the metallic twang of the resonator guitar, reminiscent of classic country music songs. You'll later add distortion to this track to give it a modern rock sound.

9   Click the **Gtr Harmonics** track header (track 4).

10   Press **Shift-Space** bar.

You hear a clean guitar arpeggiating harmonics. You'll later distort that guitar using a guitar amp patch from the Library.

11   Click the **Lead Synth** track header (track 5).

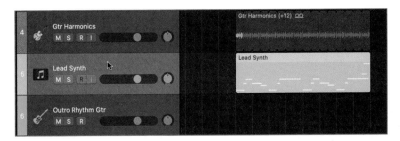

The Lead Synth MIDI regions on the track are soloed. Remember to press Shift-Space bar as needed to play the selected regions.

You hear nothing. Note that in the inspector, the Lead Synth channel strip doesn't have an instrument plug-in. You'll later add a synth plug-in that will be triggered by the notes inside the MIDI regions on that track.

12   In the Outro, drag to select all the regions on tracks 6 and 7.

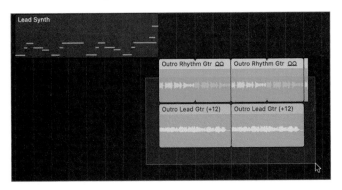

Both guitar tracks play at the same time. They sound great together, and you'll process them through modulation and distortion plug-ins to give them movement and character.

Let's select the two tiny regions on tracks 8 and 9. There's not much room to the left of the regions, so it's easier to drag from right to left.

13 In the intro, drag to select the two regions on tracks 8 and 9.

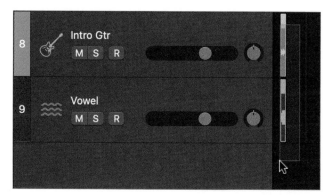

The two regions play short samples and stop abruptly. Later, you'll use delay plug-ins on both tracks to make the two samples echo throughout the intro.

14 In the control bar, click the **Solo** button.

The Solo button is off, and all regions are colored again to indicate they're no longer muted.

Using the Solo button in conjunction with the Play From Selection key command is a great technique for identifying the sound of individual regions in a project you're hearing for the first time. Remember to use these tools throughout this lesson (and beyond) when you need to focus on an instrument while dialing the plug-ins on its channel strip.

Use Audio Effect Plug-ins Settings

Now that you are familiar with all the tracks in the song, you'll insert plug-ins on channel strips and choose settings (factory presets) or adjust plug-in parameters to give the desired sounds to your instruments.

First, you'll add character to the two guitars in the Outro section, using a phaser plug-in to add movement to the first one and a fuzz pedal to distort the other. You'll then adjust their volume and pan to balance them out nicely in the stereo field, widening the mix to give it dimension in that section.

1   Select the **Outro Rhythm Gtr** track (track 6).

The Outro Rhythm Gtr regions are selected, and the Outro Rhythm Gtr channel strip is displayed on the left in the inspector.

Now, you'll solo the track and create a cycle area for the Outro section to be able to experiment with plug-in settings while focusing on the sound of the guitar and not have to be concerned with navigation.

2   In the track header, click the **Solo** button (or press S).

The track is soloed and all other tracks in the workspace are muted. An advantage of using the Solo button on track headers over using the Solo button in the control bar is that the track remains soloed independently of region selection.

3   In the ruler at bar 37, drag the first Outro arrangement marker into the ruler.

Cycle mode is on, and the cycle area corresponds to the marker you dragged. From now on, use the Space bar to toggle playback on and off, and you'll always hear only the Outro Rhythm Gtr region below the cycle area.

4   Listen to your guitar.

5 In the inspector, on the Outro Rhythm Gtr channel strip, click the **Audio FX** slot, and in the plug-in pop-up menu, choose **Modulation** > **Microphaser**.

> **NOTE ▶** When inserting a plug-in, there is no need to go all the way down the hierarchy in the plug-in pop-up menu to choose a format—such as Stereo or Dual Mono. Simply choose the plug-in name, and Logic Pro picks the most appropriate format for the channel strip—Stereo in this case.

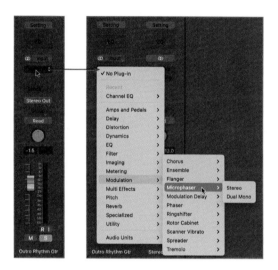

> **TIP ▶** The five most recent plug-ins you've inserted are listed at the top of the Plug-in menu.

The Microphaser is inserted in the Audio FX area of the channel strip (McrPhas) and the Microphaser plug-in window opens.

You hear the effect on the guitar creating a swooshing filter modulation. Let's open the Library to choose settings for the Microphaser.

6 In the control bar, click the **Library** button (or press Y).

The Library opens. On the left channel strip, a blue triangle points from the Library to the Setting button at the top, and the Library displays patches for the channel strip. Let's find the Microphaser plug-in settings.

7   Click to the left of the Microphaser plug-in.

The blue triangle now points to the Microphaser plug-in, and the Library displays Microphaser settings.

8   In the Library, click the **Underwater** setting.

In the plug-in window, the knobs turn to recall this setting's values, and the setting name is displayed in the plug-in header. This setting creates a very fast twirling effect. It's way too much for this guitar!

9   In the Library, click **Slow Heavy**.

This setting creates a slower yet deeper phasing effect. Let's compare the guitar with and without the phaser.

10 At the upper left of the plug-in window, click the **On/Off** button.

On the channel strip, the plug-in is dimmed to indicate it's off, and you can hear the original guitar sound without the phaser effect. You can turn the plug-in on or off directly on the channel strip, which is useful when the plug-in window is not open.

11 Close the Microphaser plug-in window.

12 On the channel strip, move the pointer over the Microphaser plug-in and click the **On/Off** button that appears on the left.

The phasing effect is back on. Keep track 6 soloed for now; you'll unsolo it in the next exercise. Don't forget to regularly save your work!

13 Choose **File** > **Save As**.

14 In the **Save As field**, enter **03 Fast Jam in progress** and choose a location where you want to save this project.

In the Save dialog, keep this new copy organized as a package and copy only the audio files into the project. In the Finder, a package is displayed as a single file that you can open in Logic Pro, and the audio files are contained inside the package.

15 Click **Save** (or press Return).

For the rest of this lesson, you'll be working on this new copy of the project, leaving the original 03 Fast Jam untouched should you want to start this lesson over from the beginning in the future.

You have inserted a phaser plug-in in the Audio FX area of a channel strip to process the sound of a guitar track. You also know how to point the blue triangle to the desired insert on a channel strip to choose among the settings for that plug-in in the Library.

Dial Audio Effect Plug-ins Settings

Loading a setting from the Library is a quick way to find a pre-made sound effect. However, if you have something more precise in mind, you'll want to tweak the knobs to dial your own sound. On the lead guitar track in the outro, you'll insert a guitar pedal plug-in to dial in just the right fuzz distortion sound.

1 Select the **Outro Lead Gtr** track (track 7).

The Outro Lead Gtr channel strip is displayed on the left in the inspector. Track 6 is still soloed from the previous exercise. Now, you need to turn your attention to track 7. To solo a track while unsoloing all other tracks, you can Option-click the track's Solo button.

2   On the Outro Lead Gtr track, **Option**-click the **Solo** button.

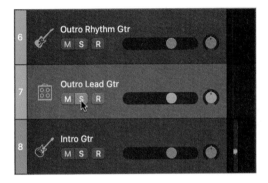

Track 6 is unsoloed, and track 7 is soloed.

3   In the inspector, click the **Audio FX** slot and choose **Amps & Pedals** > **Stompboxes** > **Distortion** > **OctaFuzz**.

The over-the-top buzzing distortion is just what the doctor ordered for this lead guitar riff, but it's a bit shrill.

4   On the Octafuzz pedal, drag the **Tone** knob all the way down.

The distortion is still intense, but the high frequencies are rounded off, and the tone is warmer.

5   Close the **OctaFuzz** plug-in window.

6 On track 7, click the **Solo** button to unsolo the guitar.

The plug-ins you added on the two guitar tracks in the outro affect their loudness, and you need to readjust their volume. You'll also pan them on either side of the stereo field to widen the mix in that section.

7 On the Outro Rhythm Gtr track (track 6), drag the **volume fader** up to *-1.0 dB* and the **pan** knob down to *-28*.

8 On the Outro Lead Gtr track (track 7), drag the **volume fader** down to *-4.0 dB* and the **pan** knob up to *+40*.

This outro sounds powerful. The phasing modulation on the rhythm guitar on track 6 gives it movement and grabs the attention while the heavy distortion on track 7 gives the lead guitar a commanding tone.

9 In the ruler, click the cycle area (or press C).

Cycle mode is off.

10 Choose **File** > **Save** (or press Command-S) to save your project.

You have inserted individual effect plug-ins on channel strips to give different tracks a unique sound and help them stand out in the mix. You used the Library to choose a setting for one plug-in, dialed your own sound manually in the other, and balanced the volume and pan of both tracks to give the guitars a nice wide stereo mix at the end of the song.

Use Software Instrument Plug-ins

In the previous exercises, you worked with guitar loops on audio tracks and added audio effect plug-ins to process the audio signal coming from the audio regions on the track. You'll now move your attention to the Lead Synth track (track 5) that has MIDI regions on a software instrument track and insert a software instrument plug-in in the Instrument slot.

1   Click the **Lead Synth** track header (track 5).

The track and its regions are selected. In the inspector, the Lead Synth software instrument channel strip is on the left, and the Library displays software instrument patches.

2   In the control bar, click the **Solo** button.

The selected Lead Synth regions are soloed. For the MIDI regions to produce any sound, they need to trigger a software instrument. Let's try a couple of different instruments.

3   On the Lead Synth channel strip, click the **Instrument** slot and choose **Studio Horns**.

Use Shift-Space bar to listen to the instrument. The notes in the MIDI region trigger the Studio Horns instrument plug-in, which plays a nice realistic-sounding trumpet, but it's not quite what you're after for this modern rock song.

4   Move your pointer over the **Instrument** plug-in slot and click the **double-arrow symbol** that appears on the right.

You can choose a different instrument from the pop-up menu.

TIP ▶ To remove a plug-in from a channel strip, in the plug-in pop-up menu, choose No Plug-in.

5   Choose **Alchemy**.

The Alchemy instrument plug-in is inserted, and its window opens. You'll work with settings and don't need to keep the plug-in window open.

6   Close the **Alchemy** plug-in window (or press Command-W).

Alchemy plays a rather generic-sounding synth sound with a modulated filter. Let's display Alchemy settings in the Library.

7   Click to the left of the Alchemy plug-in.

The blue triangle points to the Alchemy plug-in, and the Library displays Alchemy settings.

8   In the Library, choose **Basic > Leads > 80s Sync Lead**.

When the Library has key focus, you can use the Up Arrow and Down Arrow key commands to select the previous and next setting in the Library.

9   Press the **Down Arrow** a few times to listen to a few different Alchemy settings.

10   Scroll all the way down and click **Wobble Lead**.

Alchemy now produces a rich and complex, expressive lead synthesizer sound. The synth is quite loud, so you need to turn it down.

11   On the Lead Synth channel strip, turn the **volume fader** down to *-15.0 dB*.

When working with software instrument tracks, the Library makes it easy to browse different patches. Don't forget to use the arrow keys to browse through consecutives patches during playback.

Use MIDI Effect Plug-ins

On software instrument channel strips, the MIDI data from the track goes through the MIDI FX area before it's routed to the Instrument slot. MIDI data is performance data, and the MIDI effect plug-ins affect the incoming notes, their timing, pitch, and velocity—for example, creating transposing or echoing effects. In this next exercise, you'll use an Arpeggiator MIDI effect plug-in to make the synthesizer melody arpeggiate notes in different octaves.

1   On the Lead Synth channel strip, click the **MIDI FX** insert and in the plug-in pop-up menu, choose **Arpeggiator**.

The Arpeggiator plug-in window opens. The MIDI regions on the track contain a single voice melody, so the Arpeggiator simply repeats the same note at 1/16 note intervals. Let's slow it down.

2   Drag the **Rate** knob down to *1/8*.

To spread the arpeggio effect over a wider pitch range, let's raise the octave range.

3   Drag the **Octave Range** slider up to *3*.

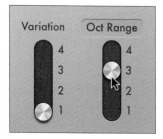

The notes are arpeggiated over a three-octave range and go quite high in pitch. To make the performance more legato, you can lengthen the individual notes generated by the Arpeggiator.

4   Click the **Options** button.

5   Drag the **Note Length** knob up to *105 %*.

The notes now slide in pitch from one octave to the next, producing an exhilarating portamento effect. Let's hear the synth in the context of the whole mix.

6   Close the Arpeggiator plug-in window.

7   In the control bar, click the **Solo** button to turn it off.

The arpeggiated synth adds a captivating melody to this section.
You've inserted an Arpeggiator MIDI effect plug-in to arpeggiate a rather simple single voice melody and spread the repeating eighth notes over a three-octave range. You've adjusted the note length inside the Arpeggiator to make sure the arpeggiated note pitches slide from one octave to the next, generating an expressive performance.

Load and Edit Patches

Patches store multiple plug-ins and their parameter values. Patches also store Smart Control knob mappings to quickly dial different parameters. When you are looking for a complete sound processing solution for a track, selecting a patch from the Library is a quick and easy way to get started.

MORE INFO ▶ Patches can contain more complex signal routing involving multiple channel strips, as you'll explore later in this lesson.

Use Patches from the Library

In this exercise, you'll load two different-sounding guitar amp patches for the guitar tracks in the verses and in the choruses. Let's turn the Solo button back on.

1 In the control bar, click the **Solo** button.

2 Select the **Gtr Harmonics** track (track 4).

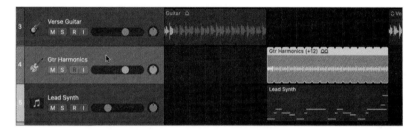

The regions on the track are selected and soloed.

3 Listen to Gtr Harmonics regions in the chorus.

The guitar arpeggiates harmonics with a clean sound. Let's choose a distorted guitar patch.

4 In the Library, choose **Electric Guitar and Bass** > **Crunch Guitar** > **Big Brute Blues**.

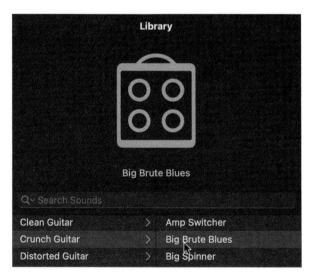

On the Gtr Harmonics channel strip, five audio effect plug-ins are inserted to re-create the Big Brute Blues patch sound. A bus send is created that routes the audio signal to an auxiliary channel strip (often abbreviated as Aux) to add a reverb effect to the guitar. Later in this lesson, you'll set up your own bus sends to add reverb to a synthesizer channel strip.

5   On the Gtr Harmonics channel strip, drag the **volume fader** down to *-7.4 dB*.

6   Select the **Verse Guitar** track (track 3).

7   In the Library, choose **Electric Guitar and Bass** > **Crunch Guitar** > **Old School Punk**.

That patch is a little aggressive. On the channel strip, let's turn off some of the effect plug-ins to go back to a somewhat more basic sound.

8   On the Verse Guitar channel strip, move the pointer over the **Pedalboard** plug-in and click the **On/Off** button that appears on the left.

The plug-in is turned off, and the guitar has a little less distortion.

9   Three slots below, turn off the **Compressor** plug-in.

The guitar sounds a bit rawer and a bit louder too. You need to readjust its volume.

10   On the Verse Guitar channel strip, drag the **volume fader** down to *-12.4 dB*.

11   Turn off **Solo** mode and listen to the mix.

The guitars in the verses and the choruses now have a crunchy vintage amp tube distortion sound and bring a rock sound to the ensemble.

You have selected patches for two guitar tracks and turned off the superfluous effect plug-
ins that weren't needed for their sound. As you load patches or turn effect plug-ins on or
off on a channel strip, the change in signal processing often results in a different volume,
so make sure you readjust the volume faders to keep the instrument levels balanced.

Edit Patches with Smart Controls

Smart Controls are fully programmable knobs and switches that are mapped to various
controls in a patch: channel strip controls, such as the volume fader, pan knob, or Send
Level knobs, and plug-in knobs and sliders. When in a pinch, the Smart Controls offer
you quick access to the main patch parameters, avoiding the need to open multiple plug-
in windows to hunt for the right knob.

1 Select the **Gtr Harmonics** track (track 4).

2 In the control bar, click the **Smart Controls** button (or press B).

The Smart Controls pane opens, showing controls for the Big Brute Blues patch you
loaded earlier in this lesson.

Let's open the Amp Designer plug-in to see how the Smart Controls affect the amp
settings.

3   On the Gtr Harmonics channel strip, click the **Amp Designer** plug-in (Amp).

The Amp Designer plug-in opens.

4   On the Smart Controls, drag the **Gain** knob all the way down, and then all the way up.

In Amp Designer, the Gain knob moves from *4* to *8.5*. The Smart Control knob restricts the range of gain it controls to what was determined as being the most useful gain range for that specific patch.

5   Set the **Smart Control Gain** knob about halfway up (12 o'clock position).

This corresponds to a Gain value of about *6.1* in Amp Designer, and the guitar is a little more distorted.

6   On the Smart Controls, drag the **Tone** knob up, and then down.

In Amp Designer, both the Treble and the Presence knobs move at different rates. A single Smart Control knob can control multiple patch parameters at various rates and even in different directions.

7   Set the **Tone** knob to *7.5*.

8   Close the **Smart Controls** pane.

9   Close the **Amp Designer** plug-in window.

You've used the Smart Controls pane to quickly adjust the sound of one of the plug-ins in the guitar patch. You'll later assign controllers to Smart Controls to dial your sound with hardware knobs or sliders, and use Logic Remote to adjust Smart Controls from your iPad.

Set Up Parallel Processing

Blending some of the dry audio of an instrument with some of the processed audio is a technique called *parallel processing*. To set it up, you can use the Sends section of a channel strip to route some of the instrument's audio signal to a bus. A *bus* is like a virtual audio cable inside Logic Pro; it routes audio from one point to another in the Mixer. The bus routes the audio to an auxiliary channel strip (a channel strip that is used solely to process the audio you route through it) where you insert the effect plug-in. The track channel strip (dry audio) and the auxiliary channel strips (processed audio) are both routed to the Stereo Out.

Send an Audio Signal to a Bus to Route It to an Aux

In this exercise, you'll send some of the lead synthesizer audio signal to a bus routed to an auxiliary channel strip to add a reverb effect. Using parallel processing for reverbs is quite common, because it allows you to mix some of the reverberated signal (wet) with the original signal (dry). After you've inserted the reverb plug-in on an Aux, you can send multiple instruments to that Aux, making them sound like they're together in the same space.

1   On the Lead Synth channel strip, click the **Send** slot, and in the send pop-up menu, choose **Bus** > **Bus 1**.

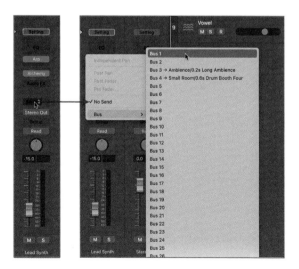

NOTE ▶ Depending on the patches you loaded earlier, you may see different names in your bus pop-up menu, and a different Aux number may be used on the right channel strip in the inspector.

In the inspector, the right channel strip is a new Aux channel strip (Aux 3) with its input set to Bus 1. The bus is just a way to route some of the Lead Synth audio signal to the input of the Aux 3 channel strip. Let's rename Aux 3.

2   At the bottom of the Aux 3 channel strip, double-click the name (Aux 3) and enter **Reverb**.

Let's find a reverb patch.

3   At the top of the Aux channel strip, move your pointer to the left of the Setting button and click the **triangle** that appears.

The blue triangle points to the Setting button at the top of the Reverb channel strip, and the Library displays auxiliary patches.

4   In the Library, choose **Reverb** > **Large Spaces** > **Rooms** > **3.7s Metallic Room**.

On the Reverb channel strip, three plug-ins are inserted: a Chorus (turned off), a Space Designer (Space D), and a Channel EQ plug-in. Space Designer is the reverb plug-in. On the Lead Synth channel strip, you need to dial in the amount of signal you want to send to Bus 1 to be processed by Space Designer.

5   On the Lead Synth channel strip, drag the **Bus 1 Send Level** knob up.

The more synth signal you send to Bus 1, the more the synth is reverberated, and the farther away from you it sounds. Notice that while the track is playing, the meters on the Reverb channel strip reach higher.

TIP Option-click a knob or a slider to set it to its default value.

6   Set the **Bus 1 Send Level** knob to *-2.1 dB*.

To compare the sound of the synth with and without reverb, you can toggle the bus send on and off.

7   On the Lead Synth channel strip, move the pointer over the **Bus 1** send and click the **On/Off** button that appears on the left.

You hear only the dry synth, without reverb. On the Reverb channel strip, the meters show no signal.

8   On the Lead Synth channel strip, turn the **Bus 1** send back on.

In the inspector, to determine which channel strip is displayed on the right, you can Shift-click different destinations on the left channel strip.

9   On the Lead Synth channel strip, **Shift**-click the **Stereo Out** slot.

The Stereo Out channel strip is displayed on the right.

10   On the Lead Synth channel strip, **Shift**-click the **Bus 1** send.

The Reverb aux is displayed on the right.

Using parallel processing allows you to use the bus Send Level knob to balance the amount of reverb you are summing with the dry signal, which lets you adjust the perceived distance of the instrument in the mix.

Merge Patches

Now that you've set up an Aux channel strip with a reverb patch, you can place other instruments in the same virtual space by routing them to the same Aux so they're processed by the same reverb plug-in. In this exercise, you'll duplicate the synth track to layer its sound with a different sounding synth. To get the desired sound for that new synth, you'll merge the bus send from one patch with the instrument of another.

1   **Option**-drag the **Lead Synth** track header (track 5) down.

The MIDI regions on track 5 are duplicated onto track 6. The Alchemy instrument plug-in inserted on track 5 is duplicated on track 6; however, you'll now choose a different patch for the duplicate track.

2   Rename track 6 to **Synth Double**.

3   In the Library, choose **Synthesizer** > **Lead** > **Slip and Slide Lead**.

This patch uses the Retro Synth instrument plug-in (RetroSyn) and a whopping 10 effect plug-ins and two bus sends. For this double, you prefer a synth without all these effects. As for the bus sends, you would rather process that new synth through the same reverb plug-in you set up in the previous exercise so that both synths appear to be in the same space.

Let's take a step back and load the patch again, this time without any of its effect plug-ins and bus sends.

4   Choose **Edit** > **Undo Load Patch** (or press Command-Z).

The channel strip goes back to its previous settings with the Arp and Alchemy plug-ins. To load only specific settings from a patch, you'll enable patch merging in the Library.

5   In the Library, click the action pop-up menu and choose **Enable Patch Merging**.

You can deselect the buttons corresponding to the types of settings you do not wish to load from the patches you select.

6   Click the **Audio Effects** and **Sends** buttons to disable them.

Selecting a patch in the Library will now load only its instrument and MIDI effect plug-ins on the channel strip.

7   In the Library, choose **Synthesizer** > **Lead** > **Slip and Slide Lead**.

On the Synth Double channel strip, only the Retro Synth instrument plug-in is inserted. The send to Bus 1 that was present before you loaded the patch remains untouched, so this synth has the same reverb as the Lead Synth.

Let's fine-tune the sound of the synths in the chorus.

8   On the Synth Double channel strip, drag the **volume fader** to *-13.2. dB*.

9   Drag the **Bus 1 Send Level** knob up to *-3.5 dB*.

> **TIP** ▶ Double-click a slider or knob in Logic Pro to enter a value.

To finish mixing your choruses, let's spread out the synth tracks in the stereo field.

10   On the Lead Synth track header (track 5), drag the **pan** knob to *-28*.

11   On the Synth Double track header (track 6), drag the **pan** knob to *+45*.

The wide mix of reverberated layered synths and crunchy guitar harmonics make the choruses sound big and spacious—a nice contrast from the more intimate ambiance of the verses.

You've duplicated the synth track and used patch merging to load only the desired types of settings from the patch you chose in the Library. You then took advantage of the parallel processing you had set up in the previous exercise to add the same reverb to that new synth track, and panned the two synths, lifting your song section to another dimension.

Layer Patches with Summing Track Stacks

The two synthesizer tracks play the same MIDI regions and are meant to sound like a single layered patch. Packing the two tracks into a summing track stack lets you fold the two tracks into a single one. You can place your MIDI regions on a single track—the main track of the stack—and the MIDI data is routed to all subtracks inside the stack.

1 In the Tracks view, **Shift**-click the **Lead Synth** track header (track 5).

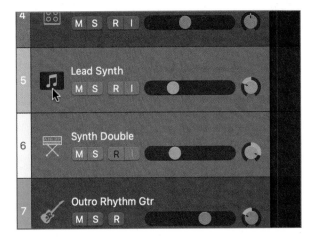

Tracks 5 and 6 are selected.

2 Choose **Track** > **Create Track Stack** (or press Command-Shift-D).

The Track Stack dialog opens, giving you a choice of a folder or summing stack. You can see more details about each option under the disclosure triangle. Summing stacks allow you to mix multiple software instruments and save the stack as a patch, which is what you'll do here.

3 In the Track Stack dialog, select **Summing stack** and click **Create**.

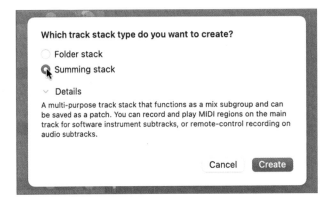

The two synth tracks are packed in a summing stack. Let's first rename the main track of the stack.

4   Double-click the name of the main track and rename it **Layered Arp**.

When multiple software instruments tracks are in a summing stack, MIDI regions on the main track trigger all instrument subtracks inside the stack. You'll move one set of MIDI regions to the main track and delete the other.

5   In the Tracks view, select both **Lead Synth** regions in the Lead Synth track.

6   Drag the selected regions to the main track of the summing stack.

TIP ➤   After you start dragging regions in the workspace, and while you are still holding down the mouse button, press and release Shift to limit the dragging motion to one direction (vertical or horizontal). Press and release Shift again to unlock this limitation.

You no longer need the duplicated regions on the Synth Double subtrack.

7   Select both **Lead Synth** regions in the Synth Double track and press **Delete**.

The MIDI regions on the main track trigger the instruments in both subtracks. You'll open the Mixer to take a quick look at the signal routing of the summing stack you created.

8   In the control bar, click the **Mixer** button (or press X).

9   Listen to the chorus.

The output of the two subtracks (the two synthesizer tracks) are set to Bus 2, and their signal is routed to the input of the main track (Layered Arp), also set to Bus 2. The main track then routes the sum of the two synths to the stereo out (St Out).

10 On the Arp Layers track header, click the **disclosure triangle**.

The track stack closes and appears as one single track. In the Mixer, the disclosure triangle for the stack closes, and the subtracks are hidden.

11 Close the **Mixer**.

You packed two software instrument tracks into a summing track stack, and moved MIDI regions to the main track of the track stack so that they trigger the two instruments on the subtracks. Later you'll save that layered instrument summing stack as a single patch for easy recall.

Reorder and Copy Plug-ins

When using multiple plug-ins to process an audio signal, the order of the plug-ins on the channel strip affects the resulting sound. In the Audio FX area of a channel strip, the audio signal is routed from top to bottom. Distorting a signal and then echoing it, for example, produces a different sound than echoing the signal first and distorting it afterward.

Process a Track with Multiple Plug-ins

On the two tracks at the bottom of the Tracks view (tracks 10 and 11) are two short audio regions in the intro of the song. You'll process the Intro Gtr on track 10 through three different effects: a delay, a distortion, and a flanger (a sweeping motion effect). You'll then change the order of the plug-ins to make sure you get the desired sound. Later you'll copy the delay plug-in on the Vowel track to give it the same echoing effect as the Intro Gtr.

1   Listen to the beginning of the intro.

You can select the regions and press Shift-Space bar (Play from Selection) to make it easy to listen to the tracks. The Intro Gtr and Vowel tracks are very short, one-hit samples. Let's turn them into delayed sound effects that echo throughout the song intro to give them an intriguing quality.

2   Select the **Intro Gtr** track (track 10).

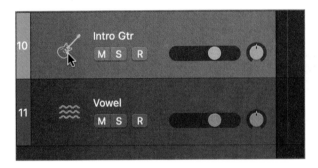

The Intro Gtr channel strip appears on the left in the inspector.

3   On the Intro Gtr channel strip, click the **Audio FX** area and choose **Delay** > **Tape Delay**.

The guitar chord echoes a couple of times and dies out quickly. To make the delay effect last longer, you'll make the sound repeat a few more times throughout the intro.

4   In the Tape Delay plug-in, raise the **Feedback** to *78 %*.

NOTE ▸ Feedback values above 100% create infinite sustain effects. The repeated signal is constantly fed back into the input of the effect, and the echoes never die. This effect is often used in dub music.

Now the guitar echoes multiple times, sustaining the effect longer throughout the intro.

5   In the inspector, click the thin gray slot below the Tape Delay plug-in and choose **Amps and Pedals** > **Amp Designer**.

The Amp Designer plug-in window opens. The default amp sounds rather mid-range and almost nasal. Let's find a better setting.

TIP ▶ To hide or show all open plug-in windows, press V.

6   In the inspector, click to the left of the Amp Designer plug-in.

The Library displays Amp Designer settings.

7   In the Library, choose **02 Crunch** > **Brown Stack Crunch**.

This amp setting sounds deeper and has more body. You can compare the sound of this setting with the default setting that was loaded when you first opened the Amp Designer plug-in.

8   In the Amp Designer plug-in header, click the blue **Compare** button.

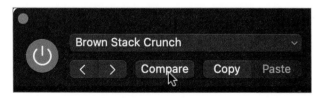

The Compare button is black. You hear the default amp setting again and clearly hear the difference in frequency range. Let's go back to Brown Stack Crunch.

9   Click the **Compare** button.

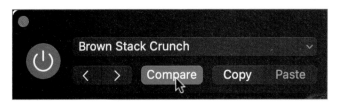

The Compare button is blue again, and Amp Designer reverts its parameter values to the Brown Stack Crunch setting.

NOTE ▸ When you save your project and then edit a plug-in's parameters, the Compare button toggles between the parameter values saved in the project (the button is black) and the edited values (the button is blue).

On a guitar amp, the amount of distortion applied to the guitar depends on the level of the guitar at the input of the amp. The Tape Delay plug-in produces echoes that slowly decrease in level throughout the intro and feeds them into the Amp Designer plug-in. The result is a series of repeats that are less and less distorted throughout the intro. You'll later change the order of the plug-ins to get a different result, but first let's add one more effect.

10   In the inspector, click below the Amp Designer plug-in and choose **Modulation > Flanger**.

MORE INFO ▸ Hold down Option while clicking an empty Audio FX slot to access Legacy plug-ins or more plug-in format options (for example, a mono plug-in on a stereo channel strip).

The Flanger creates a frequency filtering effects that evolves continuously throughout the repeating echoes, evoking the whoosh of a jet airplane.

11 In the control bar, click the **Library** button (or press Y).

The Library closes.

Let's change the order of the plug-ins on the channel strip to first process the short sample with a frequency modulation effect, and then repeat the same modulated sample throughout the intro.

When moving a plug-in on the channel strip, a white horizontal line in the Audio FX area indicates a position in the effect chain where you can insert a plug-in.

12 Drag the **Flanger** to the very top of the Audio FX area until you see a white line above the Tape Delay plug-in.

The Flanger moves to the first slot and the Tape Delay and Amp Designer plug-ins both move one slot down. You now hear the same very short modulation echoed multiple times.

Because the Tape Delay is before the Amp Designer, you still hear the first few notes distorted, and then the following ones incrementally clean up as the sound is repeated. Let's first distort the sound and then echo it to get a consistent distortion on the sample.

When moving a plug-in, a white frame around another plug-in means you're swapping the positions of the two plug-ins. Let's swap the positions of the Tape Delay and Amp Designer plug-ins.

13 Drag the **Tape Delay** over the Amp Designer until you get a white frame around the Amp Designer plug-in.

The plug-ins swap places. Let's listen attentively to the guitar.

14 Select both regions on tracks 10 and 11.

15 In the control bar, click the **Solo** button.

Listen to the intro. The Intro Gtr track has a consistent-sounding flanged and distorted sample echoing throughout the intro. However, the sample on the Vowel track plays only once. To make it repeat along with the guitar, you'll copy the Tape Delay plug-in from the Intro Gtr to the Vowel channel strip.

16 In the control bar, click the **Mixer** button (or press X).

The Mixer opens, and the Intro Gtr channel strip is selected.

17 **Option**-drag the **Tape Delay** plug-in to the **Vowel** channel strip on the right.

The plug-in is copied (with the same parameter values). The sample on the Vowel track now echoes along with the guitar on the track above.

18 Pan the Intro Gtr and Vowel tracks left and right to get a wide mix.

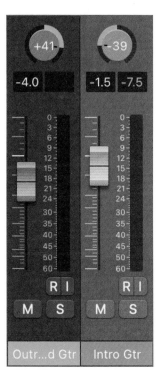

The sound effects in the intro are now spread out in the stereo field.

19 Click the **Solo** button to turn it off.

20 Close the Mixer.

TIP ▶ To insert the same plug-in on several channel strips, in the Mixer, first drag the pointer over the name of consecutive channel strips (or Command-click separate channel strips to select them), and then insert the plug-in on one of the selected channel strips.

With the help of a few plug-ins, you've created a nice echoing effect that gives the song's introduction a mysterious feel and captures the attention of the listener from the start. Moving plug-ins on the channel strip allows you to determine precisely in what order they process the audio signal to produce the desired effect. Copying plug-ins in the Mixer makes it easy to reproduce an effect from one instrument to another.

Save User Patches and Settings

While working on your songs, you may spend a good amount of time editing patches or plug-in settings, or inserting multiple individual plug-ins on a channel strip and dialing each plug-in to get a specific sound you're after. When you're happy with the way you've dialed a plug-in or a patch, you can save your own user plug-in setting or patches in the Library. Later you can recall them on other tracks in the same project or other projects.

Save Your Customized Plug-in Settings and Patches

You'll now save the Tape Delay parameters you adjusted earlier as a custom Tape Delay setting. You'll then save the effect plug-in chain you created earlier on the Intro Gtr track (Flanger, Amp Designer, and Tape Delay) as a patch that can be recalled on any audio track. Finally, you'll save the Layered Arp synth summing stack as a software instrument patch.

1   Make sure the Intro Gtr track (track 10) is selected.

To open the Library and display a specific plug-in's settings, you can click to the left of that plug-in.

2   In the inspector, on the Intro Gtr channel strip, click to the left of the Tape Delay plug-in.

The Library opens and displays the Tape Delay settings.

Let's save your user Tape Delay setting.

3   At the lower right in the Library, click **Save**.

The Save Setting dialog opens. Note that the location is set to the Tape Delay folder inside the Plug-in Settings folder. To make settings and patches accessible in the library on your Mac, do not change the location in the save dialog.

The Save As field is selected, so all you need to do is enter a name for your user setting.

4   Type **Long Delay**, and click **Save** (or press Return).

The setting is saved and appears at the root in the Library, while a new folder named App Presets is created that contains the factory settings. Your setting is now displayed whenever the Library is open and the blue triangle points to a Tape Delay plug-in.

Let's save the whole patch now.

5   At the top of the Intro Gtr channel strip, click to the left of the **Setting** button.

The Library displays audio patches.

6   At the lower right in the Library, click **Save**.

The Save Patch dialog opens. Note that the location is set to the Audio folder inside the Patches folder on your hard drive.

7   Type **Flangey Echoes**, and click **Save** (or press Return).

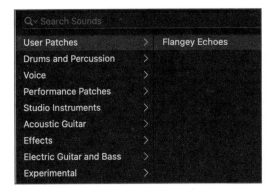

The patch is saved. A new User Patches folder appears at the root of the Library, and the Flangey Echoes patch is inside. Your new custom patch is now accessible in the Library when an audio channel strip is selected and the blue triangle points to its Setting button. Let's save another patch.

TIP ▶ To delete a patch, select it in the Library and press the Delete button in the lower right.

8   Select the **Layered Arp** track (track 5).

9   At the lower right in the Library, click **Save**.

The Save Patch As dialog opens and the Save As field is populated with the name of your track (Layered Arp), so you'll save it under that name.

10   Click **Save** (or press Return).

The software instrument patch is saved. When a software track is selected and you select that patch in the Library, the summing stack and its subtracks are re-created.

The user patch and settings you've saved are available in the Library on your Mac as long as the appropriate channel strip type (audio or software instrument) is selected and the blue triangle points from the Library to the desired button or insert slot on a channel strip.

Your newly found plug-in management skills will greatly improve your sound design and mixing workflows. Selecting and saving settings and patches, as well as moving and copying plug-ins on your channel strips, allow you to be in total control over your sound processing.

Key Commands

Keyboard Shortcuts	Description
Library	
Up Arrow	Selects the previous patch or setting
Down Arrow	Selects the next patch or setting
General	
Command-W	Closes the active window
V	Hides or shows all plug-in windows
Shift-Space bar	Plays from Selection
Tracks view	
Command-Shift-D	Creates a track stack
B	Toggles Smart Controls

4

Lesson Files	None
Time	This lesson takes approximately 60 minutes to complete.
Goals	Adjust recording level
	Record a single region
	Record takes
	Record in Cycle mode
	Punch on the fly
	Punch automatically
	Delete unused recordings
	Record MIDI
	Merge record MIDI

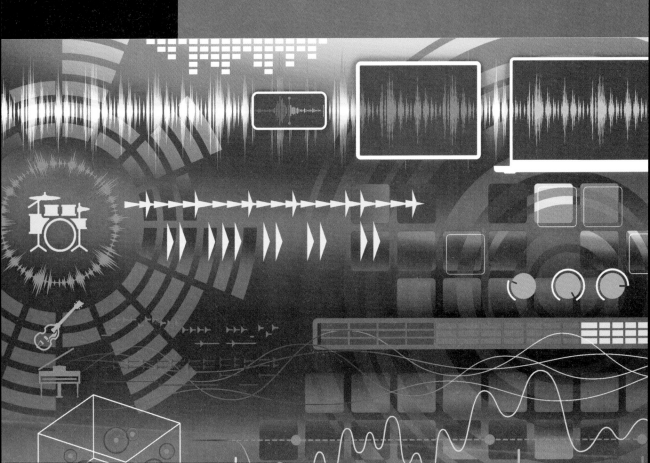

Record Audio and MIDI

In this lesson, you'll record audio and MIDI and explore situations that you'll typically come across when working with live musicians: record an instrument, record additional takes of the same instrument, record in Cycle mode, punch on the fly, punch automatically, and merge MIDI recordings. After experimenting with these recording techniques, you'll clean up the project folder to delete unused audio files.

Record Audio

In this example, you'll record a single instrument. The exercise describes recording your voice with a microphone, but feel free to record a guitar or any instrument you have.

Adjust the Recording Level and Record Audio

You'll start a new project with one audio track and record your instrument on that track.

1   Choose **File** > **New** (or press Command-Shift-N).

2   In the Create New Track dialog, click **Audio**.

3   In the Audio button, make sure **Mic or Line** is selected.

4   In the Details area, from the Audio Input menu, choose the input number where you connected your microphone on your audio interface. If you are using the Mac microphone, choose **Input 1**.

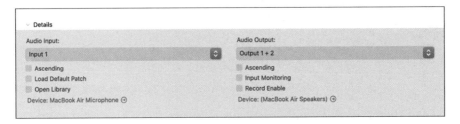

5   Keep all the checkboxes unselected.

At the bottom of the details area, the audio devices used are listed. If you need to use a different device, click one of the arrow buttons to the right of the device names to open the Audio preferences.

NOTE ▶ If your Mac does not have a built-in microphone, you'll need to connect a compatible audio input device (USB audio interface, USB microphone, your display's microphone, or a headset with a built-in microphone) to record audio.

TIP ▶ To record multiple sources onto multiple tracks simultaneously, assign the different input numbers where your sources are connected to different tracks, record-enable them, and click Record. To make sure you don't process live audio through plug-ins that add latency, choose Record > Low Latency Monitoring Mode while recording.

6   Click **Create** (or press Return).

A new audio track (Audio 1) is created. In the inspector, Input 1 is selected at the top of the Audio 1 channel strip.

If the track has a custom name, Logic Pro assigns that name to the audio files recorded on that track. To help identify your audio files, let's rename the track before you start recording.

7   In the track header, double-click the name, and type **Vocals**.

To avoid losing the audio files you record, it's good practice to save your project before you start recording in it.

8   Choose **File** > **Save** (or press Command-S) to save your project.

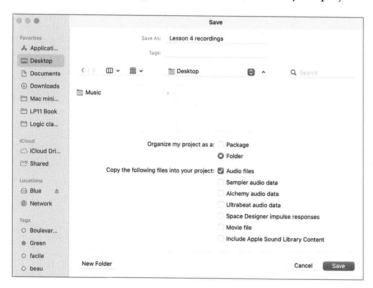

Choose a name for your project, save it on your Desktop, organize your project as a folder, and copy audio files into your project.

NOTE ▶ To prevent feedback and avoid re-recording the playback from the speakers, use headphones to monitor the output of Logic Pro while recording.

9   Click the **R** (Record Enable) button in the Vocals track header.

The track is record-enabled. You can hear the sound of your microphone, and in the inspector, you see the level of the incoming audio signal on the channel strip meters. Let's adjust your recording level to make sure your recording isn't distorted.

NOTE ▶ For audio recording to work as expected, click the microphone icon in your menu bar, and set Mic Mode to Standard for Logic Pro.

NOTE ▶ If you're using macOS Sonoma, make sure to click the microphone icon in your menu bar and set Mic Mode to Standard for Logic Pro to ensure audio recording works as expected.

TIP ▶ To monitor your microphone or instrument processed by effect plug-ins, insert plug-ins on the track's channel strip. You're still recording the dry (unprocessed) audio signal on the track, and you can always readjust or remove the plug-ins later.

10 Watch the meters while you sing into the microphone.

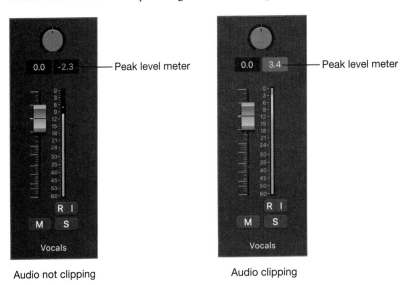

Audio not clipping   Audio clipping

In the peak level meter, values below *-2.0 dBFS* are green, values between *-2.0* and *0 dBFS* are yellow, and the meter turns orange to indicate clipping when the signal exceeds *0 dBFS*.

11 On your audio interface, adjust the input gain so the peak stays below *0 dBFS* even when you sing the loudest part of the performance you're about to record.

TIP ▶ To tune your guitar, click the Tuner button in the control bar.

Tuner button

12 In the control bar, click the **Record** button (or press R).

The playhead and the LCD display in the control bar both turn red to indicate that Logic Pro is recording. The playhead jumps one bar earlier and gives you a four-beat count-in with an audible metronome click before the recording starts. A new red region is created behind the playhead on the record-enabled track, and you can see the recording's waveform created as you sing.

TIP ▸ To set the count-in length, choose Record > Count-in, and then choose the number of bars from the submenu. To change the Metronome settings, choose Record > Metronome Settings.

13 After you've recorded a few bars, in the control bar, click the **Stop** button (or press the Space bar).

A new Vocals#01 audio region is created. Let's listen.

14 Press **Shift-Space** bar.

The playhead jumps to the beginning of the selected region and playback starts.

15 Press the **Space** bar to stop playback.

If you are not happy with your new recording, you can delete it and start over.

16 Press **Delete**.

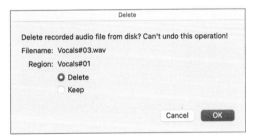

A Delete alert appears with two choices:

▶ **Delete**—The audio file is deleted from your storage device.

▶ **Keep**—The audio region is removed from the Tracks area. The audio file is kept on your storage device, and you can always drag it back from the Project Audio Browser if you need it.

Let's cancel this dialog to keep the audio region on the track for the next exercise.

17 Click **Cancel** (or press esc).

18 Choose **File** > **Save** (or press Command-S).

You've adjusted the recording level and recorded your first audio region in Logic Pro. Simple enough! You'll now explore more complex scenarios that involve more advanced recording techniques.

Record Multiple Takes

During a recording session, you can record several takes of the same performance, and later choose the best take, or even combine the best parts of each take to create a *comp* (composite take).

When you record over an audio region, Logic Pro packs the recordings into a take folder (you can change that behavior under Record > Overlapping Audio Recordings).

1 Make sure the Vocals track is still record-enabled.

2 Position the playhead at the beginning.

3 In the control bar, click **Record** (or press R) to record a second take that is slightly longer than the first.

The new recording (in red) appears to be recorded over the previous blue audio region.

4 Stop the recording.

A take folder is created. Inside the take folder, on subtracks below the Vocals track, the original recording (Take 1) is muted, and the new recording (Take 2) is selected.

On the Vocals track, the take folder shows the waveform of the selected take (Take 2) and is named Vocals: Take 2, which is the name of the track appended with the name of the take it's playing.

NOTE ▶ If Take 2 is shorter than Take 1, the take folder is named Guitar: Comp A, and plays a comp made of Take 2 and the end of Take 1.

5 Record a third take.

6 In the Vocals track header, click the **R** (Record Enable) button to disable it.

The track is disarmed, and you can no longer hear the live sound from your mic.

Take 1 and Take 2 are muted, and the take folder plays the most recent recording, Take 3.

7 Click **Take 1**.

Listen to the take folder; you hear Take 1.

8 Click **Take 2**.

Listen to the take folder; you hear Take 2.

9 At the upper left of the Vocals take folder, click the **disclosure triangle** to close the folder.

TIP ▶ You can also double-click a take folder to open or close it.

Let's clean up the track so we can start the next exercise with an empty track. You'll keep the audio files on your storage device—you'll use another method to delete outtakes later in this lesson.

10 Click the take folder on Track 1 to select it.

11 Press **Delete**.

12 In the Delete dialog, select **Keep** and select the **For all** checkbox.

The "For all" option applies your choice to keep the files for all the selected files (in this case, the three recordings inside the take folder).

13 Click **OK** (or press Return).

Record Takes in Cycle Mode

Switching from playing your instrument to operating Logic Pro between each take isn't always practical and can disrupt your creative vibe. When recording in Cycle mode, Logic Pro creates a new take for each pass of the cycle and packs them in a take folder.

1 In the upper half of the ruler, click the dimmed cycle area (or press C).

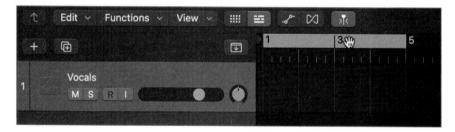

The cycle area is yellow to indicate that Cycle mode is on.

TIP You don't have to position the playhead when recording in Cycle mode. After the count-in, Logic Pro starts recording at the beginning of the cycle.

2 In the control bar, click **Record** (or press R).

The Vocals track is automatically record-enabled. The playhead jumps a bar ahead of the cycle for a one-measure count-in and starts recording the first take. When it reaches bar 5—the end of the cycle area—it jumps back to bar 1 and starts recording a new take.

NOTE ▸ If no track is record-enabled, Logic Pro automatically record-enables the selected track during recording.

Logic keeps looping the cycle area, recording new takes until you stop recording.

3   Record two or three takes.

4   Click **Stop** (or press the Space bar).

All the takes recorded in Cycle mode are packed into a take folder. The Vocals track is automatically disabled for recording. Feel free to click a take to select it and listen to it.

NOTE ▸ When you stop recording, if the most recent recording is shorter than a bar, Logic Pro automatically discards it. To keep the last recording during a cycle recording, make sure you stop the recording more than one bar after the beginning of the cycle area.

5   At the upper left of the take folder, click the **disclosure triangle**.

The take folder closes. Let's discard the take folder so that you can experiment with punching techniques on the Vocals track in the next exercises.

6   Click the take folder to select it and press **Delete**.

7   In the Delete alert, make sure **Keep** is selected and click **OK** (or press Return).

Because you clicked Record only once and recorded all three takes successively while in Cycle mode, all the takes are contained in a single audio file. There's only one audio file to delete, which is why there is no "For all" checkbox.

8 In the ruler, click the cycle area (or press C) to turn off Cycle mode.

You have recorded your voice onto an audio track. You have recorded additional takes into a take folder on the same track, and used cycle recording to record a take folder while repeating a cycle area. In the next section, you'll explore techniques to re-record over specific sections in an existing recording—for example, to fix mistakes.

Punch In and Out

When you want to correct a specific section of a recording—usually to fix a mistake—you can start playback before the mistake, punch in to engage recording at the beginning of the section you wish to fix, and then punch out to stop recording at the end of the section while playback continues. A take folder is created, containing a comp that combines the old recording outside the punch-in/punch-out range with the new recording inside that range. This technique allows you to fix smaller mistakes in a recording while still listening to the continuity of the performance.

> **NOTE** ▶ Punching is nondestructive. At any time, you can open the take folder and select the original recording.

There are two punching methods: on the fly (using key commands to punch in and out in real time) and automatic (positioning punch locators before you start recording). Punching on the fly is fast but requires someone to operate Logic Pro while the musician is performing. Automatic punching is ideal for the musician-producer who is working alone.

Punch on the Fly

Let's make a new recording, and then you'll punch on the fly to re-record a specific area of that new recording. Remember to zoom in or out as necessary to get a closer look at the waveforms.

1 In the Vocals track header, click the **R** (Record Enable) button to record-enable the track.

2 Click **Record** (or press R).

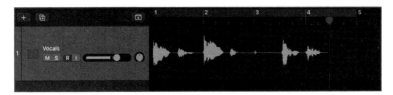

Record at least five bars of vocals and purposefully make a mistake in a specific spot.

3 Click the **Space** bar to stop recording.

Feel free to listen to the recording to determine which section needs to be re-recorded and to be ready to punch in and out at the desired locations.

You can click Record to punch in, and click Play to punch out. However using the Record Toggle key command to punch in and out is faster and allows for greater precision. That key command is unassigned by default, so let's assign it.

4 Choose **Logic Pro** > **Key Commands** > **Edit Assignments** (or press Option-K).

The Key Commands Assignments window opens.

5 Click the **Record Toggle** command to select it.

6 In the right column, click the **Learn by Key Label** button.

7 Press **Option-1**.

Option-1 is now listed in the Key column next to Record Toggle, indicating that the command was successfully assigned.

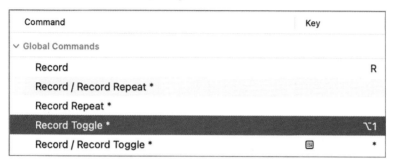

Command	Key
∨ Global Commands	
Record	R
Record / Record Repeat *	
Record Repeat *	
Record Toggle *	⌥1
Record / Record Toggle *	▣ *

8 Close the Key Command Assignments window.

9 In the control bar, click **Go to Beginning** (or press Return).

NOTE ▶ To be able to punch on the fly, make sure Record > Allow Quick Punch-In is selected.

10 Start the playback.

Get ready to press your Record Toggle key command when you reach the point where you want to punch in.

11 Press **Option-1** (Record Toggle).

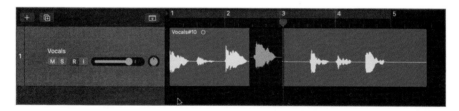

The playhead continues moving, but Logic Pro is now recording a new take on top of the previous recording. Keep your fingers in position to punch out.

12 Press **Option-1** again.

The recording stops while the playhead continues playing the project.

13 Stop the playback.

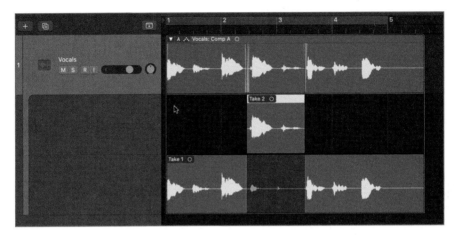

On the Vocals track, a take folder was created and a comp is automatically created (Comp A) that combines the original recording (Take 1) up to the punch-in point, the new take (Take 2) between the punch-in and punch-out points, and the original recording (Take 1) after the punch-out point. Fades are automatically applied at the punch-in and punch-out points.

14 Listen to your Vocals track.

In the next exercise, you'll examine another punching technique, so let's undo this last recording (the new take) but keep the longer five-bar recording with your mistake.

15 Choose **Edit** > **Undo Recording** (or press Command-Z).

The take folder disappears, and you once again see the longer region you recorded at the beginning of this exercise.

Punching on the fly is a great technique that allows musicians to focus on their performance while the engineer takes care of punching in and out at the right times. On the other hand, if you worked alone through this exercise and tried to punch in and out while playing your instrument or singing, you realize how challenging it can be. When working alone, punching automatically is recommended.

Punch Automatically

To prepare for automatic punching, you enable the Autopunch mode and set the autopunch area. Setting the punch-in and punch-out points in advance allows you to focus entirely on your performance during recording.

1   **Option**-**Command**-click the ruler (or press Command-Control-Option-P).

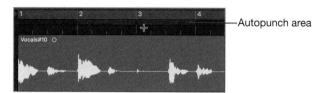

The ruler becomes taller to accommodate the red autopunch area that defines the section to be re-recorded.

2   Adjust the autopunch area so that it encompasses the area you want to re-record.

You can manipulate the Autopunch area the same way you edit the cycle area: drag the edges of the autopunch area to resize it, or drag the entire area to move it. Red vertical guidelines help you align the punch-in and punch-out points with the waveform. You can zoom in to make sure you're re-recording exactly what you want.

3   **Control**-**Option**-drag to zoom in on the area you want to re-record.

4   If needed, adjust the autopunch area.

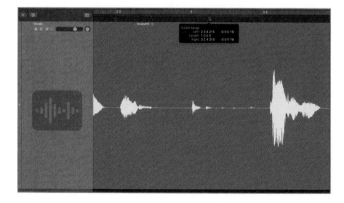

5   **Control**-**Option**-click to zoom out.

6   Click **Go to Beginning** (or press Return).

7   Click **Record** (or press R).

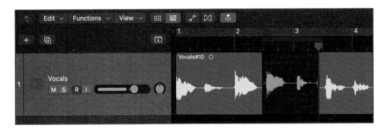

Playback starts. In the control bar, the Record button blinks; Logic Pro isn't yet recording.

TIP ▶ To hear the live instrument outside the autopunch area, deselect Record > Auto-Input Monitoring.

When the playhead reaches the punch-in point (the left edge of the autopunch area), the Record button turns solid red, and Logic Pro starts recording a new take.

When the playhead reaches the punch-out point (the right edge of the autopunch area), the recording stops, but the playback continues.

8   Stop playback.

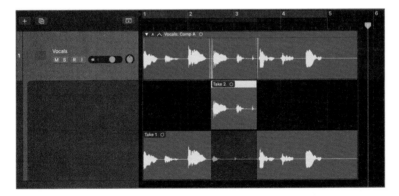

A take folder, Vocals: Comp A, is created on the track.

Just as when you punched on the fly in the previous exercise, a comp is created that plays the original recording up to the punch-in point, inserts the new take between the punch-in and punch-out points, and continues with the original recording after the punch-out point.

9   Click the **R** button on the Vocals track to disable it.

10   **Option**-**Command**-click the ruler (or press Command-Control-Option-P) to disable Autopunch mode.

11   Click the take folder's **disclosure triangle** to close it.

12   Save your work.

> **TIP** ▸ To speed up the Autopunch recording process, select the section you want to re-record with the Marquee tool and start recording. Logic Pro automatically turns on the Autopunch mode, and the autopunch area matches the marquee selection.

Delete Unused Audio Files

During a recording session, the focus is on capturing the best possible performance, and you may forget to delete the bad takes. The unused recordings take up unnecessary storage space and make the project folder bigger than it needs to be.

In this exercise, you'll select and delete all the audio files that are no longer needed in your project. You'll work in the Project Audio Browser, which lists all the audio files and audio regions that have been imported or recorded in your project.

1   In the control bar, click **Browsers** (or press F) and ensure that the **Project** tab is selected.

The Project Audio Browser opens, listing all the audio files you've recorded during this lesson. You can even see all the files that you removed earlier from the Tracks view but elected to keep in the Delete alert.

For each audio file, the browser shows:

▶ Filename

▶ Sample rate (48000 Hz)

▶ Bit depth (24 Bit)

▶ Tempo (120.0 bpm)

▶ Region length (in hours:minutes:seconds:frames.subframes)

TIP ▶ To change the units used to display time, choose Logic Pro > Settings > View and choose a unit format in the Display Time As pop-up menu.

Clicking the disclosure triangle in front of the audio filename toggles the display of audio regions referring to that audio file.

NOTE ▶ Editing regions in the Tracks area is nondestructive. The audio data in the audio file stays intact, and the regions merely point to different sections of the audio file.

2   From the Project Audio Browser menu, choose **Edit** > **Select Unused** (or press Shift-U).

All the audio files that do not have an associated region in the workspace are selected.

TIP ▶ To preview a region, select it and click the Preview button (or press Option-Space bar). While the region plays, a small white playhead travels through the regions. To start previewing from a specific point, hold down the mouse button over the desired location on the waveform.

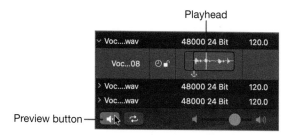

Once you feel satisfied that the selected audio files do not contain any useful material, you can delete them.

3   From the Project Audio Browser menu bar, choose **Audio File** > **Delete (X) File(s)** (where X is the number of selected files).

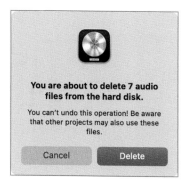

An alert asks you to confirm the deletion.

4   Click **Delete**.

The files are deleted.

5   In the control bar, click **Browsers** (or press F) to close the Project Audio Browser.

In some cases—for example, if you chose Edit > Undo Recording (or pressed Command-Z) earlier—you may still have audio files inside the project folder that aren't listed in the Project Audio Browser. Let's clean them up.

6   Choose **File** > **Project Management** > **Clean Up**.

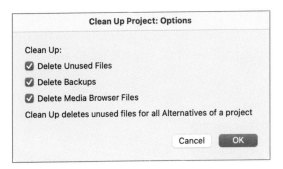

The Clean Up Project: Options dialog opens.

7   Keep all three checkboxes selected and click **OK**.

A Clean Up Project dialog opens, listing all audio files inside the Audio Files folder of the project folder that are not listed in the Project Audio browser.

NOTE ▸ If there are no files to clean up, the Clean Up Project dialog does not open.

8   Keep all the files selected and click **OK**.

The files are deleted.

Record MIDI

In Logic Pro, the basic techniques used to record MIDI are similar to the techniques you used to record audio, and the punching in and out techniques you learned earlier can be used when recording MIDI. One unique aspect of MIDI recording is that you can merge multiple MIDI recordings into the same MIDI region. For example, when recording piano, you can record just the left hand, and then in a second pass, record the right hand in the same MIDI region.

Record a MIDI Region

First, let's record a simple part. You'll observe the MIDI In display in the control bar as you send MIDI events to Logic Pro from your MIDI keyboard.

1   On the Vocals track, click the **M** (Mute) button.

2   Choose **Track > New Software Instrument Track** (or press Option-Command-S).

3   In the control bar, click the **Library** button (or press Y).

4   In the Library, choose **Piano > Concert Grand**.

The Concert Grand patch is loaded on the track.

NOTE ► If no MIDI controller keyboard is connected to your Mac, you can choose Window > Show Musical Typing (or press Command-K). That window turns your Mac keyboard into a polyphonic MIDI controller. Press Z or X to transpose the octave range down or up, and press C or V to decrease or increase note velocities. Keep in mind that you may need to close the Musical Typing window to use some key commands.

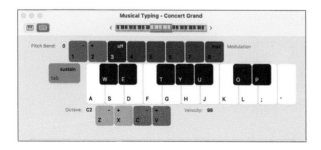

5   Play a few notes on your MIDI keyboard while observing the LCD display.

A small dot appears at the upper right of the LCD display to indicate that Logic Pro is receiving MIDI events. These small dots can be useful to quickly troubleshoot MIDI connections.

NOTE ▶ When Logic Pro sends MIDI events to external MIDI devices, a small dot appears at the lower right of the LCD display.

6   Play a chord on your MIDI keyboard.

The chord name appears in the LCD display.

Logic can provide a more detailed view of the incoming MIDI events.

7   To the right of the LCD display, click the small arrow and choose **Custom**.

The Custom LCD display appears, with a MIDI input activity monitor that shows incoming MIDI events in more detail.

8   Hold down a key on your MIDI keyboard.

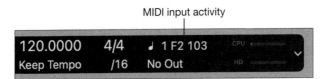

A note icon indicates that the event received is a MIDI note on event. The following values are the note's MIDI channel number, pitch, and velocity. In the previous image, the note's MIDI channel is *1*, its pitch is *F2*, and its velocity is *103*.

NOTE ▶ MIDI events can be sent on up to 16 different MIDI channels, which allows you to control different timbres on different channels when using multi-timbral instruments.

9 Release the key on your MIDI keyboard.

Depending on your controller, in the LCD display, you may see a note on event with a velocity of zero, or you may see a note with a strike through it, which represents a note off event.

NOTE ▸ Pressing and releasing a key on a MIDI keyboard sends two events: a note on event and a note off event. In its MIDI editors, Logic Pro represents the two events as a single note event with a length attribute.

You could start recording a piano part now, but first let's open the Piano Roll so that you can watch the MIDI notes appear on the grid as they are recorded.

10 In the control bar, click the **Editors** button, and at the top of the Editors pane, ensure that **Piano Roll** is selected (or press P).

The Piano Roll opens at the bottom of the main window.

11 Position the playhead at the beginning of the project and click the **Record** button (or press R).

The LCD display and the playhead turn red to indicate that Logic Pro is recording. The playhead jumps back one bar, giving you a four-beat count-in, and you can hear the metronome.

12 When the playhead appears, play quarter notes for a couple of bars to record a very simple bass-line melody on the piano.

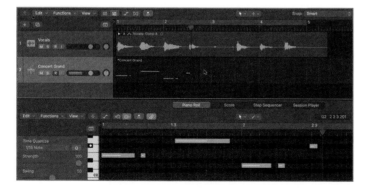

When you play the first note, a red MIDI region appears on the record-enabled track. The region's length continually updates to include the most recent MIDI event received.

The MIDI notes appear in the Piano Roll and on the region in the workspace as you record them.

13 Stop recording.

The region is now shaded green. It is named Concert Grand. You can see the recorded notes in the Piano Roll.

TIP ▶ To see all the notes in the Piano Roll, make sure they are all unselected and press Z.

14 In the Piano Roll at the upper left of the Concert Grand region, click the small **Play** button.

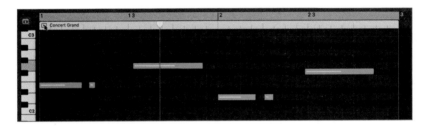

The MIDI region plays in solo and Cycle mode. If you are not happy with your performance, you can undo it (Command-Z) and try again.

If you are mostly happy but one or two notes need correction, you can quickly fix them in the Piano Roll:

▶   Drag a note vertically to change its pitch.

▶   Drag a note horizontally to change its timing.

▶   Click a note and press Delete to remove it.

▶   Select notes and in the local inspector, click the Q button (or press Q) to correct their timing.

MORE INFO ▶ You'll learn how to edit MIDI events in more detail in Lesson 9.

TIP ▶ If you want to keep a performance you played while Logic Pro was not recording, click Stop and press Shift-R (Capture as Recording). A MIDI region containing your last performance is created on the track.

You've recorded MIDI notes into a MIDI region to trigger a software instrument and learned the basics of editing the notes in Piano Roll. You can use the same recording techniques you used earlier to record MIDI, but as you'll see, you won't always get the same results as when recording audio.

Merge Recordings and Record Takes

In Logic Pro, when recording MIDI events on top of an existing MIDI region, you can choose to merge the new recording with the existing MIDI region.

In the previous exercise, you recorded a simple bass-line onto a piano track. Now you'll record chords as you listen to your bass line, merging the new chords with that bass line inside the same MIDI region. When recording over an existing MIDI region, the default behavior is to merge the new notes with the existing region on the track. Then you'll change your settings to record takes into a take folder, the same behavior you experienced earlier on audio tracks.

1   Move the playhead to the beginning and start recording.

This time, play only a couple of chords that complement the bass line you previously recorded.

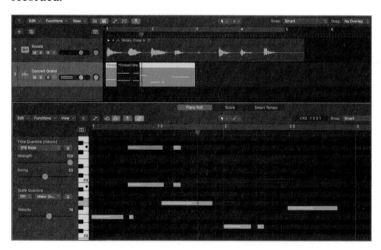

2   Stop recording.

3   If needed, zoom out to see all your notes.

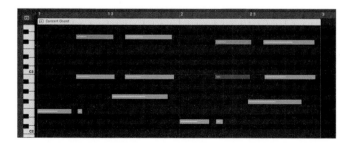

In the Concert Grand region, the chords you just recorded are merged with the bass notes that you recorded in the previous exercise.

Now let's try to record take folders.

4   Choose **Logic Pro** > **Settings** > **Recording**.

You can change the behavior independently for MIDI and Audio overlapping recordings, depending on whether Cycle mode is on or off.

5   Under MIDI, click the **Cycle Off** pop-up menu, and choose **Create Take Folder**.

6   Close the Settings window.

7   Move the playhead to the beginning and start recording a new piano melody.

8   Stop recording.

A take folder is created. Logic Pro records your new performance as a new take while the previous take is muted. Feel free to open the MIDI take folder, select the desired take, and listen to your project.

9   Choose **File** > **Save** (or press Command-S).

10   Choose **File** > **Close Project** (or press Option-Command-W).

The various settings for overlapping recordings for both MIDI and audio provide a lot of flexibility. For example, try the Merge preference for overlapping MIDI recordings in Cycle mode to record a drum kit, one drum kit piece at a time for each pass of the cycle (first the kick, then the snare, then the hi-hat, and so on).

Key Commands

Keyboard Shortcuts	Description
Recording	
R	Starts recording
Q	Quantizes selected MIDI notes
Command-Control-Option-P	Toggles Autopunch mode
Option-Command-click the ruler	Toggles Autopunch mode
Key Command Assignments	
Option-K	Opens the Key Command Assignments window
Project Audio Browser	
F	Opens or closes the Browser pane
Shift-U	Selects unused audio files
macOS dialogs	
esc	Cancels the dialog
Windows	
Command-K	Opens or closes the Musical Typing window
P	Opens or closes the Piano Roll

5

Lesson Files	None
Time	This lesson takes approximately 50 minutes to complete.
Goals	Create a new project with a Drummer track
	Preview Session Player presets
	Choose a drummer type and style
	Edit the Drummer performance in the Session Player Editor
	Select preset patterns and create custom patterns
	Convert Drummer regions to MIDI regions
	Create, name, and color markers for song sections

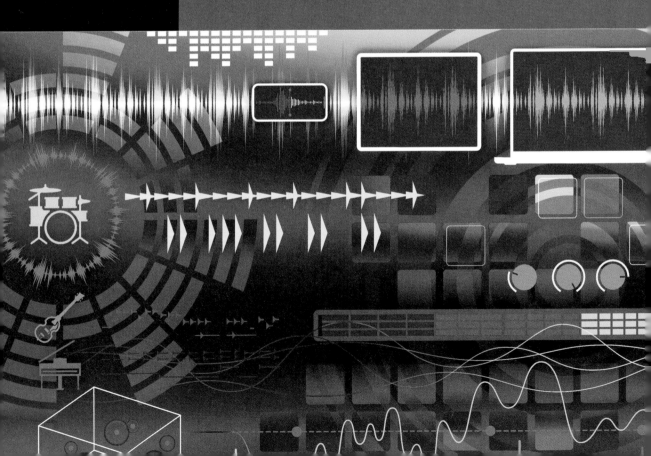

Lesson 5

Create a Virtual Drum Track

In most popular modern-music genres, drums form the backbone of the instrumentation. They provide the foundation for the tempo and groove of the piece, and they are often recorded or programmed first so they can provide a rhythmic reference for the other musicians to listen to when they record their instrument.

In Logic Pro, you can leverage the virtual Session Players to quickly lay out a drum track. You can choose which kit pieces the Drummer plays, how busy or how hard to play, how many fills to add, and so on. It's almost like communicating with a real drummer to detail the style of playing you need for your song.

In this lesson, you'll edit and arrange Session Player regions that contain a variety of drum performances to lay the foundations for a new song that you will continue to build in the following lessons.

Select a Drummer Style

To get started, you'll create a *Session Player track*, which is a software instrument track where you arrange Session Player regions. You'll then select a style for the performances contained in these regions in the Session Player Editor pane at the bottom of the main window.

Create a Session Player Track with a Drummer Region

Let's open a new project, add a Drummer track, and examine the display of the drum performance in the Drummer region.

1   Choose **File** > **New** (or press Command-Shift-N).

2   In the Create New Track dialog, click the **Session Player** button and make sure **Drummer** is selected.

In the Drummer Style pop-up menu, keep Pop Rock selected. You'll change the style later.

3   Click **Create** (or press Return).

A software instrument track (SoCal) is created along with an 8-bar Session Player region (Drummer - Pop Rock). In the inspector, the *SoCal* patch (a drum kit patch that uses the Drum Kit Designer software instrument) is loaded on the SoCal channel strip.

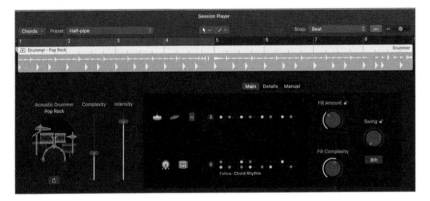

At the bottom of the main window, the Session Player Editor opens, allowing you to edit the performance contained in the selected Session Player region.

At the top of the main window in the LCD display, the project tempo is set to *110 bpm*, which suits the pop rock music genre.

4   Press the **Space** bar to listen to the Session Player region.

The Drummer plays a straightforward rock pattern—a simple drum fill in the middle of the region (before bar 4) and a second, more complex fill at the end.

Let's take a closer look at the Session Player region.

5   In the workspace, **Control-Option**-drag around the first bar of the Session Player region.

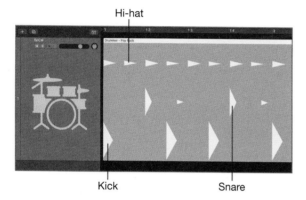

The Drummer region displays drum hits as triangles on lanes, roughly emulating the look of drum hits on an audio waveform. Kicks are shown on the bottom lane, snares are shown on the middle lane, and cymbals are shown on the top lane. When toms or hand percussions are used, they're on the top lane along with the cymbals.

To create a cycle range of the desired length, you can drag the ruler horizontally.

6   In the upper-half of the ruler, drag from bar 1 to bar 2.

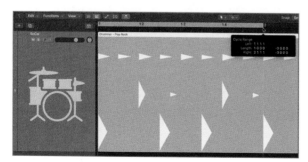

A cycle range is created for the section you drag, and Cycle mode is turned on.

7 Listen to the first bar a few times while looking at the drum hits in the Session Player region.

Although you cannot edit individual drum hits in the Session Player region, the region display gives you a quick glance at the Drummer's performance.

8 Click the cycle area to turn off Cycle mode.

9 Press **Z** to zoom out so that you can see the entire Session Player region.

10 Choose **File > Save** (or press Command-S) to save your song with a name and in a location of your choice.

Remember to save your work at regular intervals throughout this lesson. You'll continue working on this file in the next lessons.

Now, you can read the Drummer region. In the next exercise, you'll listen to presets in different styles. Later, you'll watch the pattern update in the Drummer region as you adjust its settings in the Drummer Editor.

Choose Styles and Presets

When you select a style in the Session Player Editor, Logic Pro loads the software instrument patch that is best suited for that genre. Let's preview a few styles and presets and select one that works for your song.

1 In the Session Player Editor, click the little **Play** button at the upper left of the Drummer - Pop Rock region.

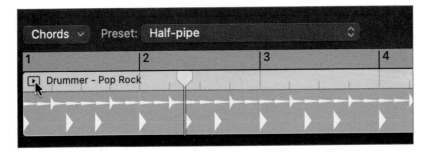

The region starts playing in Solo and Cycle modes.

Throughout this lesson, continue to stop and start playback as needed to hear the results of your adjustments. Now that the Session Player has key focus, you can press Option-Space bar to toggle this Play button.

2   In the Session Player Editor menu bar, click the **Preset** pop-up menu and choose **Mixtape**.

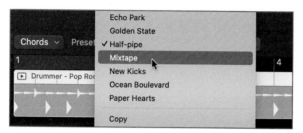

In the Session Player Editor, the knobs and sliders adjust to reflect the values of the preset, and in the Session Player region, the performance updates.

The Drummer plays a busier groove with a ride cymbal, more kicks, and more ghost notes on the snare (*ghost notes* are lower volume syncopated notes that add a subtle rhythmic feel around the stronger notes).

3   In the Session Player Editor, click the **Session Player** button.

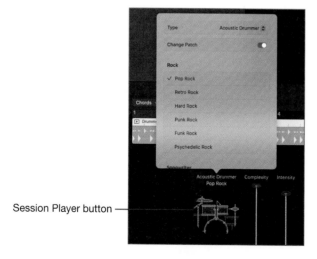

Session Player button

The Session Player dialog opens. You can change the type of Session Player and select a style. The styles displayed depend on the type of player selected. For the Acoustic Drummer type, you can select styles from four main categories: Rock, Songwriter, Alternative, and R&B.

TIP ▶ To keep the current patch when selecting a new style, disable the Change Patch switch.

4   In the Session Player dialog, click the **Type** pop-up menu and choose **Electronic Drummer**.

In the Session Player dialog, the style categories update to Electronic, Hip Hop, and Alternative.

5   In the Hip-hop category, select **Modern Hip Hop**.

In the inspector, the patch associated with that style (Platinum Cuts) is loaded to the track's channel strip. That patch uses DMD (Drum Machine Designer), and the Drummer plays a swung, half-time hip hop groove played on a drum machine. In the Session Player Editor, the controls update to display electronic drum parameters.

The project tempo is set to *95 bpm*.

NOTE ▶ In the LCD display, if the tempo does not automatically update when you choose a style, double-click the tempo value to enter the desired tempo.

Feel free to explore more Session Player types, styles, and presets before moving on.

6   Select the **Acoustic Drummer** type and the **Funk Rock** style.

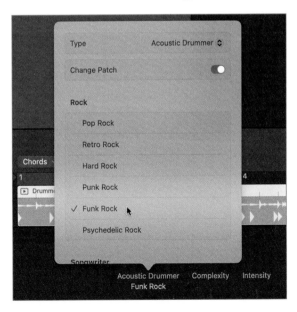

The Smash patch is loaded on the track. The Drummer plays an energetic funky groove on a powerful drum kit. In the LCD display, the tempo is set to *95 bpm*.

You have found a Drummer that plays the funky groove you want for this project on a punchy-sounding drum kit and set a tempo that works well for the genre. You're now ready to customize the performance.

Edit Session Player Regions

In the Session Player Editor, editing a performance is almost like communicating to a real musician the parts you want them to play. For each Session Player region, you select preset patterns (or create your own) and adjust various parameters. Then the Drummer produces a performance that follows your instructions.

Adjust the Drum Fills and Select a Hi-Hat Pattern

In this exercise, you'll ask the Drummer to rein in the energy, stop playing fills, and hit the ghost notes harder on the snare to accentuate the syncopated groove.

1   In the Session Player Editor, drag the **Fill Amount** knob all the way down to *0%*.

The Drummer no longer plays any drum fills. Let's select a new hi-hat pattern.

2   Next to the **hi-hat Kit Piece** button, click the **Pattern** button.

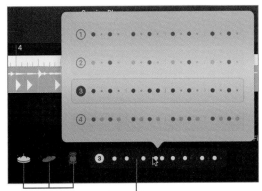

Kit Piece buttons   Pattern button

In the Patterns dialog, patterns are represented on a grid of dots grouped as four beats of four sixteenth notes each. These dots show a rough idea of what the Drummer may play depending on other settings such as the Complexity slider.

Pattern 2 shows that the hi-hat plays every eighth note but the dots on the beat are dimmer while the dots on the upbeats are darker, indicating that the Drummer will accent the upbeats.

3   In the Patterns dialog, click pattern **2**.

The hi-hat plays eighth notes, and the Drummer accents the upbeat. Let's listen to the hi-hat in isolation.

4   Click both the **kick** and **snare Kit Piece** buttons.

Follow: Chord Rhythm

The kick and snare Kit Piece buttons are dimmed to indicate that they are muted. Inside the region, only the hi-hat notes remain in the top lane, and you can clearly hear the hi-hat groove. It sounds like a disco beat, which will work great for this song.

5   Click the **kick** and **snare Kit Piece** buttons to unmute them.

Next to the kick and snare Kit Piece buttons, you can choose a pattern for the kick and snare. In the next exercise, you'll create your own custom pattern.

Create a Custom Pattern

To really make this drum groove your own, you'll now create a custom pattern, clicking steps on rows to sequence the kick and the snare individually.

1   In the Session Player Editor, click the **Manual** button.

You can create individual kick and snare patterns on two rows of 16 steps.

2   On the kick row, click the first and third steps, and on the snare row, click the first step of beat 2.

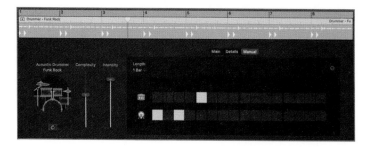

The Drummer plays the pattern you've started to create. On the Session Player region, you can see the kick and snare notes match the steps you've turned on.

3   On the kick row, turn on the fourth step of beat 3 and the second step of beat 4. On the snare row, turn on the first step of beat 4.

The Drummer keeps repeating your custom 1-bar pattern. To add variety, let's turn your pattern into a 2-bar pattern and switch things up in bar 2.

4   Click the **Length** pop-up menu and choose **2 Bars**.

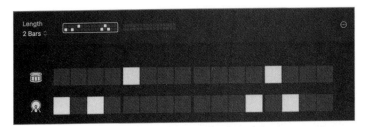

Next to the Length pop-up menu, two overviews appear for the two bars.

5   Click the overview of bar 2 (which is currently empty).

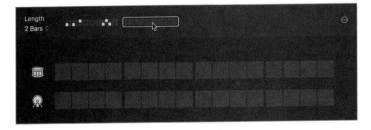

Let's turn on steps in bar 2 to complete the pattern.

6   On the kick row, click the following steps:

▶   beat 1, step 1

▶   beat 3, step 3

7 On the snare row, click the following steps:

▶ beat 2, step 1

▶ beat 4, steps 1, 3, and 4

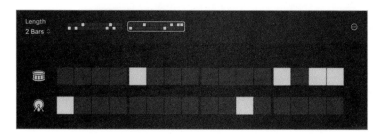

Now, you have a unique kick and snare pattern. Let's make the Drummer play a bit more and hit the drums a little harder.

8 Drag the **Complexity** slider so it's about three quarters up and drag the **Intensity** slider all the way up.

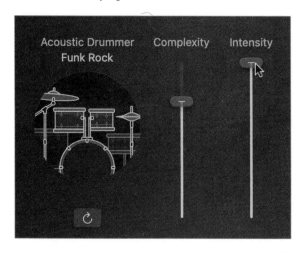

The difference is subtle, but the Drummer now plays some sixteenth notes on the hi-hat and plays slightly louder.

TIP ▶ To compare the results before and after changing a parameter in the Session Player Editor, press Command-Z to undo, and then press Shift-Command-Z to redo.

9 Click the **Details** button and drag the **Dynamics** knob all the way down.

Reducing the dynamic results in less volume difference between the stronger and the softer notes. The ghost notes on the snare are now louder, and the syncopation they create is accentuated.

You've created your own unique custom pattern that will form the basis of the groove used for your song. In the following exercises, you'll create, edit, and arrange a few more Session Player regions to complete the drum track.

Arrange the Drum Track

To continue arranging your drum track, you'll create more Session Player regions to add sections to your song and continue editing their performance to produce different drum grooves for each section.

Create the Intro

To create an intro, you'll create a copy of the Session Player regions in the workspace and edit the first copy to create an intro.

1 Choose **Edit** > **Repeat** > **Once** (or press Command-R).

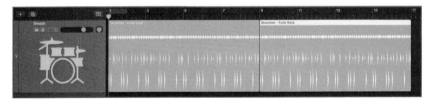

In the workspace, a copy of the Session Player region is created at bar 9.

2 Click the first Session Player region at bar 1.

The region is selected, and you can edit it in the Session Player Editor.

3   Drag the **Complexity** and **Intensity** sliders all the way down.

The Drummer is much quieter in this new intro, playing *side sticks* (hitting the rim of the snare to create a softer sound, almost like a woodblock). At bar 7, the Drummer switches back to hitting the center of the snare and progressively raises the intensity to reach the level required to play the second region at bar 9.

Let's use the Marquee tool (your Command-click tool) to split the first region into two regions of equal lengths so you can make the performance evolve during the intro.

4   Command-double-click at bar 5.

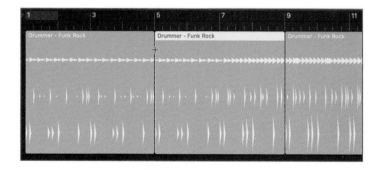

The region splits in two. Let's edit the first region's custom pattern.

5   Click the region at bar 1 to select it.

6   In the Session Player Editor, click the **Manual** button.

7   Click the **Length** pop-up menu and choose **4 Bars**.

To the right of the Length pop-up menu, four overviews allow you to access the 16 steps in each one of the four bars.

8   At the upper right, click the action menu and choose **Reset**.

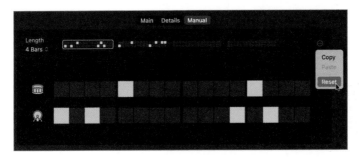

The kick and snare rows are emptied. To start the song, you'll create a simple pattern without kick drum.

9   In the snare row, in each of the four bars, click the first steps of beats 1 and 2.

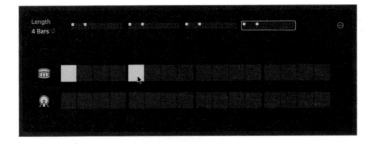

10 In bar 4, beat 4, click steps 1, 3, and 4.

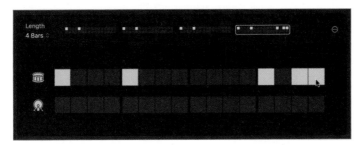

11 Click the **Details** button.

12 Drag the **Ghost Notes** knob all the way up to *100%*.

The Drummer plays many more side-stick notes, which adds complexity to this part of the intro. Let's make the hi-hat ring a little more.

13 Click the **Hi-Hat** pop-up menu and choose **Open**.

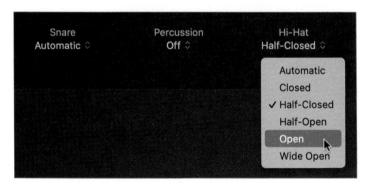

Now you'll work on the second part of the intro.

14 Click the second region at bar 5.

At bar 7, the Drummer starts playing regular snare hits; however, you want to keep side sticks throughout the entire intro.

15 Click the **Details** button.

16 Click the **Snare** pop-up menu and choose **Side Stick**.

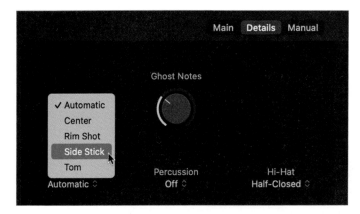

Now the Drummer plays the side stick throughout the entire intro. Let's add some shaker to this second half of the intro.

17 Click the **Percussion** pop-up menu and choose **Shaker 3**.

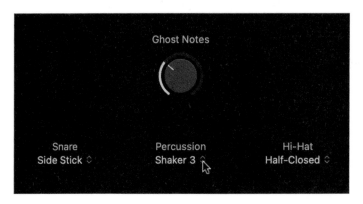

The shaker is very quiet; let's turn it up.

18 In the control bar, click the **Smart Controls** button (or press B).

19 In the Smart Controls pane, turn up the **Percussion** knob to about 3 o'clock.

You can now better hear the shaker, which adds a nice texture to this second part of the intro.

TIP For more control over the sound of your drums and the effects used to process them, open the plug-ins on the Smash channel strip in the inspector.

You've used the Session Player Editor to adjust the complexity and intensity of the Drummer's playing. You've selected different drum kit pieces, added hand percussions, and adjusted the number of fills and ghost notes in different regions. Now that you have a good grasp on the Session Player Editor, you'll add a few more regions to continue building the drum track.

Create Markers for Song Sections

To make it easier to navigate the arrangement and identify song sections, you'll create markers for the intro and verse you've already created as well as for the remaining sections you'll create later.

1 At the top of the track headers, click the **Global Tracks** button (or press G).

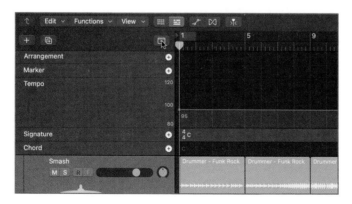

The global tracks open. You need to see only the Marker track.

2 **Control**-click a global track header and choose **Configure Global Tracks** (or press Option-G).

3 Turn on **Show Single Track** and select **Marker**.

To create markers for the existing song sections, you can drag your regions into the Marker track.

4 Click the **Smash** track header (or press Command-A).

All the regions on the track are selected.

5 Drag the selected regions to the **Marker** track.

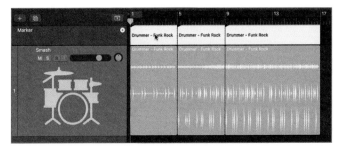

Three markers are created. They have the same color and name as the regions you dragged. Let's create more markers for the remaining song sections.

6 Click the background (or press Shift-D) to deselect the markers.

You can copy and resize markers in the Marker track the same way you edit regions in the workspace.

7 In the Marker track, **Option**-drag the marker from bar 9 to bar 17.

8 Resize this new marker so it's 4 bars long.

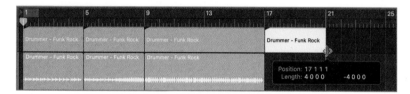

9 **Option**-drag this new 4 bar-long marker to bar 21.

10 **Option**-drag this last marker to bar 25.

11 Resize this marker at bar 25 to make it 8 bars long.

Now that you have all the markers you need, let's rename them and give them custom colors.

12 Double-click the first marker, enter **Intro 1**, and press **Tab**.

The marker is renamed, and the text field opens on the next marker.

13 Continue this procedure to rename the following markers:

> ▶ Marker at bar 5 = **Intro 2**

> ▶ Marker at bar 9 = **Verse**

> ▶ Marker at bar 17 = **Bridge**

> ▶ Marker at bar 21 = **Rise**

> ▶ Marker at bar 25 = **Outro**

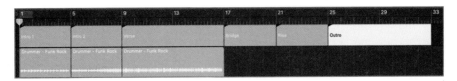

14 Choose **View** > **Show Colors** (or press Option-C).

The Color palette opens.

15 Choose different colors for your markers.

Adding markers helps identify song sections and later will help you navigate the song. Your song structure is now complete, and you are ready to start working on the Bridge, Rise, and Outro sections.

Convert Session Player Regions to MIDI Regions

Now, you'll create a new Session Player region for the bridge. After you start editing the new region and realize that your edits affect how the Drummer plays the verse, you'll convert the verse region to MIDI to prevent it from changing.

1   Position the pointer to the right of the last Session Player region and click the + sign that appears.

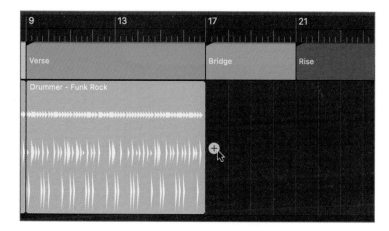

A new 8-bar Session Player region is created at bar 17.

2   Resize the new region to a length of 4 bars.

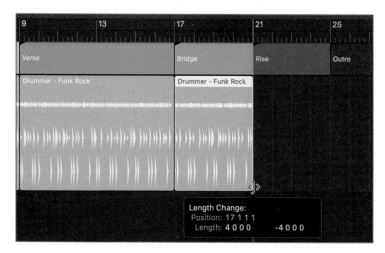

3   Double-click the new 4-bar region (or press E) to open the Session Player Editor.

During this bridge, let's make the Drummer perform a simple and quiet pattern.

4   In the Session Player Editor, drag the **Complexity** slider all the way down.

5   Drag the **Intensity** slider all the way down.

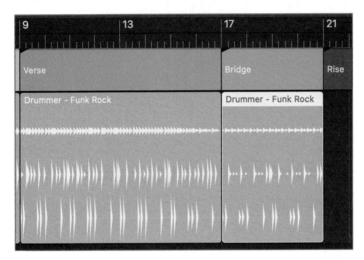

Listen to the transition from the verse to the bridge and look at the regions. At the end of the verse, the Drummer progressively lowers his intensity to ensure a smooth transition to the bridge. However, for this song, you want an abrupt transition from the intense groove in the verse to the quiet bridge.

6   Press **Command-Z**.

The Intensity slider goes back up, and the Drummer performance stays intense until the end of the verse. To prevent that Session Player region in the verse from updating when you edit other regions, you'll convert it to a MIDI region.

7   **Control**-click the region in the verse and choose **Convert** > **Convert to MIDI Region** (or press Control-Option-Command-M).

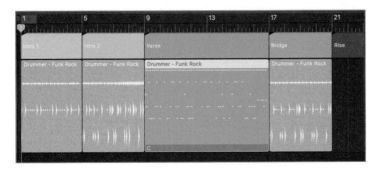

The Session Player region is converted to a MIDI region that plays the same notes. At the bottom of the main window, the Piano Roll shows the MIDI notes inside the region.

8   Click the Session Player region in the bridge to select it.

9   In the Session Player editor, drag the **Intensity** slider all the way down.

Now the Drummer keeps the intensity up throughout the entire verse and suddenly shifts to play a quiet pattern in the bridge.

A Session Player region can sometimes update its performance to adapt to other Session Player regions immediately before or after it on the track. Converting the region to MIDI allows you to keep the performance intact no matter how you edit other regions around it.

Complete the Bridge

Let's continue editing the performance in the bridge to make the Drummer play a softer, more open part and give that section more space.

1   In the Session Player Editor, click the **Main** button.

2   Click the **hi-hat Pattern** button and choose pattern **4**.

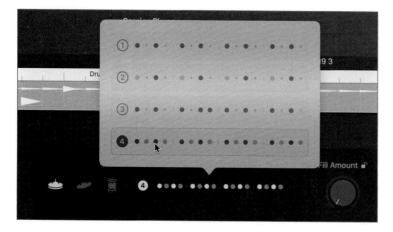

To make this bridge breathe and create an impression of space, you'll remove all ghost notes to make room for the reverb tails of the remaining notes.

3   Click the **Details** button and turn the **Ghost Notes** knob all the way down to *0%*.

Now, you'll make the Drummer play a tom rather than a snare.

4 Click the **Snare** pop-up menu and choose **Tom**.

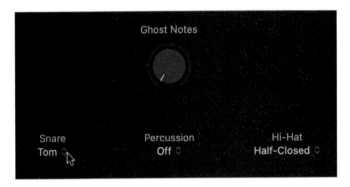

To really give a different color to this bridge, let's add a shaker and close the hi-hat.

5 Click the **Percussion** pop-up menu and choose **Shaker 3**.

6 Click the **Hi-Hat** pop-up menu and choose **Closed**.

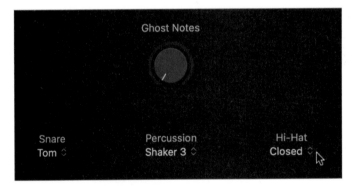

The hi-hat notes no longer ring as much, which leaves more room to hear the shaker. Increasing the volume range between the softer and louder notes will open this quiet section even further.

7 Drag the **Dynamics** knob up to *130%*.

Let's edit the custom pattern to get a simple, straightforward drum beat.

8 Click the **Manual** button.

9 Edit the pattern so that the kick plays beat 1 and 3 and the snare plays beat 2 and 4.

10 In bar 1, beat 1, make the kick play step 3.

You've created a quiet part for your bridge, where the Drummer plays the tom instead of the snare. The pattern is sparser, and a shaker adds texture to this section. All these edits produce a striking contrast with the verse before.

Complete the Rise and Outro Sections

To end the song, you'll make the Drummer switch from the toms back to a snare, and progressively bring the intensity back up.

1 Choose **Edit** > **Repeat** > **Once** (or press Command-R).

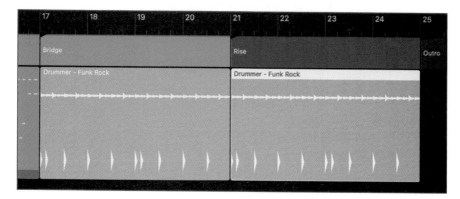

The Session Player in the Bridge section is copied to the Rise section.

2 Drag the **Complexity** slider a third of the way up.

3   Drag the **Intensity** slider halfway up.

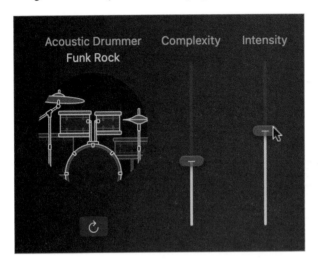

4   Click the **Details** button and set the **Ghost Notes** to *20%*, **Snare** to **Automatic**, and **Percussion** to **Off**.

The Drummer plays a more complex and more intense groove with a regular snare. Let's add a very subtle drum fill at the end of the Rise section.

5   Click the **Main** button and drag the **Fill Amount** knob up to *1%*.

A fill is added at the end of the region; however, it's way too busy.

6 Drag the **Fill Complexity** knob all the way down to *1%*.

Now the Drummer simply hits the toms a couple of times at the end of the region. Let's move on to the Outro section

7 Move the pointer to the right of the last region in the workspace and click the **+** sign.

A new 8-bar region is created with the same subtle fill at the end. To end the song, you'll add a more complex fill.

8 Drag the **Fill Complexity** knob up to *50%*.

TIP ▶ To try different fills, click the Perform Again button, and the Drummer produces a new subtle variation of the performance.

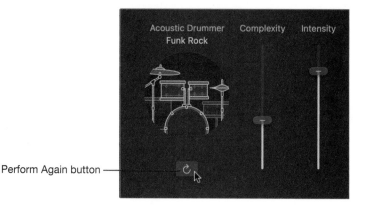

9 Drag the **Intensity** slider almost all the way up.

10 Click the **Details** button and from the **Percussion** pop-up menu, choose **Claps 2**.

The hand claps in this section really help lift the groove and give it a human feel. It almost makes you want to get up and clap along!

Let's add one last Session Player region and make it small to end the drum track on a downbeat.

11 To the right of the region in the Outro section, click the + sign to create a new region.

12 Resize the region to shorten it so that it contains notes only on the first beat.

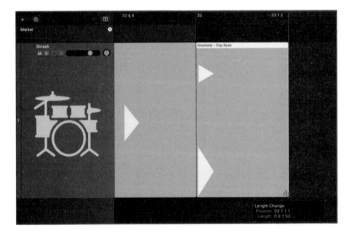

To resize the region, you can pick one of two methods:

▶ Use the Help Tag to make sure the length of the region is *0 0 1 0*.

▶ Work in broad strokes, resizing the region, zooming in, and repeating the operation until you see notes only on the first downbeat.

13 Save your project and keep it open for the next lesson.

You have previewed different drum styles and produced a variety of patterns for the different sections of a funk rock song. With Drummer, Drum Kit Designer, and Drum Machine Designer, Logic Pro allows you to quickly lay down a rhythmic foundation for a wide range of modern music genres. In the next lesson, you'll continue building upon this foundation by adding a bass track to your song.

Key Commands

Keyboard Shortcuts	Description
Tracks area	
G	Toggles the global tracks
Option-G	Opens the Global Tracks Configuration dialog
Control-Option-Command-M	Converts the selected region to MIDI
Command-R	Repeats the selection once
Option-C	Toggles the Color palette

6

Lesson Files	Logic Book Projects > 06 Funky Drums (or continue working from the file you saved at the end of Lesson 5)
Time	This lesson takes approximately 45 minutes to complete.
Goals	Create a Bass Player track
	Preview Bass Player styles
	Edit the Bass Player performance in the Session Player Editor
	Adjust the number of melodic notes, octave jumps, and note lengths
	Adjust dead notes, pickup hits, and slides
	Make the Bass Player follow the rhythm of the Drummer

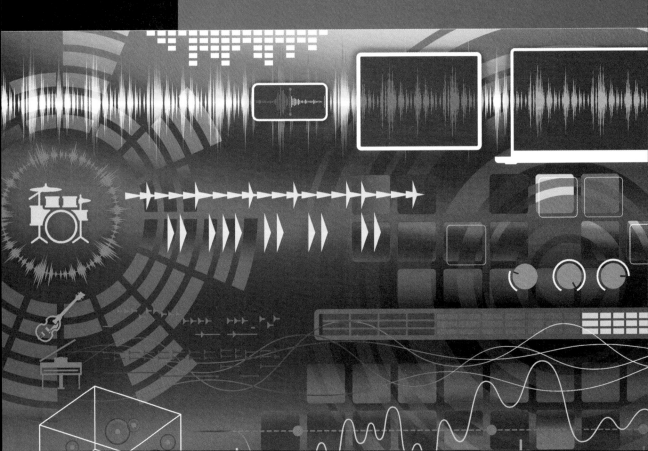

Lesson 6

Create a Virtual Bass Track

In this lesson, you'll create a Bass Player track to go along with the Drummer track that you produced in Lesson 5. The Bass Player can produce nearly any kind of performance, from simple, sustained whole notes playing only the root of the chord, to complex melodies with various percussive effects that can create rhythmic accents in the groove.

Although the Bass Player comes up with the performances, you have control over a vast array of parameters to precisely define the result you're looking for.

Loop Chord Progressions and Preview Bass Player Styles

First, you'll make sure the chord progression you use covers the entire song, and then you'll preview a few bass styles. Different styles can use a variety of playing techniques, such as slapping, playing double stops, and playing with fingers or with a pick. Selecting a style loads the associated bass guitar, amp, and effects in the form of a software instrument patch.

Loop a Chord Progression in the Chord Track

You'll create a Bass Player track along with a default chord progression. In the Chord track, you'll loop the chord progression throughout all the song sections to make sure the Session Player regions you'll create in this lesson all follow those chord changes.

1   To start this first exercise, continue working in the file you saved at the end of Lesson 5 or open Logic Book Projects > **06 Funky Drums**.

2   Choose **Track** > **New Tracks** (or press Option-Command-N).

3   Click the **Session Player** button and click **Bass Player**.

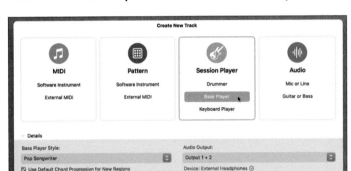

4   In the Details area, keep **Pop Songwriter** selected in the **Bass Player Style** pop-up menu and keep **Use Default Chord Progression for New Regions** selected.

5   Click **Create** (or press Return).

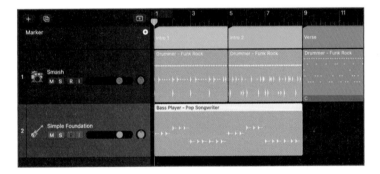

A new software instrument track is created with an 8-bar Session Player region at bar 1. The Simple Foundation bass patch is loaded onto the channel strip.

6   Press the **Space** bar.

The bass repeats one note for the first bar, another for the second bar, a third note for bars 3 and 4, and then repeats that line in the Intro 2 section. Let's look at the Chord track.

7   Stop playback.

8   **Control**-click the Marker track header and choose **Configure Global Tracks** (or press Option-G).

9   In the Global Tracks Configuration dialog, select **Chord Track**.

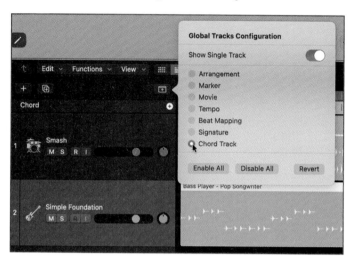

10   Click outside the dialog to close it.

In the Chord track, you see the default C, D minor, and A minor chord progression that you heard the bass line follow. Let's loop that chord progression.

11   In the Chord track at bar 9, bring the pointer to the upper-right edge of the chord progression to get the Loop tool and drag to bar 34.

The chord progression now keeps looping for the entire song.

12   **Control**-click the Chord track header and choose **Configure Global Tracks** (or press Option-G).

13   Select **Marker Track** and click outside the dialog to close it.

Remember to save your work at regular intervals throughout this lesson. You'll continue working on this file in the next lessons.

You've created a new Session Player track for your bass, and you briefly opened the Chord track to loop the default chord progression throughout your song. In Lesson 8, you'll explore the Chord track further and create your own chord progressions.

Preview Bass Player Styles

Let's listen to different styles. As with Drummer, selecting a style loads the associated bass patch on the track. To preview different bass styles, you'll work in the verse.

1   Drag the Bass Player region to the verse.

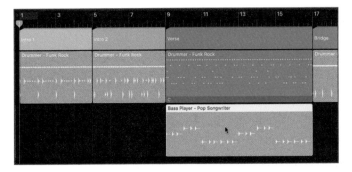

2   Choose **Navigate > Set Rounded Locators by Selection and Enable Cycle** (or press U).

The cycle area matches the Verse section. From now on, use the Space bar to toggle playback when you want to hear the drums and the bass play together. The bass plays a simple pattern with three notes per bar.

3   In the Session Player Editor menu bar, click the **Presets** pop-up menu and choose **Fleeting Glances**.

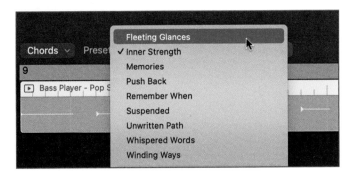

The Bass Player plays more notes over a greater pitch range and reaches higher notes.

4   From the **Presets** pop-up menu, choose **Whispered Words**.

The Bass Player plays *double-stops* (two notes at a time).

5   Click the **Session Player** button.

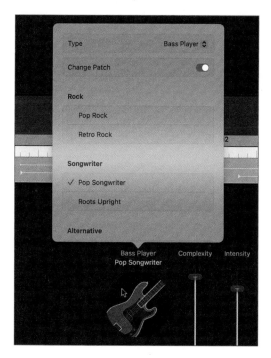

The Session Player dialog opens.

6   In the **Rock** category, select **Retro Rock**.

After a moment, the Session Player region updates, and the Rock Legend patch is loaded on the track. The bass sounds like it's distorted through a tube amp.

7   In the Session Player dialog, select **Disco Slap**.

The Bass Player uses a slapping technique, striking the strings against the fretboard to get a percussive sound. Take a moment to explore more styles and presets. When you're ready, let's select a style that will go along with your funk rock drum groove.

8   In the Session Player dialog, select **Indie Disco**.

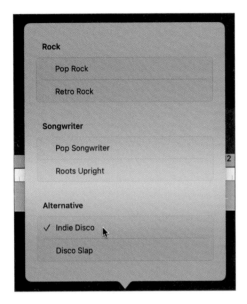

The Bass Player plays a syncopated bass line with staccato notes that works perfectly with your drums.

You've previewed a few of the styles that the Session Player Editor has to offer. The styles span a vast array of genres and bass playing techniques, as well as bass sounds that can suit many of your music productions.

Edit and Arrange Bass Player Regions

Editing Bass Player regions in the Session Player Editor is similar to editing Drummer regions, only some of the parameters are specific to bass-line arranging and bass-playing techniques. For example, you can vary melodic elements (play higher or lower notes, keep playing the root note, play more notes in the scale, or even add octave jumps) and carefully calibrate playing techniques (slides, dead notes, pickup hits, and more).

Edit the Bass Player Performance

Let's start fine-tuning your bass line. To quickly return any knob or slider to its default value, you can Option-click it.

1 **Option**-click the **Complexity** slider.

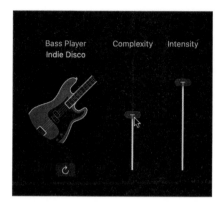

The Complexity slider jumps to a value that's almost halfway up.

2 Drag the **Intensity** slider up all the way.

Although the difference is subtle, the Bass Player plays just a bit louder. There are fills in the middle and end of the region, but they're a bit too much for this song.

3 Drag the **Fill Amount** knob all the way down to *0%*.

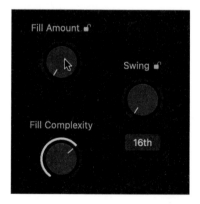

The fills disappear. The bass line is composed of only the root note of each chord in the Chord track, played in different octaves, but you'll make the Bass Player be more adventurous.

4 Click the **Melody** pop-up menu and choose **Some Notes**.

The bass line is a little more melodic. Let's reduce the number of octave jumps.

5   Click the **Octaves** pop-up menu and choose **Some**.

Now that you have a solid bass line, you can fine-tune more subtle playing technique nuances that will elevate the performance even more. To focus on those details, let's solo the bass.

6   On the Dancefloor track header, click the **S** (Solo) button (or press S).

Some of the bass notes are muted so that you hear only the percussive attack part but no pitch. These notes are called dead notes (or ghost notes), and they contribute to add a syncopated groove to the bass line.

7   In the Session Player Editor, click the **Details** button.

8   Drag the **Dead Notes** knob all the way down to *0%*.

Only non-muted, pitched notes remain. The groove suffers from the lack of dead notes, and you'll dial them back later. But first, let's try another percussive technique.

9   Click the **Pickup Hits** button.

The Bass Player uses a flat hand to hit the strings against the pickups to make percussive sounds. The pickup hits are placed on beat 2 and beat 4—the same beats where drummers usually play the snare.

10   Drag the **Dead Notes** knob up to *91%*.

The pickup hits and the syncopated dead notes both help the bass line really groove.

11 On the Dancefloor track header, click the **S** button (or press S).

You've helped the Bass Player come up with a solid groove for your verse that plays along nicely with your drums. To complete the song, you'll create more Session Player regions and edit them to give each section its own bass line.

Edit the Intro

To start working on the intro, you'll copy the verse region to bar 1 and edit that copy to create a softer, quieter bass line that plays sustained notes in a higher pitch range.

1 **Option**-drag the Session Player in the verse to bar 1.

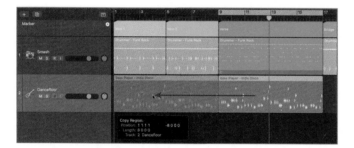

2 Press **U**.

The cycle area matches the new region at bar 1. Let's first edit this 8-bar region. You'll split it in two later to fine-tune the Intro 1 and Intro 2 sections individually.

3 In the Session Player Editor, drag the **Complexity** slider all the way down.

4 Drag the **Intensity** slider so that it's halfway up.

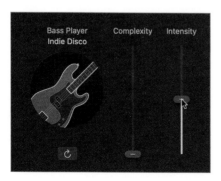

Apart from a few dead notes, the Bass Player plays only one note per bar, and the notes are rather short.

5   Click the **Main** button.

6   Click the **Phrasing** pop-up menu and choose **Long**.

The sustained notes now fill the intro nicely. Let's make the Bass Player play higher notes.

7   Drag the **Lowest Note** slider all the way up to C3.

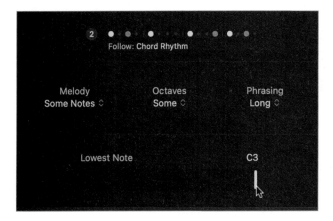

You'll make the bass line a little more engaging by adding only a few notes.

8   Drag the **Complexity** slider up slightly and wait for the Bass Player region overview to update. The slider needs to come up just enough that a single high note appears at the end of bar 1.

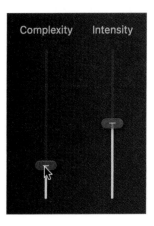

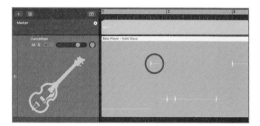

If necessary, drag the Complexity up or down by small amounts (or click the Perform Again button) until you get only one new high note at the end of bar 1. After you've achieved that, let's make the Bass Player slide from the first note into that high note.

9   Click the **Details** button.

10   Drag the **Slides** knob all the way up to *100%*.

The Bass Player adds more slides to the playing, which really helps draw attention during this intro. Now let's make the bass line evolve in the Intro 2 section.

11   In the workspace, Command-double-click the Session Player region at bar 5.

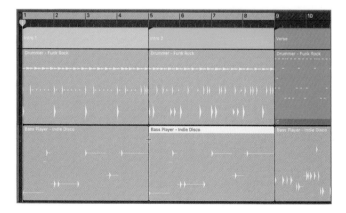

The Session Player region is split in two, and the region in Intro 2 is selected, ready to be edited.

12 In the Session Player editor, drag the **Lowest Note** slider down to *E2*.

13 Drag the **Fill Amount** knob up to *28%*.

14 Click the **Peform Again** button until you get a fill that you like at the end of bar 8.

The sustained sliding notes create a captivating intro, and making the bass play higher notes leaves the listener craving more. When the main bass line finally kicks in at the beginning of the verse, the strong contrast with the intro produces a compelling effect.

Edit the Bridge

Now that you've established a strong groove during the verse, let's tone things down in the bridge to create a lot of space before bringing the energy back up in the outro.

1 On the Dancefloor track, click the + sign after the Session Player region in the verse.

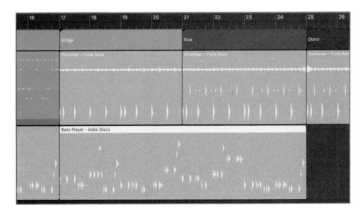

A new 8-bar Session Player region is created at bar 17, and the new region is selected.

2   Press **U**.

The cycle area matches the selected region.

3   In the Session Player editor, drag the **Complexity** slider all the way down.

4   Drag the **Intensity** slider all the way down.

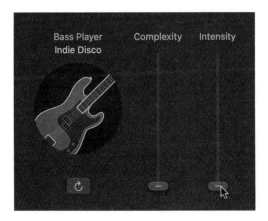

Now that you have a much simpler pattern, you can make the notes sustain more.

5   Click the **Phrasing** pop-up menu and choose **Long**.

This works great to bring the energy level down during this section. You could use a little melodic movement.

6   Drag the **Fill Amount** knob to *68%*.

The Bass Player keeps playing mostly whole notes while adding a few melodic fills in a couple of places in the region. Let's make the fills a bit richer.

7   Drag the **Fill Complexity** knob all the way up to *100%*.

Now to start the bridge quietly, let's make sure there are no fills in the first bar. You'll use the Marquee tool to split that first bar into a new region.

8 On the Dancefloor track, Command-drag the first bar of the Bridge region from bar 17 to bar 18.

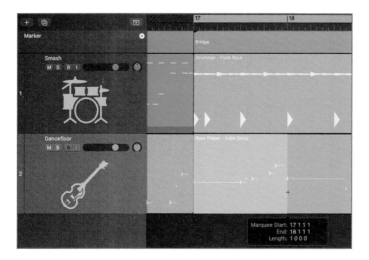

9 Click the marquee selection with the Pointer tool.

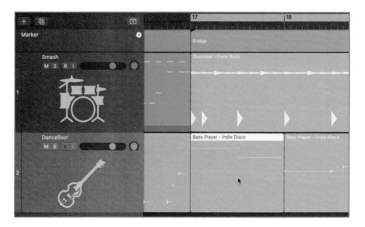

The marquee selection is split into a new 1-bar region, and that region is selected.

10 In the Session Player Editor, drag the **Fill Amount** knob all the way down to *0%*.

In bar 17, the Bass Player plays only one sustained high note with a slide. Let's transpose the note down.

11 Drag the **Lowest Note** slider all the way down to *B0*.

Coming off a powerful verse, that note appears a bit quiet, so let's turn it up.

12 Drag the **Intensity** slider a quarter of the way up.

For the bass to sound tight with the drums in the rest of the bridge, let's make the Bass Player performance follow the rhythm of the Smash track (your drum track).

13 In the workspace, click the 7-bar region at bar 18 to select it.

14 In the Session Player Editor, click the **Pattern** button.

15 Under Follow Rhythm Of, click the **Track** pop-up menu and choose **Smash**.

Some of the bass notes move to play in time with the notes in the Drummer region on track 1, and the bass and drums sync up.

You created a quiet bass line for your bridge, based on whole notes along with a few melodic fills. Making the bass follow the rhythm of the drum track ensures that the rhythm section is locked in.

Edit the Outro

To end the song in beauty, you'll make the Bass Player come up with a busier, more melodic bass line, with a groove similar to the one you used for the verse.

1   On the Dancefloor track, click the + sign after the Session Player region in the Rise section.

    A new 8-bar region is created in the outro, and the region is selected.

2   Press **U**.

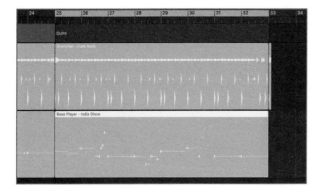

    The cycle area matches the selected region.

3   In the Session Player region, drag the **Complexity** slider up to a third of its range.

4   Drag the **Intensity** halfway up.

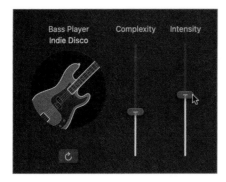

This busier bass line will groove more if the Bass Player plays slightly shorter notes.

5 Click the **Phrasing** pop-up menu and choose **Medium**.

Let's add more octave jumps.

6 Click the **Octaves** pop-up menu and choose **More**.

This is the last section of the song, so for a grand finale, let's make the Bass Player play as many notes as possible.

7 Click the **Melody** pop-up menu and choose **Most Notes**.

A few notes are added to the melody. Even if it may not seem like a lot of new notes, this choice will impact new performances the Bass Player comes up with as you further edit the region or click the Perform Again button.

8 Click the **Details** button and drag the **Slides** knob up to *100%*.

9   Click the **Perform Again** button.

Keep clicking the Perform Again button (maybe 10 times) until the Bass Player plays high notes around beat 3 of the outro (25 3).

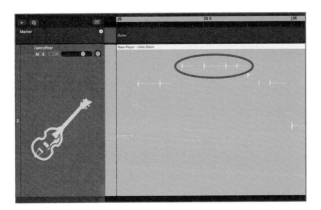

Now let's finish the bass track on a downbeat right after the outro. You'll use the 1-bar region you've created at the beginning of the bridge earlier.

10 **Option**-drag the 1-bar region at the beginning of the bridge (at bar 17) to bar 33.

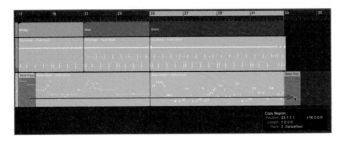

11 Press **C** to turn off Cycle mode and listen to your ending.

The bass and drums play the last note together on the downbeat right after the outro, and the bass notes slides down while the cymbal rings, producing a smoothly executed and musical ending.

12 Save your project and keep it open for the next lesson.

You've produced a bass track that nicely complements the drums, using a variety of bass-line patterns and playing techniques to musically enrich the song. In the next lesson, you'll produce Keyboard Player tracks to further refine your mastery of the Session Players.

Key Commands

Keyboard Shortcuts	Description
Tracks	
S	Solos the selected track

7

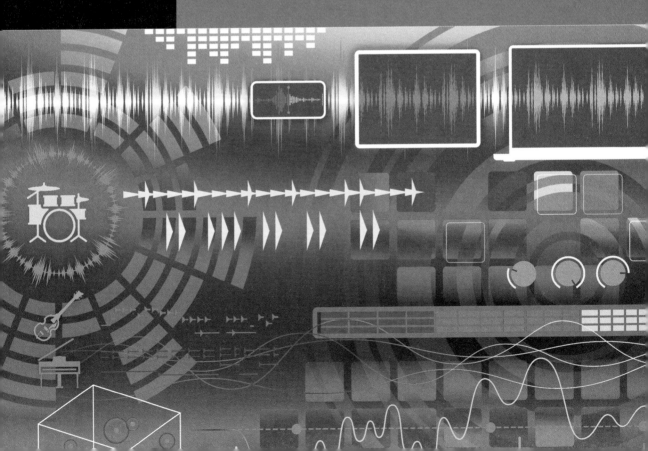

Lesson 7

Create a Virtual Keyboard Track

In Logic Pro, the Session Players generate performances that trigger a software instrument. When you choose a style, an associated patch that is appropriate for that style is loaded on the track. You are, however, free to change the patch to make the Session Player play any instrument you can think of, which can lead to creative results.

To complete your arrangement, you'll use Logic Pro's Keyboard Player to create a couple of different tracks: a piano track and a string section.

Preview Keyboard Player Styles

Let's create a Keyboard Player track and preview all five playing styles, comparing them to the classic keyboard patterns heard in a few popular examples.

To start this first exercise, continue working in the file you saved at the end of the previous lesson, or open Logic Book Projects > **07 Funky Drums and Bass**.

1 Choose **Track** > **New Tracks** (or press Option-Command-N).

2 In the Session Player button, click **Keyboard Player**.

3 Keep the **Keyboard Player Style** pop-up menu set to **Freely** and the **Use Default Chord Progression for New Regions** checkbox selected.

4   Click **Create** (or press Return).

A new software instrument track is created with an 8-bar Session Player region at bar 1. The Studio Grand piano patch is loaded onto the channel strip.

5   Press the **Space** bar.

Chords are already present in the Chord track, so the Session Player region on this new track follows those chords and plays in harmony with the bass.

Let's preview Keyboard Player styles.

6   At the upper left in the Session Player editor, click the **Play** button (or press Option-Space bar).

The Keyboard Player region plays in Solo and Cycle modes.

7   Click the **Session Player** button and select the **Broken Chords** style.

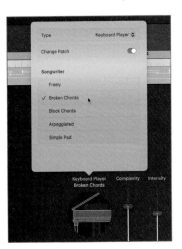

The left hand plays the root of the chord as whole notes while the right-hand alternates chord notes in an eighth-note pattern played on a vintage upright piano. This creates a rhythmic pattern reminiscent of John Lennon's song *Imagine*.

8   In the Session Player dialog, select **Block Chords**.

Now, the right hand repeats whole chords every eighth note, as in the song *Stay* by Rihanna and Mikky Ekko.

9   Click the **Session Player** button and select the **Arpeggiated** style.

The right hand plays the notes of the chords in sequence, one after the other, a little like in *Someone Like You* by Adele.

10   Click the **Session Player** button and select the **Simple Pad** style.

This time the Keyboard Player ditches the piano for a reverberated synth sound and plays sustained chords as whole notes to create a lush atmosphere, like the mellotron string sound during the chorus in David Bowie's *Space Oddity*.

You've previewed a wide range of keyboard playing styles from piano to synths. When previewing Keyboard Player styles, keep a creative mind and imagine the results you could produce if you load another kind of patch from the Library, such as an organ, a mellotron, strings, or even a horn section.

Edit and Arrange Keyboard Player Regions

Now, you'll leverage a range of playing style options to give each song section its own musical identity.

Edit the Intro and the Verse

You'll use a rhythmic broken chord pattern for the verse, and then you'll resize a region so that the Piano Player comes in only in the second half of the intro to play simple whole-note chords.

1   In the Session Player Editor, click the **Session Player** button and choose **Broken Chords**.

On the channel strip in the inspector, the Vintage Upright patch is loaded. The rhythmic pattern of the broken chords works great for your verse, so let's repeat that region.

2 Press **Command-R**.

A copy of the region is created in the verse.

3 Press **U**.

From now on, use the Space bar to toggle playback when you want to hear the drums, bass, and keyboard simultaneously.

This piano performance is good the way it is; you just need a little more energy in this section.

4 In the Session Player Editor, drag the **Intensity** slider almost all the way up.

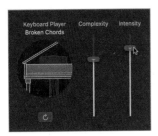

You may see the performance update in the first region on the track (in the Intro 1 and Intro 2 sections). As you've experienced with the Drummer in Lesson 5, editing a Session Player sometimes affects the performance in adjacent Session Player regions.

The piano works perfectly for your verse. When a part sounds right for the song, there's no need to tinker with it endlessly, so let's move on! For the intro, you'll keep only the drums and bass during the first four bars, and make the piano come in at bar 5.

5 In the Intro 1 section, move your pointer to the lower-left corner of the first keyboard region and drag to bar 5 to shorten it.

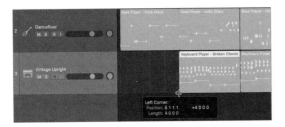

The first Keyboard Player region now covers only the Intro 2 section. For this intro, you'll use whole-note chords like you heard earlier in the Simple Pad style; however, you want to keep the Vintage Upright patch.

6   Click the **Session Player** button.

7   In the Session Player dialog, click the **Change Patch** switch to turn it off.

From now on, selecting a new style will not load its associated patch.

8   Select **Simple Pad**.

9   At the upper left in the Session Player Editor, click **Play** (or press Option-Space bar).

You hear the piano in solo. The Keyboard Player plays whole-note chords. Let's make it play lower bass notes with the left hand.

10 Drag the **Left Hand** slider to the left.

The Keyboard Player plays lower root notes with the left hand.

Remember to save your work at regular intervals throughout this lesson. You'll continue working on this file in the next lesson.

The first half of the intro features the rhythm section alone. The Keyboard Player comes in only in the second half, playing simple whole-note chords, and then moves on to a more rhythmic pattern for the verse.

Edit the Bridge and Rise Sections

For the Bridge and Rise sections, you'll make the Keyboard Player expand the range of notes to achieve a wider tessitura. The left hand will move lower on the keyboard to play deep, mysterious chords, and a bit later, the right hand will move up to make arpeggios reach higher notes.

1   Click the **Keyboard Player** region in the Verse section.

2   Press **Command-R** to repeat it.

3   Press **U**.

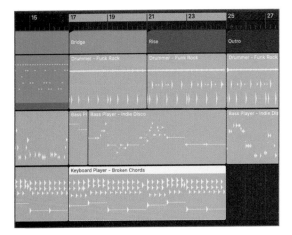

The cycle area covers the Bridge and Rise sections. You'll start by selecting an arpeggio pattern.

4   Click the **Session Player** button and choose **Arpeggiated**.

To fine-tune the arpeggios, let's hear the piano in solo.

5   At the upper left in the Session Player Editor, click **Play** (or press Option-Space bar).
    With the left hand, the Keyboard Player plays a single root note.

6   Click the **Left Hand Voicing** pop-up menu and choose **Root & Octave**.

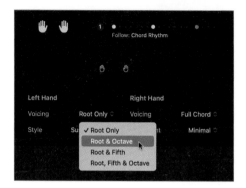

Now the left hand plays octaves, producing a richer sound in the lower range of the
piano. Let's move the right hand a little further up.

7   Drag the **Right Hand** slider up slightly.

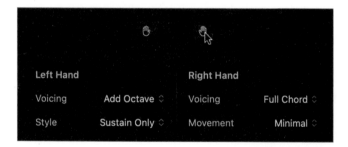

The arpeggios are played on higher keys. Now let's create a custom arpeggio pattern.

8   Click the **Manual** button.

9   Click the following steps:

    ▶   Beat 1, steps 1, 3, and 4

    ▶   Beat 2, steps 1, 3, and 4

    ▶   Beat 3, steps 1, 2, 3, and 4

    ▶   Beat 4, step 4

The arpeggios are really driving this bridge now. If you listen carefully, you might notice that the Keyboard Player is sometimes speeding up or slowing down. You don't need machine-like timing, but this is a little too erratic.

10 Click the **Details** button and drag the **Humanize** knob down to *11%*.

The timing of the performance tightens up. Since the drums and bass leave a lot of room in these two sections, you can let the piano take center stage, so let's turn up the intensity a notch.

11 Drag the **Intensity** slider up to about two thirds of the range.

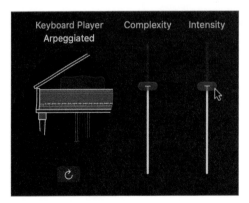

You've created your own custom arpeggio pattern that will form the basis for this section; however, it's a little repetitive. In the next exercise, you'll divide up this Session Player so that you can add variety to the performance.

Split Regions to Fine-Tune the Performance

To make the Bridge and Rise sections evolve, you'll split the region and further edit the parameters of the new, smaller regions to obtain whole-note chords in the bridge, and arpeggios ascending through an expansive range in the Rise section.

1   Command-double-click the region at bar 21.

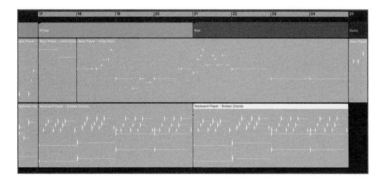

During the bridge, you'll make the Keyboard Player stop playing the arpeggios on the right hand and play only low keys with the left hand.

2   Click the region in the Bridge section to select it.

3   In the Session Player Editor, click the **Right Hand**.

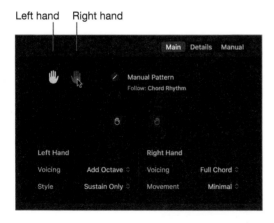

The right hand is muted. The Keyboard Player plays octaves on the left hand. To make the piano sound richer in that section, let's add the fifth.

4   Click the **Left Hand Voicing** pop-up menu, and choose **Root, Fifth & Octave**.

The fifth has a resonant quality that adds depth to the octaves. Now you'll split the last bar of the Rise section into a new region to make the Keyboard Player expand the range of the arpeggios and reach higher up on the keyboard.

5   Command-double-click the Keyboard Player region in the Rise section at bar 24.

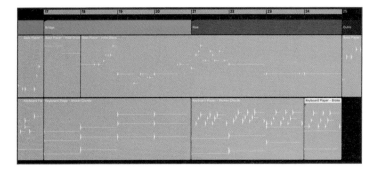

The new 1-bar region is selected. Let's make the arpeggios cover a wide range of keys here.

6   In the Session Player Editor, click the **Movement** pop-up menu and chose **Large Range**.

The Keyboard Player starts playing with a large range at the end of the previous region (in bar 23). Let's make the arpeggios at bar 24 reach even higher.

7   Drag the **Right Hand** slider three increments to the right.

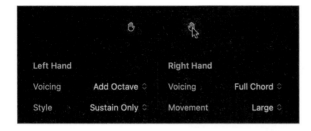

Now the last note of the Rise section has the highest pitch.

With the right hand taking a break, the bridge departs from the rhythmic broken chords in the verse. The sustained lower chords infuse a breath of fresh air before the Rise section where the arpeggios soar, reaching increasingly higher notes.

Edit the Outro

To end the piano track, you'll continue using arpeggios for the outro, add a few fills, and refine the custom pattern to make the Keyboard Player play nearly every sixteenth note.

1   After the last region in the Rise section, click the + sign.

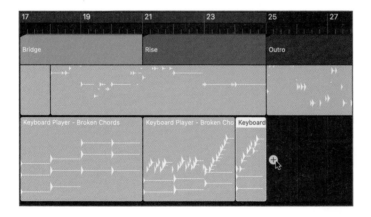

An 8-bar Session Player region is added in the Outro section.

2   Press **U**.

The cycle area matches the Outro marker. Let's make the left hand play a single bass note in a lower register.

3   Click the **Left Hand Voicing** pop-up menu and choose **Root Only**.

4   Drag the **Left Hand** slider a little to the left so the bass notes of the keyboard are played on lower keys.

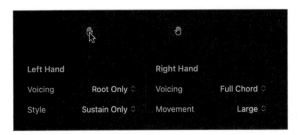

The Keyboard Player's hands are spread further apart, which makes this part take more space. Let's change the voicing of the right hand.

5   Click the **Right Hand Voicing** pop-up menu and choose **4+ Voice (Fixed Inversion)**.

Since the chords in the Chord track are simple chords with only three voices, the same notes are played; however, the arpeggios follow a different pattern. Let's add some fills.

6   Drag the **Fill Amount** knob up to *36%*.

7   Drag the **Fill Complexity** knob up to *36%*.

The performance is straying away from the straight arpeggios at the end of some bars in the region, adding variety.

8   Click the **Manual** button and make sure all the steps in beats 1 and 2 are on.

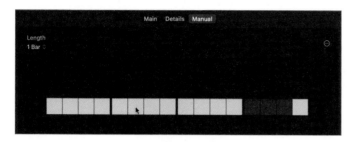

Some of the notes are a little too high.

9   Click the **Main** button and drag the **Right Hand** slider a couple of increments to the left.

Now the arpeggios stay in a more reasonable pitch range.

10   Press **C** to turn off Cycle mode.

Let's add a sustained chord on the downbeat after the outro. You'll try a different method for copying the bridge region to the end of the track.

11   In the bridge, click the **Keyboard Player** region to select it.

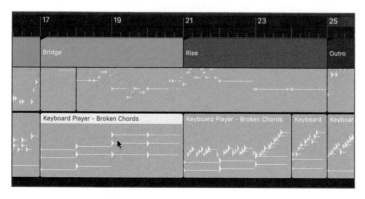

12 Press **Command-C** to copy the selected region.

13 In the ruler, click at bar 33 to position the playhead.

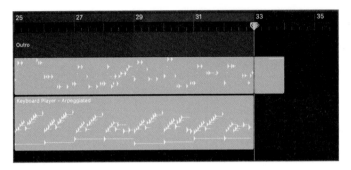

14 Press **Command-V** to paste the bridge region.

The copied region repeats the same chords because after the outro, there are no more chord changes in the Chord track.

15 Resize the region so that it's 1 bar long.

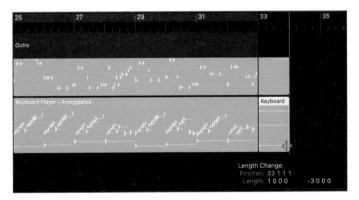

Now the piano ends the song on the downbeat of bar 33 along with the drums and bass.

To give each section of your song its unique identity, you employed a variety of keyboard playing techniques, from whole-note block chords to rhythmic eighth-note broken chords and arpeggios. Positioning the hands on the keyboard while adjusting the voicings and playing ranges gave you a lot of control to fine-tune your custom parts.

Create a String Pad Track

Now, you'll add one more Keyboard Player track, this time to play a string section in the outro. The sustained string chords underline the harmony, and their thick sound fills the space, giving a lush texture to the finale of your song.

1   Choose **Track** > **New Track** (or press Option-Command-N).

2   In the Create New Track dialog, make sure the **Session Player** button is selected and **Keyboard Player** is selected, and then click **Create** (or press Return).

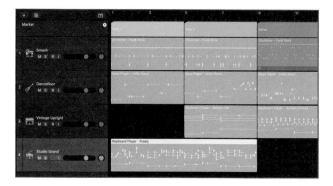

A new software instrument track is created with an 8-bar Keyboard Player at the beginning. Let's cut that region and paste it in the outro.

3   Press **Command-X** to cut the region.

4   In the Marker track, **Option**-click the **Outro** marker to position the playhead at bar 25.

5   Press **Command-V** to paste the region.

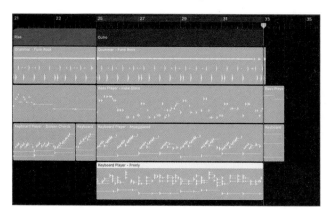

The region is pasted at the playhead position on the selected track.

6   Press **U**.

The cycle matches the outro, and Cycle mode is turned on.

7   In the Session Player Editor, click the **Session Player** button and choose **Simple Pad**.

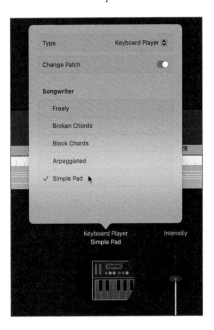

A heavily reverberated synth patch is loaded, and the Keyboard Player plays sustained whole-note chords. This patch is not quite the sound you're looking for, so let's select another one from the Library.

8   In the control bar, click the **Library** button (or press Y).

9   In the Library, scroll to the left to see the root of the folder hierarchy and choose **Studio Horns > 7-Piece Section Instruments > Sugar Hill**.

The Keyboard Player is adding a full horn section to your song. Let's try something else.

10 Scroll to the left and choose **Vintage B3 Organ** > **Hard Rock Organ**.

A distorted vintage organ could add a grainy texture to the right arrangement. Let's finally settle for a string section.

11 In the Library, scroll to the left to see the root of the folder hierarchy and choose **Studio Strings** > **Section Instruments** > **King's Cross**.

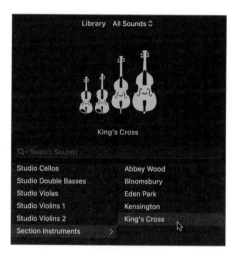

This string section is what you're looking for; however, it's too loud. Let's adjust the instrument balance.

12 Press **Y** to close the Library.

13 On the King's Cross track header, drag the volume fader down to *-20.0 dB*.

14 On the Vintage Upright track header, drag the volume fader down to *-7.0 dB*.

The string pads move to the background, and the piano is a little less up-front and center, which leaves more room for the rhythm section to shine. Let's finish the song with a sustained chord from the string section.

15 On the King's Cross track, click the + sign to the right of the Keyboard Player region.

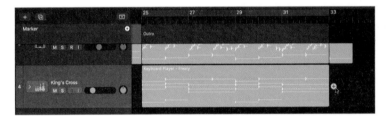

An 8-bar region is added at bar 33 that sustains a single chord.

16 Resize the last region so that its length is *1 2 0 0*.

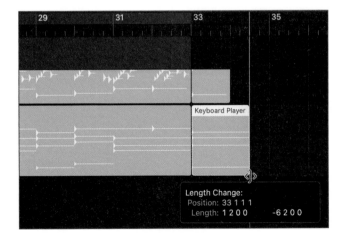

Now the string section plays the last chord of the song along with the other instruments.

17 Save your project and keep it open for the next lesson.

You've completed the drums and bass arrangement with two different Keyboard Player tracks: one to play a vibrant piano part, and the other to add a string section to your outro. In the next lesson, you'll create your own custom chord progressions in the Chord track to develop the harmony in the different parts of your song.

8

Lesson Files   Logic Book Projects > 08 Funky Song
(or continue working from the file you saved at the end of Lesson 7)

Time   This lesson takes approximately 40 minutes to complete.

Goals   Preview chord progressions

Move chords from regions to Chord track and vice versa

Edit chords in the Chord track

Edit and arrange chord groups

Edit chords in the Session Player Editor

Change the scale used for fills

Change a region's Pitch Source parameter

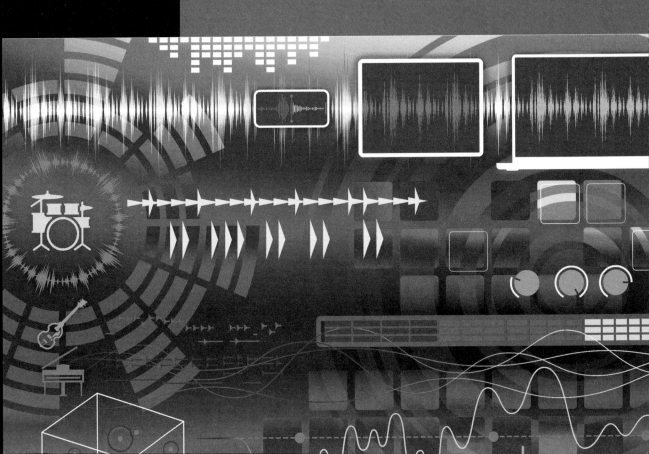

Work with Chords

In a piece of music, the chords played by the melodic and harmonic instruments form the foundation of the harmonic structure. Each chord progression conveys its own emotion, and you might want to vary them between different sections of the song.

In the Chord track, chord progressions are contained in chord groups that can be resized, copied, looped, and more—just like regions. Session Players all follow the Chord track to play in perfect harmony, although you can choose to give certain regions their own chords if you want them to play chord progressions independently of the Chord track.

Preview Chord Progressions

Before you start to create your own chord progressions, let's preview some preset chord progressions that are included in Logic Pro. These are popular progressions that are widely used throughout various music genres. When inspiration doesn't strike, they can provide a starting point to begin new compositions.

Set Up the Project

To prepare your main window to work with chords, let's make sure you can see both the Marker and Chord tracks.

1   To start this lesson, continue working in the file you saved at the end of Lesson 7 or open Logic Book Projects > **08 Funky Song**.

2   **Control**-click the Marker track header and choose **Configure Global Tracks** (or press Option-G).

3 Turn off **Show Single Track**.

Let's keep only the Marker and Chord tracks visible.

4 Deselect the **Arrangement**, **Tempo**, and **Signature** checkboxes.

Only the Marker and Chord Track checkboxes remain selected. Let's make the global tracks taller.

5 Move your pointer to the bottom edge of the Chord track and drag the divider down.

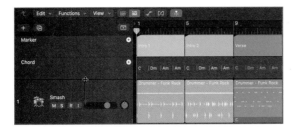

Now, you are ready to preview chord progressions and see how to paste them in the Chord track.

Preview Preset Chord Progressions

To hear the chord progressions included with Logic Pro, you'll open the verse piano region in the Session Player Editor. You'll preview a couple of different chord progressions, select one, change its rhythm, and copy and paste it to the Chord track to make the bass follow along.

1 On the Vintage Upright track (track 3), double-click the **Keyboard Player** region in the verse.

2   At the upper left in the Session Player Editor, click the **Chords** menu.

In the Chords pop-up menu, Follow Global Chord Track is selected.

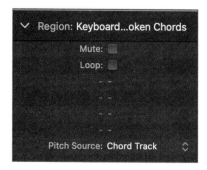

In the Region inspector, Pitch Source is set to Chord Track.

3   In the Chords pop-up menu, choose **Follow Region Chords**.

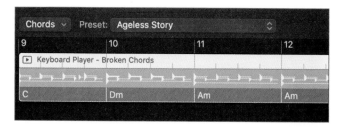

The default chord progression appears at the bottom of the Keyboard Player region, and in the Region inspector, Pitch Source is set to Region Chords.

4   In the Session Player Editor, choose **Chords** > **Chord Progressions** > **ii - V - I**.

In the verse, the instruments no longer play together—the Bass Player region follows the chords in the Chord track while the Keyboard Player region follows its own chord progression.

MORE INFO ▶ Roman numerals indicate the position of the chord's root relative to the key signature. Uppercase numerals represent major chords, and lowercase numerals represent minor chords.

5   In the Session Player Editor, click **Play** (or press Option-Space bar).

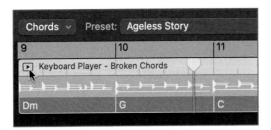

The piano plays in Solo and Cycle modes.

6   In the Session Player Editor, choose **Chords** > **Chord Progressions** > **I - V - vi - IV**.

Let's make the chords switch twice as fast.

7   Choose **Chords** > **Double Chord Rhythm**.

The chords change every two beats. Your chord progression is starting to sound like the Beatles' *Let It Be*! Let's make the bass join in on the fun.

8   Choose **Chords > Paste Region Chords to Global Track**.

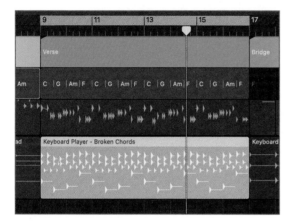

TIP ▶ To paste a region's chords in the Chord track, drag the region into the Chord track.

The chord progression disappears from the bottom of the Keyboard Player region and is pasted as a chord group in the Chord track (in the verse). In the Region inspector, the Pitch Source is set to Chord track.

9   Stop previewing the Keyboard Player in Solo mode and listen to the verse.

TIP ▶ To move the playhead and the locators to the previous or next marker, press Option-, (comma) or Option-. (period).

Both the bass and the piano follow the Chord track. Let's clear the Chord track so you can create your own custom chord progressions from a blank canvas.

10   Click the Chord track header.

All the chord groups on the Chord track are selected.

11 Press **Delete**.

All chords are deleted. In the workspace, the Session Player regions update to play the entire song over a C chord.

Consider using preset chord progressions to kickstart new compositions, where your initial focus is on the groove or the sound of the instruments rather than the harmony. You can later edit the chord progression to introduce change or wipe it out and write your own chord progressions, which you'll do in this lesson.

Create Custom Chord Progressions

To create the chord progressions for the various sections of your song, you'll edit chords in the Chord track. You'll also edit chords in the Session Player Editor for the verse region so the piano can play a slightly different chord progression without affecting what the bass plays.

Create a Chord Group

When you enter chords in the Chord track, an associated scale is automatically selected according to the position of the chord's root relative to the key signature. The Session Players use notes from that scale when they play non-chord tones—for example, during fills or for passing tones. To ensure that the correct scales are selected when entering chords, let's select a key signature for your project.

1 In the LCD display, click **Cmaj** (the key signature display) and in the pop-up menu, choose **F Minor**.

An alert asks if you want to transpose chords.

2   Click **Don't Transpose**.

Fmin appears in the key signature display.

3   Press **Return** to position the playhead at bar 1.

4   In the Chord track header, click the + (Add Chord) button.

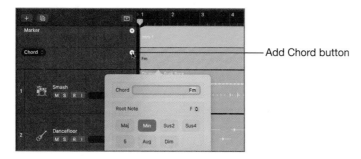

An 8-bar chord group is created with an Fm chord, and the Edit Chord dialog opens.

5   In the Edit Chord dialog, click the **Root Note** pop-up menu and choose **D♭**.

6   Click the **Maj Chord Type** button.

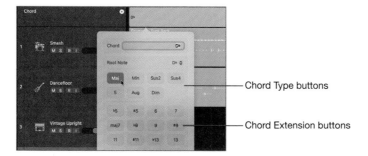

7   Click outside the Edit Chord dialog (or press esc) to close it.

8   Listen to the intro.

The bass follows the Chord track and plays a simple bass line in D♭.

9 In the Chord track, double-click the **D♭** chord.

The Edit Chord dialog opens.

10 Press **Tab**.

A new chord (Fm) is created in the next bar, and the Edit Chord dialog is ready for you to edit that chord. Let's keep the F minor chord in bar 2 and move on to the next chord.

11 Press **Tab**.

TIP ▸ To select the previous chord, press Shift-Tab.

A third chord is created at bar 3. In the Edit Chord dialog, the Chord field is selected. To speed up the chord entry, you can type the chord name, entering chord symbols as text—for example, b = ♭.

12 In the Edit Chord dialog, type **Eb** and press **Return**.

TIP ▸ There's no need to use caps when entering a chord name.

13 Click outside the Edit Chord dialog to close it.

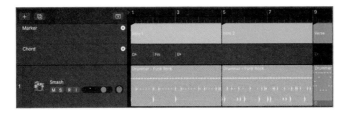

The 4-bar chord progression in the Intro 1 section sounds good. The rest of the song keeps playing over an E♭ chord.

You've created a chord group with your own custom chord progression that will form the basis for the first part of the song.

Edit Chord Groups and Choose Scales

Now let's edit the Chord track to make your 4-bar chord progression repeat every four measures throughout the song. You'll need to shorten the chord group to last only 4 bars.

1 Click any chord in the Chord track.

The entire chord group is selected. You can edit chord groups in the Chord track the same way you edit regions in the workspace.

> **TIP** In the Chord track, you can Control-click a chord group, choose Chord Progressions, and then choose a chord progression from the submenu.

> **TIP** To color chord groups, choose View > Show Colors (or press Option-C), select a chord group, and then click a color in the palette.

2 Move the pointer to the lower-right edge of the chord group to see a Resize pointer, and drag to the left to resize the chord group to 4 bars long.

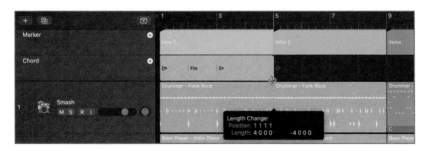

3   Move the pointer to the upper-right edge of the chord group to see a Loop pointer, and drag to the right to loop the chord group until bar 34.

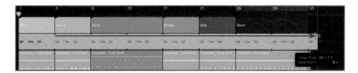

The new chord progression works well for most of the song. In bar 7, the Bass Player plays a D♭ note under the E♭ chord, which isn't your first choice. Let's make sure the bass line is limited to notes from the major pentatonic scale.

4   In the chord group at bar 3, double-click the **E♭** chord.

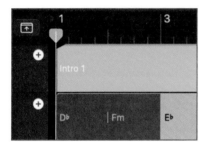

The E♭ chord is selected.

5   Double-click the **E♭** chord.

The Edit Chord dialog opens.

6   In the Edit Chord dialog, click the **Scale** pop-up menu and choose **Major Pentatonic**.

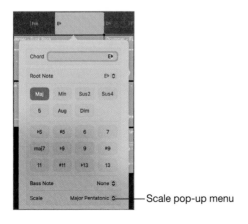

Scale pop-up menu

The Bass Player no longer plays a D♭ in bar 7.

TIP ▶ To ungroup chords, Control-click a chord group and choose Ungroup Chords. To group chords, Shift-click chords to select them, Control-click them, and then choose Group Chords.

You've created a chord group that contains your custom chord progression. Editing a chord group allows you to move, loop, or copy a chord progression to different parts of the song.

Edit Region Chords

To spice up the piano part during the verse, you'll make the Keyboard Player play different chord extensions in the last two bars of the chord progression. To ensure these changes impact only the piano track, you'll leave the Chord track untouched and edit the chords at the region level.

1 **Control**-click the Keyboard Player region in the verse and choose **Chords** > **Paste Chords from Global Track**.

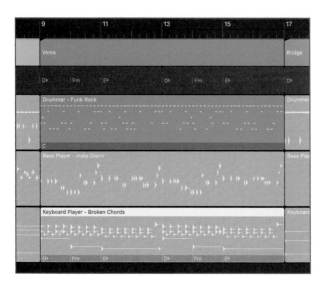

The chord progression from the Chord track is copied to the region and displayed at the bottom. In the Region inspector, the Pitch Source is set to Region Chords.

2 Double-click the selected Keybord Player region (or press E).

3   In the Session Player Editor, double-click the **E♭** chord at bar 11.

The Edit Chord dialog opens, and the Chord field is selected. Let's enter an E♭6sus4 chord.

4   Enter **eb6s4** and press **Return**.

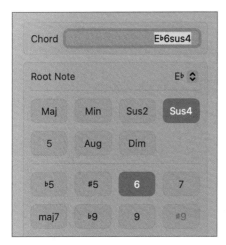

In the Edit Chord dialog, the Chord field displays E♭6sus4, the Root Note pop-up menu is set to E♭, and both the Sus4 Chord Type button and the 6 Chord Extension button are selected.

5   At the bottom in the Chord Edit dialog, click the **Preview** button.

You hear an E♭6sus4 played on a piano. The suspended chord creates a tension that you'll resolve to a more stable E♭ chord in the next bar.

6   **Control**-click the bottom of the region at bar 12 and choose **Create Chord**.

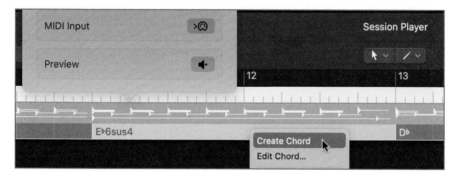

An Fm chord is created, and the Edit Chord dialog moves to the new chord.

TIP   To enter a chord, click the MIDI Input button in the Edit Chord dialog and play the chord on your MIDI keyboard (or the Musical Typing window).

7   Enter **Eb** and press **Return**.

8   Click outside the Edit Chord dialog to close it.

Let's copy the two chords from bars 11–12 to bars 15–16.

9   Click the **E♭6sus4** chord (bar 11).

10 **Shift**-click the E♭ chord (bar 12).

Both chords are selected. Let's copy and paste them to bar 15.

11 Press **Command-C**.

12 Click the E♭ chord (bar 15).

13 Press **Command-V**.

The two chords are pasted in bars 15 and 16. The more complex harmony in this chord progression makes the verse sound richer. Let's compare the result of the piano following the simpler progression in the Chord track to the richer one you just edited in the region.

14 In the Region inspector, click the **Pitch Source** pop-up menu and choose **Chord Track**.

The chord progression disappears from the Keyboard Player region, and the piano plays a simple E♭ chord in bars 11–12 and 15–16.

15 Click the **Pitch Source** pop-up menu and choose **Region Chords**.

The region chords reappear, and you can hear your richer chord progression with the E♭6sus4 chord in bars 11 and 15.

You've used the Session Player Editor to edit the chords inside a region and used the Pitch Source parameter to make the region follow the Chord track or its own chords. Another useful application for region chords is a bass line that plays notes other than the chords' root notes.

Edit Chord Groups

Let's edit the chords in the bridge, keeping an F minor chord throughout the entire section. To get ready to enter the first chord of a section, you'll Option-click the corresponding marker to position the playhead at the beginning of that marker.

1 **Option**-click the Bridge marker.

The playhead is positioned at the beginning of the Bridge marker (at bar 17).

2 In the Chord track header, click the + (Add Chord) button.

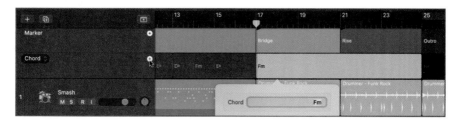

A new 8-bar chord group is created with an F minor chord, and the Edit Chord dialog opens. You want the instruments to play over F minor chords throughout the entire bridge. To make the Bass Player play more fills throughout the part, you'll enter chords on each bar.

3 Make sure the Edit Chord dialog is open and press **Tab** three times.

4 Click outside the Edit Chord dialog to close it.

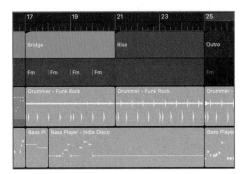

Now the Bass Player plays fills throughout the bridge.

The bridge provides a suspension in your song, and maintaining the same chord for the entire section accentuates this calming feeling before the Rise section takes off again.

Edit Chords in the Rise and Outro Section

Now in the Rise section, let's create a chord progression that uses chord inversions to produce a chromatically ascending bass line, lifting the energy to lead the listeners into the outro.

1 **Option**-click the Rise marker.

The playhead is positioned at the beginning of the Rise marker (at bar 21).

2 In the Chord track header, click the + (Add Chord) button.

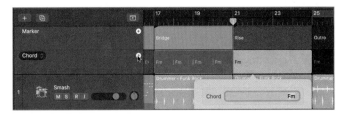

An F minor chord is added at bar 21, and the Edit Chord dialog is open.

3 Enter **Db** (at bar 21) and press **Tab**.

Now, you'll enter the first inversion of a **B♭** chord—a **B♭** chord with its third (a D note) as the lowest note.

4   Enter **Bb/D** (at bar 22) and press **Tab**.

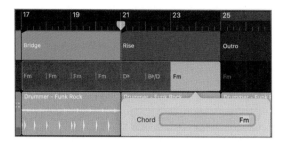

5   Enter **Eb** (at bar 23) and press **Tab**.

6   Enter **C7** (at bar 24) and press **Return**.

7   Click outside the Edit Chord dialog to close it.

8   Double-click the C7 chord.

The C7 chord is selected.

9   Move your pointer to the left edge of the C7 chord to see a Resize pointer, and drag to the right to make the C7 chord start at *24 3 1 1*.

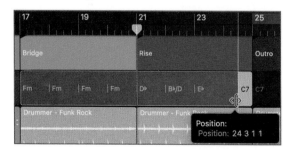

The Eb chord at bar 23 is extended to last for six beats, while C7 lasts for only two beats.

You've created an ascending chord progression to lead the audience out of the restful bridge, build the energy back up, and get everyone ready for the grand finale.

Edit Chords in the Outro

To complete the harmonic structure of your song, let's create an adventurous chord progression in the outro that takes the listeners on a journey. You'll add different chords in every bar and finish the song with an F major chord at bar 33 for the sustained notes after the outro.

1   **Option**-click the Outro marker.

The playhead is positioned at the beginning of the Outro marker (at bar 25).

2   In the Chord track header, click the + (Add Chord) button.

A new 8-bar chord group is created with an F minor chord. You'll keep that F minor chord in the first bar of the outro.

3   Press **Tab**.

4   Enter **C7** and press **Tab**.

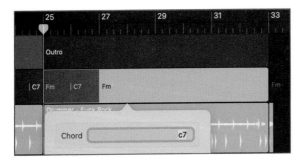

5   Continue this process to enter the remaining chords, pressing **Return** after the last chord (F).

▶ Bar 27 = A♭   ▶ Bar 31 = A♭

▶ Bar 28 = B♭   ▶ Bar 32 = C

▶ Bar 29 = B♭ minor   ▶ Bar 33 = F

▶ Bar 30 = E♭

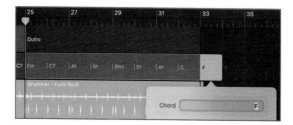

6   Click outside the Edit Chord dialog to close it.

Your song is complete. It starts with a suspenseful intro leading into a funky, energetic verse. The bridge provides a reflective pause before the harmony takes off again in the Rise section, with its ascending bass line. The string section adds a grandiose dimension to the bold and daring chord progression in your outro, and the sustained F major chord ends the song with an uplifting resolution.

Key Commands

Keyboard Shortcuts	Description
Navigation	
Option-, (comma)	Moves the playhead and locators to the previous marker
Option-. (period)	Moves the playhead and locators to the next marker
Option-click a marker	Moves the playhead to the beginning of the marker
Session Player editor	
Command-C	Copies the selected chord
Command-V	Pastes the selected chord

9

Lesson Files   Logic Book Projects > 09 Future Nostalgia

Time   This lesson takes approximately 2 hours to complete.

Goals   Program drum beats in Step Sequencer

Program plug-in step automation in Step Sequencer

Program MIDI notes and region automation in the Piano Roll

Add volume and speed fades to Audio regions

Create custom Apple Loops

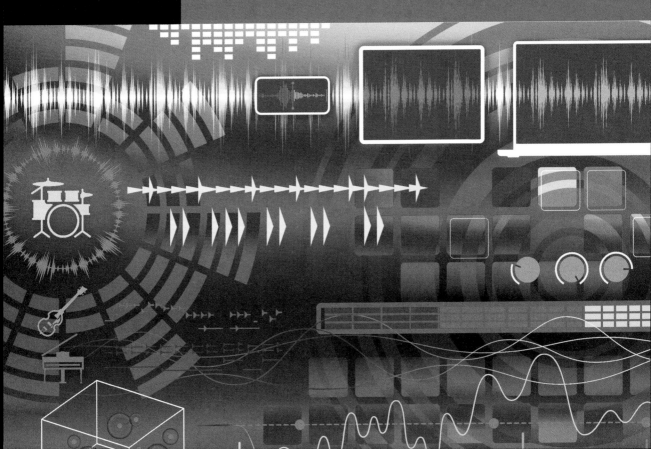

Lesson 9
Create Content

In this lesson, you'll create musical material by writing your ideas as MIDI notes in a region, toggling steps in a sequencer, or editing regions in the Tracks view. When creating content, you have the freedom to take your time and experiment with simple or complex rhythms, melodies, or harmonies. You can listen and edit notes as you work, allowing you to develop musical ideas that surpass the constraints of live performance.

You'll use Step Sequencer to program a drum beat and to create step automation to add a rhythmic filtering effect to a piano recording. You'll create notes in the Piano Roll to write a bass line and edit Audio regions in the Tracks view to slice a loop, add volume fades, and produce turntable start and stop effects. Finally, you'll make your own Apple Loop using the material you created.

Use the Step Sequencer

Among the first analog drum machines in history was the iconic Roland TR-808 (commonly referred to as the *808*), which is heard in many hit songs of the eighties. The 808 featured a row of 16 small keys to program patterns, making it quick and easy to produce a beat. Logic Pro's Step Sequencer is designed around the same basic principle but with many additional features, making it suited to program not only beats but also note patterns for melodic and harmonic instruments, or even step automation of plug-in parameters.

Turn Steps On and Off

To get a feel for creating beats in Step Sequencer, you'll toggle steps on and off, first with your mouse and then by using key commands. You'll later clear your pattern to make a specific drum beat, so in this next exercise, feel free to experiment.

1 Choose **File** > **New** (or press Shift-Command-N).

2 Click the **Pattern** button and make sure **Software Instrument** is selected.

Keep the Instrument pop-up menu set to Default Patch and keep Open Library selected.

3 Click **Create** (or press Return).

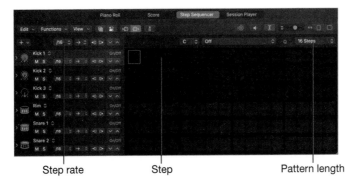

Step rate   Step   Pattern length

The Tough Kit patch is loaded on the left channel strip in the inspector, and at the bottom of the main window, the Step Sequencer opens. You can toggle steps on and off to create notes on rows for each one of the patch's kit pieces. In the Step Sequencer menu bar on the left, the Step Rate pop-up menu is set to */16* notes; on the right, the

Pattern Length pop-up menu is set to *16 Steps*. The 16 steps on the grid are grouped in four one-beat-long groups of four sixteenth notes each, which makes a one-bar-long pattern.

Let's turn on some of the steps to get a beat going.

4   On the Kick 1 row, click the first steps of beat 1 and beat 3.

On the track, a 4-bar pattern region is created to contain the pattern you've started to create. At the top of Step Sequencer, the name of the selected region (*Tough Kit*) is displayed.

5   On the Snare 1 row, click the first steps of beat 2 and beat 4.

6   In the Step Sequencer menu bar, click the **Preview Pattern** button (or press Option-Space bar).

Your pattern plays, and on each row, a white frame is around the current step. You can toggle steps while previewing the pattern, and you can drag the pointer over multiple steps to activate them.

7 On the Clap 1 row, drag the pointer over a few steps at a time (or over the entire row).

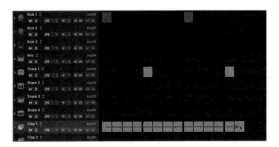

TIP ▶ Hold Shift while dragging to turn on steps in only one row.

8 While the pattern continues playing, keep toggling steps. Click inactive steps to turn them on and click active steps to turn them off.

A white frame is around the last step you clicked to indicate that it is selected. Let's use key commands to select different steps and toggle them on or off.

9 Use the Left, Right, Up, and Down Arrow keys to select a different step on the grid.

NOTE ▶ To use key commands to select steps, make sure the key focus is on Step Sequencer.

When you select a step, that row's kit piece is triggered. That can be distracting when programming a pattern while previewing it, so let's make sure you can select and toggle steps silently.

10 In the Step Sequencer menu bar, click the **MIDI Out** button (or press Option-O) to turn it off.

MIDI Out button

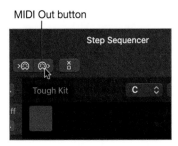

11 Use the arrow keys to select a different step.

This time, no sound is triggered as you move the white frame. Selecting a step doesn't trigger sound, so you hear the pattern you're programming without being disturbed.

12 Press ' (apostrophe) (Toggle Selected Step) to toggle the selected step on or off.

Continue experimenting, selecting steps with the arrow keys and turning them on or off with the Toggle Selected Step key command.

13 In the Step Sequencer menu bar, click the **Pattern Preview** button (or press Option-Space bar) to stop playback.

Load and Save Patterns

The Step Sequencer's Pattern Browser is where you can find preset patterns that you can use to trigger whatever instrument or patch you load on the track. There are also empty templates for drums and for a variety of musical scale modes.

1 In the Step Sequencer menu bar, click the **Pattern Browser** button (or press Option-Shift-B).

Pattern Browser button

The Pattern Browser opens to the left of the grid.

2 In the Pattern Browser, choose **Templates** > **Chromatic - 2 Oct**.

Twenty-five empty rows are created for all the notes of the chromatic scale (all 12 semitones per octave) over 2 octaves. Because the current patch is a Drum Machine Designer patch, you can see the names of all your kit pieces (plus a row for the C3 note that isn't assigned to a kit piece). In the Pattern Browser, you can find templates for many musical scales and modes, which can be useful when you're programming melodic or harmonic instruments.

3 In the Pattern Browser, choose **Patterns** > **Drums** > **Just in Time**.

Seven drum kit piece rows are displayed, and a beat is programmed on the grid. Let's use Cycle mode so you can press the Space bar to toggle playback.

4 In the Tracks area, click the **Tough Kit** pattern region and press **U**.

Cycle mode is on, and the cycle area matches the Tough Kit pattern region in the Tracks view. From now on in this lesson, use the Space bar to toggle playback on and off whenever you want.

Listen to the Just in Time pattern. It's a 32-step swung pattern, so it is divided in two pages showing 16 steps each. You're seeing only the first page. An overview of each page appears above the step grid.

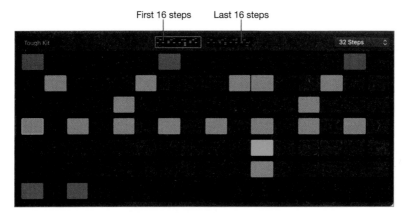

You can click an overview to see the corresponding page. Feel free to preview a few more drum patterns.

5 In the Pattern Browser, choose **Patterns** > **Drums** > **808 Flex**.

This pattern is 64 steps long. You'll clear this pattern, delete unneeded rows, and save it as a user template.

6 In the Step Sequencer menu bar, choose **Functions** > **Clear Pattern** (or press Control-Shift-Command-Delete).

All steps on the grid are off, and the pattern is now 16 steps long.

7 Click the **Hi-Hat 4** row header (fourth row) to select it.

8 Choose **Edit** > **Delete Row** (or press Command-Delete).

9 Continue deleting rows so that you keep only three rows: Kick 1, Rim, and Clap 1.

10 In the Step Sequencer menu bar, click the **Vertical Auto Zoom** button to turn it off.

11 In the upper right of Step Sequencer, click the **Pattern Length** pop-up menu and choose **32 Steps**.

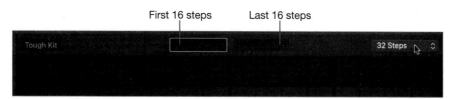

Depending on the width of your Step Sequencer, you may see your pattern divided into two 16-step pages, with two overviews appearing above the step grid. If your pattern is showing you only 16 steps, and if your Step Sequencer is wide enough to display more steps, you can zoom out horizontally to see all 32 steps at once.

12 In the upper right of Step Sequencer, click the **Minimum Step Width** button.

If your Step Sequencer is wide enough, then the steps on the grid are narrower, and you can see all 32 steps.

13 In the Pattern Browser, click the action menu, choose **Save Template**, and name the template *Basic Kit*.

14 In the Step Sequencer menu bar, click the **Pattern Browser** button (or press Option-Shift-B) to close it.

15 Chose **File** > **Save** (or press Command-S), name your project *Future Nostalgia*, save it in a location of your choice, and keep it open for the following exercises.

You have saved your own basic drum kit template with only kick, snare, and clap. The next time you want to program a drum pattern, you can load your template to reduce the clutter and see only the kit piece rows you need.

Program a Drum Beat

Let's sequence the drum beat for your song. After turning on the steps to create your pattern, you'll adjust loop lengths, use a different kit piece for one of the rows, and change step velocities to create accents on the hi-hats.

1 On the Kick row, click steps to turn on the following kick notes.

▶ Beat 1: steps 1 and 4   ▶ Beat 5: step 1

▶ Beat 3: step 3   ▶ Beat 7: step 3

▶ Beat 4: step 2

2 On the Rim row, turn on step 1 in beats 2, 4, 6, and 8.

Listen to your beat. You have a syncopated kick playing against a regular snare. The pattern is coming together. Let's find a drum kit patch that will better suit your song.

In the inspector, the blue triangle points to the Setting button of the right channel strip, used for the kit piece assigned to the selected row in the Step Sequencer, and the Library displays kit piece patches. To make the Library display full drum kit patches, you need to point the blue triangle to the Setting button at the top of the left channel strip. That Setting button displays the name of the current drum kit patch (Tough Kit).

3 In the inspector, at the top of the left channel strip, click to the left of the **Tough Kit** (Setting) button.

The Library displays Electronic Drum Kit patches.

4 In the Library, choose **Electronic Drum Kit > Silverlake**.

This kit sounds tighter and punchier. The beat sounds a little fast at the current project tempo (*120 bpm*).

5   In the LCD display, lower the tempo to *100 bpm*.

In the Step Sequencer, you can use edit modes to adjust various parameters, such as the velocity for each individual step.

6   In the Edit Mode selector in the Step Sequencer menu bar, click the **Velocity / Value** button.

Inside each step on the grid, the note velocity is displayed, and you can drag vertically in the step to adjust the velocity.

7   On the fourth kick note (in beat 4), drag down to a velocity of around *7*.

That kick sounds softer than the others, like a drummer playing a ghost note. Let's lower the velocity of all the snare notes. To raise or lower all step velocities on a row, you can use the Increment/Decrement Value buttons in the row header.

8   In the Snare 1 row header, drag the **Decrement Value** button down so all your snares have a velocity of around *40*.

The snares are softer. They also have a shorter decay and sound tighter.

For the clap, you are going to loop a 1-beat pattern, so let's adjust the loop end on that row to make the loop four steps long.

9   In the Edit Mode selector, open the menu to the right and choose **Loop**.

Colored frames appear around the steps in each row. The frames define the loop start and end positions.

10   On the Clap 1 row, drag the right edge of the frame to set the loop end after the fourth step (at the end of beat 1).

11   On the Edit Mode selector, click the **On/Off** button.

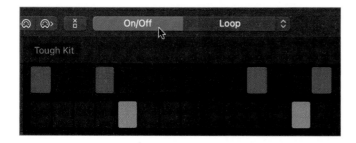

For each row, you can open subrows to edit multiple parameters.

12 On the Clap 1 row header, click the disclosure triangle.

You can now edit the Velocity, Repeat, Note, and Octave for that row as well as turn it On/Off.

TIP ▶ To open other edit modes on additional subrows, move the pointer over a subrow header, click the + sign that appears at the lower left of the subrow header, and then choose an edit mode from the pop-up menu at the upper right of the sub-row header. To remove a subrow, move the pointer to the subrow header, and click the x that appears at the upper left of the subrow header.

13 On the Clap 1 On/Off row, turn on steps 1 and 3.

On the clap, the same beat (4 steps) keeps looping, while on the kick and snare rows, the loops last the whole eight beats (32 steps) of the pattern region.

That clap sound is too obnoxious and doesn't work well for that beat. Let's replace it with a hi-hat.

14 On the Clap 1 row header, click the **Row Assignment** pop-up menu and choose **Kit Pieces > Hi-Hat 1 - Silverlake**.

This hi-hat sounds more subtle than the clap and works great. To give the hi-hat an accent, let's make sure the hi-hat played on the upbeat is softer than the downbeat.

15 On the Hi-Hat 1 Velocity subrow, lower the velocity in step 3 to around *27*.

16 On the Hi-Hat 1 row, click the disclosure triangle to hide the subrows.

You customized your own template and programmed your beat in Step Sequencer, adjusting velocities to create accents and reducing the loop length to make a shorter pattern for the hi-hat. You now have a tight, syncopated, and nuanced drum beat that will be the foundation of the song you're creating.

Add a Pattern Region to an Audio Track

To automate a plug-in on a channel strip using Step Sequencer, you need to route the pattern region's data to that channel strip. To set this up, you'll import an audio Apple Loop to the workspace—which creates an audio track—and insert the plug-in on the audio channel strip. You'll then create a new track assigned to the same channel strip and create the pattern region on that new track.

1 In the control bar, click the **Loop Browser** button (or press O).

2 In the Loop Browser, search for *Free Fall Piano* and drag it to bar 1 below the drum track.

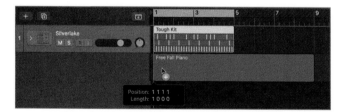

This loop contains region chords, and the loop's chords are pasted in the Chord track so that any Session Player you add to your project can follow these chords.

The Free Fall Piano region is 8 bars long. Let's double the length of the pattern region on the drum track to match the piano.

NOTE ▶ The Silverlake Drum Machine Designer track (track 1) is a track stack that contains one main track and 24 subtracks, so the new track is numbered track 26.

3 Resize the Silverlake region on track 1 to make it 8 bars long.

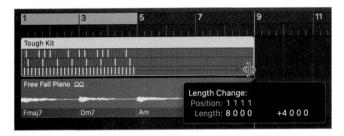

After you've resized the region, the pattern repeats for the whole length of the region. Let's make the cycle area 8 bars long as well.

4 Press **U**.

The drums and piano sound good together, but the piano is static, playing four 2-bar long sustained chords. You'll add a filter plug-in and later create step automation for its cutoff to make the frequency spectrum of the piano evolve in a rhythmic way, adding motion to the piano sound.

5 Make sure the Free Fall Piano track is selected and, in the inspector on the Free Fall Piano channel strip, click the **Audio FX** insert and choose **Multi Effects** > **Remix FX**.

6 Drag the pointer in the **Filter XY** pad while the loop is playing.

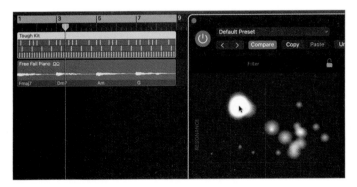

To create a pattern region at the same position as the Free Fall Piano audio region and route its data to the same Free Fall Piano channel strip, you need to create a new track assigned to the same channel strip.

7   Choose **Track** > **Other** > **New Track With Same Channel** (or press Control-Shift-Return).

A new track is created (track 27), and it is assigned to the same Free Fall Piano channel strip as the previous track (track 26).

8   On track 27, **Control**-click the workspace and choose **Create Pattern Region**.

At the bottom of the main window, Step Sequencer shows rows for the notes in the key of C major over one octave (from C2 to C3). In the Tracks view, the pattern region is shorter than the cycle area, so let's fix that.

9   Choose **Edit** > **Trim** > **Fill within Locators** (or press Option-\).

The Free Fall Piano pattern region is resized to match the length of the cycle area. You're all set to automate the Remix FX plug-in in Step Sequencer.

10 Close the Loop Browser.

Create Step Automation

Now that your pattern region is created, you'll use Step Sequencer's Learn mode to create rows for the Remix FX filter parameters that you want to automate. You'll then adjust the step rate to make the filter step through different cutoff values on every beat and adjust the loop length to create a 2-bar pattern.

1   Above the row headers, click the + (Add Row) pop-up menu and choose **Learn (Add)** (or press Option-Command-L).

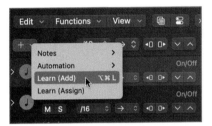

A red Learn button appears in place of the Add Row pop-up menu, indicating that you are in Learn mode.

2   In the Remix FX plug-in window, click anywhere on the Filter XY pad.

In Step Sequencer, three new rows are added: Filter Cutoff, Filter Resonance, and Filter On/Off.

3   At the top of the row headers, click the red **Learn** button to turn off Learn mode.

You'll automate only Filter On/Off and Filter Cutoff, so let's delete all other rows.

4   Select the unneeded row headers and press **Command-Delete** to keep only Filter On/Off and Filter Cutoff.

5   In the Filter On/Off row header, click the disclosure triangle.

6   In the On/Off subrow of the Filter On/Off, click the first step to turn it on.

7   In the Value subrow, click the upper half of the first step to set the value to *On*.

Next, you'll create step automation, modulating the filter value on every beat (quarter note).

8   Above the row headers, click the **Step Rate** pop-up menu and choose **/4**.

Let's adjust the loop to only eight beats to repeat the same automation loop for every 2-bar chord in the Free Fall Piano region on track 26.

9   In the Edit Mode selector, open the menu to the right and choose **Loop**.

10 On the Filter Cutoff row, drag the right edge of the colored frame to reduce the loop length to eight steps.

11 In the Edit Mode selector, click the **On/Off** button.

12 On the Filter Cutoff row, click and drag to turn on all eight steps.

13 Click the disclosure triangle on the Filter Cutoff row header.

14 Press **Command-Down Arrow** a couple of times to zoom in vertically.

15 On the Filter Cutoff Automation Value subrow, drag up or down in each step to adjust the values.

16 In the Filter Cutoff row, click a couple of steps to turn them off.

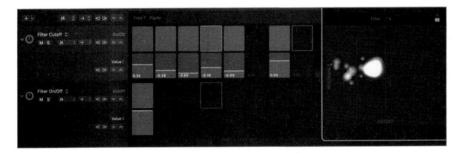

In the Remix FX plug-in window, during playback, the white light point on the Filter XY pad moves on every quarter note (or every half note in places where you turned Filter Cutoff steps off). The frequency spectrum of the Free Fall Piano changes abruptly in sync with the beat, creating an intriguing, enigmatic effect.

17 Close the **Remix FX** plug-in window.

You've used Step Sequencer to program a drum beat and to create step automation for a filter. If you enjoy this method of creation, continue exploring the various edit modes when programming drums, but also experiment with creating melody or chord-progression patterns for pitched instruments, such as basses and synthesizers.

Program MIDI in the Piano Roll

In the Piano Roll, you can precisely determine each note's position, length, pitch, and velocity. You can edit or add MIDI controller events to automate the instrument's volume, panning, pitch bend, and other parameters. Programming MIDI notes gives you a lot of freedom to create your ideas from scratch, like the way traditionally trained composers write music on staff paper.

Next, you'll program a bass line in the Piano Roll. Starting from a copy of the pattern region on the drum track, you'll use the kick drum pattern as the basic rhythm for the bass notes. Then you'll create more notes, transpose them to create a melody that complements the chord progression in the piano loop, and adjust their lengths and velocities. Finally, you'll add region automation to bend the pitch of some notes.

Convert a Pattern Region to a MIDI Region

To create a track for your bass, you'll copy the drum track and its pattern region. You'll then choose a bass patch for the new track in the Library, remove any unwanted notes from the pattern region, and convert it to a MIDI region so you can edit the notes in the Piano Roll.

1 In the Tracks view, **Option**-drag the drum track icon down.

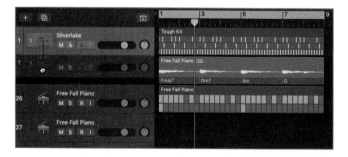

The Silverlake drum track is duplicated along with the pattern region on the track. The duplicate track (track 26) is selected so you can choose a bass patch in the Library.

2 In the Library, choose **Synthesizer** > **Bass** > **Jump Up Bass**.

Although you won't be recording the bass line in real time, you can use your MIDI keyboard to preview sounds you choose in the Library and get an idea of the bass line that you'll be programming.

3   Play a few notes on your MIDI keyboard.

That patch sounds tight and powerful. Now let's hear what it sounds like when you use the drum pattern to trigger it. Cycle mode is still on, so you can use the Space bar to preview your bass line throughout the next exercises.

4   On the Jump Up Bass track, make sure the pattern region is selected.

You can see the pattern in Step Sequencer. Listen to the bass; it sounds horrible! The drum notes are mapped to pitches that don't make musical sense when triggering a melodic instrument. They are all over the place and aren't in the right key at all. Let's clean up this pattern to get the bass line in the ballpark before you convert it to MIDI. First, you'll keep only the kick drum notes (C1).

5   In Step Sequencer, click the D1 row header to select it and choose **Edit** > **Delete Row** (or press Command-Delete).

6   Delete the F#1 row.

Only the C1 row remains. The pitch is still wrong, but the rhythm you hear sounds like it will work for the bass line. Let's try to see all 32 steps in the pattern.

7   Close the Library.

8   If your pattern is divided into only two pages, then at the upper right in Step Sequencer, click the **Minimum Step Width** button.

To get started on the right pitch, let's make the notes in the pattern region play an F—the root note of the first piano chord.

9 On the C1 row, click the C1 (Row Assignment) pop-up menu and choose **Notes > F > F1**. Make sure you don't choose F-1, which is two octaves lower.

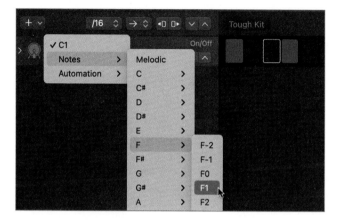

Let's turn off a couple of steps to make the rhythm even simpler.

10 On the F1 row, click the second and last active steps to turn them off.

11 On the Jump Up Bass track in the Tracks view, **Control**-click the pattern region and choose **Convert > Convert to MIDI** region (or press Control-Option-Command-M).

The pattern region is converted to a MIDI region. The Piano Roll opens at the bottom of the main window, and you can see the notes contained in the selected MIDI region. (You may need to scroll up or down to see the F1 notes.)

Copying a region from an existing instrument track to a new one is a good shortcut to create a new part in your arrangement. You could, for example, make a few copies of a violin track to create viola and cello tracks and edit their notes to produce a string ensemble part.

Transpose Notes

Now that you've converted the pattern region into a MIDI region, you can edit the notes in the Piano Roll. To follow the two bar chords in the piano track, you'll select groups of MIDI notes spanning two bars and transpose them to the corresponding root notes. Let's use Option-Up Arrow and Option-Down Arrow to transpose selected notes up or down one semitone.

1 In the Piano Roll, select all the notes in bars 3 and 4.

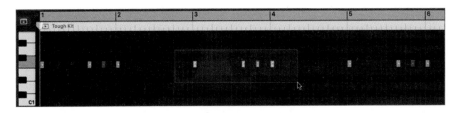

2 Press **Option-Down Arrow** three times.

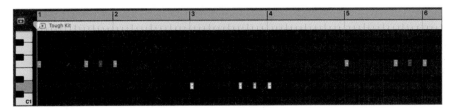

Look at the highlighted note on the keyboard on the left: The selected notes are transposed three semitones down, to *D1*. Each key press triggers a bass note, which can be useful if you need to hear the pitch you want to settle on, but it can be undesirable if you are editing the notes during playback. If you'd rather not hear bass notes triggered as you transpose them, turn off the MIDI Out button in the Piano Roll menu bar.

3 Select all the notes in bars 5 and 6.

4 Press **Option-Up Arrow** four times.

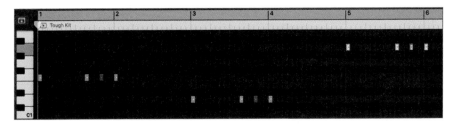

The selected notes are transposed to A1.

5 Select all the notes in bars 7 and 8.

6   Press **Option-Up Arrow** six times.

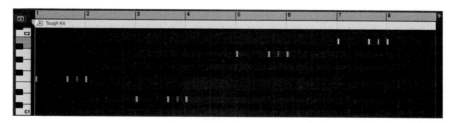

The selected notes are transposed to B1.

The notes in the bass line follow the chords on the piano track, and now they play in harmony. You'll give a little movement at the end of the bass line to make the melody lead back down toward the F note at the beginning of the region.

To transpose notes, you can drag them up or down; however, you must not shift their position. While you're dragging notes, you can press and release Shift to limit the dragging motion to only one direction: horizontal (same pitch, different timing) or vertical (same timing, different pitch). While you continue dragging, you can press and release Shift again to toggle that limit off and on.

7   Select the last two notes in the Piano Roll.

Don't hesitate to zoom in as needed.

8   Click-hold the selection and while you're holding the mouse button, press **Shift** and then continue dragging the selection down by two semitones (to A1).

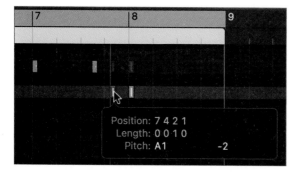

9   In the Piano Roll, click the background of the workspace to deselect all notes (or press Shift-D).

10   Click-hold the last note in the Piano Roll, press **Shift**, and then drag the note down two semitones (to G1).

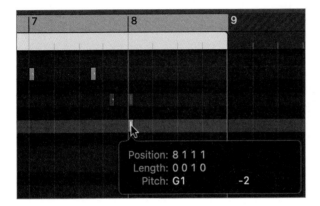

The melody of the bass line works well with the piano chords, but the notes are short, which makes the bass line sound too staccato and a little stiff. You'll fix that in the next exercise.

Change Note Length and Velocity

To make the bass line groove, you'll lengthen some of the notes to make them sustain longer. To speed up the workflow, you'll edit multiple notes at a time. First, you'll lengthen all the notes that are on downbeats.

1   In the Piano Roll, click the first note to select it.

Next, you'll select all the notes that have the same position (the downbeat) in every bar in the MIDI region.

2   Choose **Edit** > **Select** > **Same Subposition** (or press Shift-P).

All the notes positioned on a downbeat are selected.

3   Position the pointer to the right edge of the first note.

The pointer turns into a Resize pointer.

4   Drag the **Resize** pointer to lengthen the note to one quarter note (*0 1 0 0*).

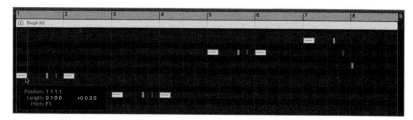

All the selected notes are one quarter-note long. Now that you have sustained notes on the downbeats alternating with shorter syncopated notes, the bass line sounds more expressive. Let's make the last note in the region even longer.

5   In the Piano Roll, click an empty area (or press Shift-D) to deselect all notes.

6   Resize the last note in the Piano Roll to approximately three quarter notes (*0 3 0 0*).

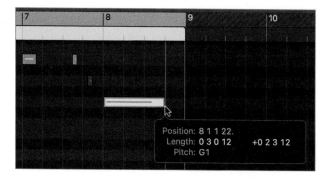

If needed while resizing the note, you can hold down Control to partially disable snapping or Control-Shift for greater precision.

In the Piano Roll, the velocity value is indicated by the color of the note, ranging from cold colors (low velocity) to warm colors (high velocity). Here, a few of the short, syncopated notes have a different color (blue), indicating they have a low velocity. They correspond to the kick drum ghost notes you adjusted in Step Sequencer earlier and sound too soft for this bass line. Let's raise their velocity.

7   Click one of the blue notes to select it.

8   Choose **Edit** > **Select** > **Same Subposition** (or press Shift-P).

All the blue notes are selected.

9 In the Piano Roll inspector, raise the **Velocity** slider to *80*.

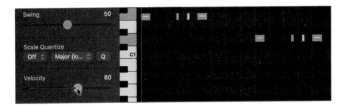

The bass line grooves much better with all the notes set at a strong velocity. The bass line and the piano are loud compared to your drums.

10 On the Jump Up Bass track header, lower the volume fader to around *−8 dB*.

11 On the Free Fall Piano track header, lower the volume fader to around *−12 dB*.

The bass and piano are lower in volume. If needed, raise the monitoring volume on your audio interface (or using the Mac computer's volume control if you're using the built-in output) to compensate. The resulting level balance of the mix should sound like you've raised the volume of your drums.

TIP ▶ While adjusting the velocities of a group of notes, hold down Option-Shift to set all selected notes to the same velocity.

TIP ▶ To adjust note velocity, Control-Command-drag the note(s) up or down.

Create Notes in the Piano Roll

Let's use the Pencil tool to create notes in the Piano Roll. You're going to create a couple of pickup notes just before the downbeat in bar 3, so feel free to zoom in around bars 2 and 3 for this exercise. In the menu bar, the info display helps you determine the exact pitch and position of the note you're about to create.

1   Position the pointer on E1 on bar 2, beat 4, third sixteenth note (the info display reads *E1 2 4 3 1*).

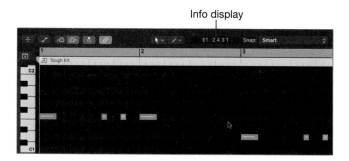

Notes you create snap to the previous sixteenth gridline so that even if your info display reads, for example, *2 4 3 193*, the note will still be created on *2 4 3 1*. To create the E1 note, you'll click at that position with the Pencil tool—your Command-click tool. Clicking the Pencil tool creates a note of the length and velocity of the last note you edited or selected.

2   **Command**-click at the pointer position.

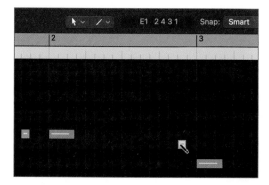

A sixteenth note is created at *2 4 3 1*. You'll create a note one semitone higher on the next sixteenth note gridline (*2 4 4 1*).

TIP ▸ Hover your pointer over a note to display a Help Tag with the note pitch and velocity.

TIP ▸ Click-hold a note to display a Help Tag with the note Position, Length, and Pitch.

3 **Command**-click to create a note on F1 on the next gridline (*2 4 4 1*).

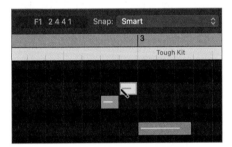

The two pickup notes sound good; however, let's lengthen them a little to make them sound legato.

4 Select the two pickup notes you just created and resize them to make them slightly longer than a sixteenth note (for example, *0 0 1 80*).

Since *Jump Up Bass* is a legato patch, overlapping the pickup notes makes their pitches slide smoothly from one note to the next. To help position the two notes as you copy them to every other bar, you'll use Snap mode.

5 In the Piano Roll menu bar, click the **Snap** pop-up menu and choose **Bar**.

6 Click one of the two pickup notes and **Option**-drag to the same pitch just before bar 5.

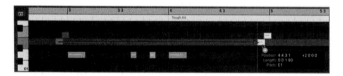

The pickup notes are copied to just before bar 5. Remember that after you start Option-dragging the notes, you can press Shift to avoid transposing them to another pitch.

7 **Option**-drag the two pickup notes to copy them just before bar 7.

The bass line sounds simple, yet it supports the harmony from the piano nicely and is tightly synced with the kick drum in your beat. And the repetitive pickup notes add just enough melodic movement to give the bass line personality and make it stand out.

Create Pitch Bend Automation in the Piano Roll

To make the bass line more expressive, let's add pitch bend automation to make it sound like a keyboard player is using their pitch bend wheel. You'll make the pitch ramp up at the beginning of the first note and the pitch ramp back down at the end of the last note. You'll also briefly open the instrument plug-in to adjust the pitch range of the automation you're creating.

1   In the Piano Roll menu bar, click the **Show Automation** button (or press A).

Show Automation button

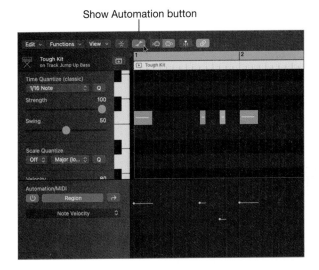

At the bottom of the Piano Roll, the automation area opens and displays the velocity of each MIDI note. Let's switch to displaying the pitch bend.

2   At the bottom left of the Piano Roll, click the **Automation/MIDI Parameter** pop-up menu and choose **Pitch Bend**.

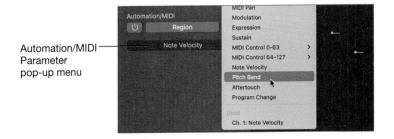

Automation/MIDI
Parameter
pop-up menu

3   In the automation area, click anywhere to create an automation curve.

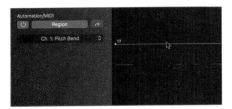

A point is created at the beginning of the region, and a green horizontal line represents your pitch bend automation curve.

4   Drag the line vertically to a value of *0*.

Let's make the pitch ramp up on the first note of the bass line.

5   In the Piano Roll workspace, **Control-Option**-drag around the first note to zoom in.

6   In the automation area, click the automation curve to create a point around the middle of the first note.

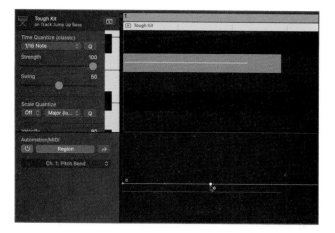

7   Drag the first automation point all the way down to *−64*.

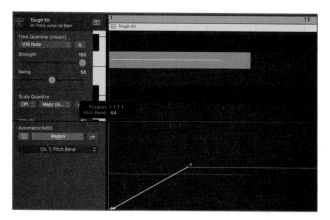

Let's adjust the zoom level to see all the notes inside the region.

8   Click the background of the Piano Roll to deselect all notes and press **Z**.

Listen to the bass line. The pitch of the first note raises two semitones. The MIDI pitch bend events do not include any pitch bend range information, so it's up to the instrument receiving the events to determine the pitch bend range. You'll now open the ES2 instrument plug-in on the Jump Up Bass channel strip in the inspector to increase its pitch bend range.

9   On the Jump Up Bass channel strip, click the middle of the **ES2** plug-in slot.

The ES2 plug-in window opens.

10   In the ES2, drag the upward **Bend** range field to *12* semitones (one octave).

Pitch bend range

The downward Bend range field is set to *link*, which means that the downward Bend range value is set the same as the upward Bend range value. Now the first note at the beginning of the bass line ramps up one octave.

11   Close the ES2 plug-in window (or press Command-W).

Continue automating the pitch bend on your bass line; for example, make the pitch drop in the middle of the last note of the bass line.

TIP Hold down Control-Shift to turn the pointer into an Automation Curve tool, and drag the lines joining two points of different values to curve them (you can't curve a horizontal line).

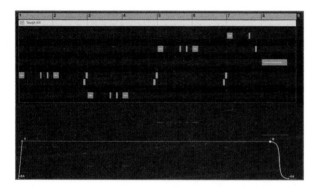

TIP To convert a MIDI or pattern region to audio, Control-click the region and choose Bounce and Join > Bounce in Place (or press Control-B).

You created a MIDI bass line in the Piano Roll. To ensure a tight groove, you used the kick drum notes as a starting point, transposed the notes to the desired pitch, created a few more notes, copied them, and adjusted their length and velocity. You then created MIDI controller data to automate pitch bend, adding expression to the performance. You now have the foundational toolset to program MIDI sequences for any instrument.

Edit Audio Regions and Add Fades

Audio regions give you a different kind of control over MIDI regions. For example, you can chop them up and slice them to create stuttering and gating effects. You can apply fades at their beginnings and ends to make the volume slowly ramp up and down, avoiding the clicks sometimes generated by cutting Audio regions. And for a bit of fun, you can apply speed fades, emulating the sounds of tape or turntables stopping and starting—a popular effect heard in many pop or hip-hop songs.

Slice a Region

Let's import an Apple Loop playing a synth melody and slice it into many smaller regions. You'll then resize the individual regions to make them shorter, creating a rhythmic gating effect.

1 Click the **Loop Browser** button (or press O).

2 Search for *yearning lead*.

3 Drag **Yearning Synth Lead** to the empty area at the bottom of the workspace at bar 1.

The synth plays a sustained, legato melody. Let's zoom in on the region and slice it up.

4 **Control-Option**-drag to zoom in on the Yearning Synth Lead region.

You need to zoom in close enough so that you can see the division lines representing sixteenth notes in the ruler.

5 Press **T**.

A floating Left-click Tool menu opens at the position of your pointer.

6 Click the **Scissors Tool** (or press I).

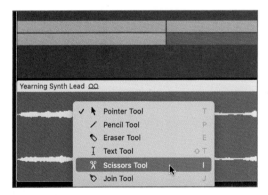

If you hold Option while you click a region with the Scissors tool, the region is divided into multiple regions of equal lengths.

7 **Option**-drag the **Scissors** tool toward the beginning of the Yearning Synth Lead region until the Help Tag displays Position: *1 1 2 1*, release the mouse button first, and then release the **Option** key.

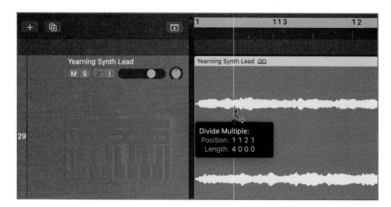

You have sliced the original region into many new regions following a sixteenth note grid. Note that the first region is not selected. You'll select them all and make them shorter to achieve the desired gating effect.

8 Click the **Tool** menu and choose the **Pointer** tool (or press T twice).

9 Click the Yearning Synth Lead track header to select all the regions on the track.

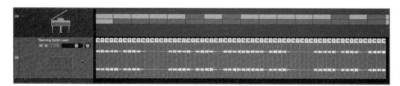

10 Choose **Edit** > **Length** > **Halve**.

You now hear a rhythmic, choppy gating effect. It is repetitive and regular for now; however, having individual Audio regions for each slice gives you a lot of editing flexibility.

Join and Repeat Regions

Now that you have small Audio regions on every sixteenth note grid line, let's delete some of them and join others together, creating silent gaps and sustained notes to produce a grooving rhythmic pattern. You'll be working mainly in bars 1 and 2, so feel free to zoom in and out as needed to perform the edits in this exercise.

1　On the Yearning Synth Lead track, select the fifth and sixth regions.

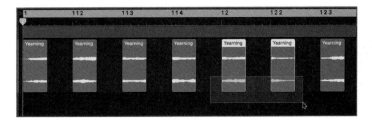

2　Choose **Edit** > **Bounce and Join** > **Join** (or press Command-J).

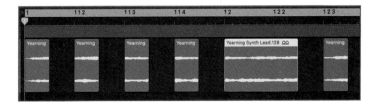

Because the two regions refer to the same audio file, the cut between the two regions is healed, and the audio material in the original audio file is used for the longer region that is now replacing the short ones you joined together. To create a rhythm pattern for this sliced synthesizer, let's remove some regions and join a few others.

3　Select the region just before the fourth beat of bar 1 (at *1 3 4 1*).

4　Press **Delete**.

5　Select the following three regions (at *1 4 1 1*).

6　Choose **Edit** > **Bounce and Join** > **Join** (or press Command-J).

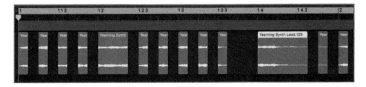

The cuts between the selected regions are healed, and you have a longer region. You'll now delete all the regions to the right of that longer region.

7 Select the region immediately to the right of the selected region (or press the Right Arrow).

8 Choose **Edit** > **Select** > **All Following** (or press Shift-F).

All the regions to the right of the selected region are also selected.

9 Press **Delete**.

You now have your chopped synth pattern. To repeat it every two bars, you'll first make a marquee selection to determine the section of the track you want to repeat. Make sure you zoom out to prepare for that next step. By default, the Marquee tool is the Command-click tool.

10 Command-drag to select *1 1 1 1* to *3 1 1 1*.

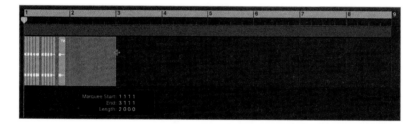

11 Choose **Edit** > **Repeat Once** (or press Command-R) three times.

The marquee selection is repeated three times.

12 Click an empty area in the workspace to clear your marquee selection and listen to your work.

The sliced synth loop adds a fun gated sound effect, which adds energy to the song. It's a little choppy right now, so in the next exercise, you'll use fades to soften the edits.

Add Fades to Audio Regions

To remove all the clicks you heard earlier and to smooth out the attack and release of all the regions, let's select all the regions on the Yearning Synth Lead track and apply fade-ins at the beginning and fade-outs at the end of all the regions at once. You'll later convert some of these volume fades into speed fades to create the classic turntable start/ stop effects.

1   Click the Yearning Synth Lead track header.

    All regions on the track are selected. When you apply a fade to one of the regions, all the selected regions will have the same fade applied.

2   Click the **Solo** button on the Yearning Synth Lead track header (or press S).

    Listen to the soloed synth track; each region starts and stops abruptly. If you pay close attention, you can hear clicking sounds at the region's start and end positions.

3   Press **T** to open the Tool menu and then press **A** to choose the Fade Tool.

4   **Control-Option** drag around two or three regions to zoom in.

    To draw fades on multiple regions, you need to make sure all the regions stay selected, so you can't start dragging by clicking an empty space between regions. You'll start dragging by clicking inside the region and drawing a fade-in from right to left over the beginning of the region.

5   On one of the Yearning Synth Lead regions, drag from inside the region to the left, outside the region.

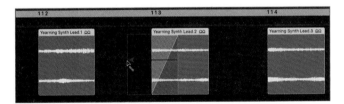

To apply a fade, always ensure that you drag over a region's boundary, or nothing will happen. You can create fades only over region boundaries. Here, the rectangular frame should cover the beginning of the region.

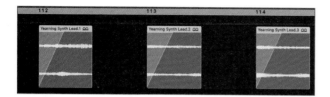

When you release your mouse button, a fade-in of the same length is applied to all selected regions on the track. Let's add fade-outs next.

TIP To remove a fade, Option-click the fade with the Fade tool.

6 Drag the Fade tool from inside the region to the right outside the region.

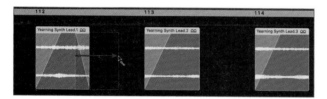

Fade-outs are created on all selected regions. You can adjust the lengths and curves of your fades to fine-tune their sound. When moving the pointer over the side or a middle of a fade, the pointer changes, indicating that you can resize or curve the fade, respectively.

7 Place the Fade tool on the right side of a fade-in (or the left side of a fade-out) and drag horizontally to resize it.

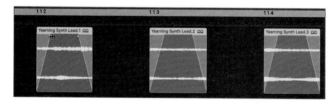

8 Place the Fade tool in the middle of a fade and drag horizontally to curve it.

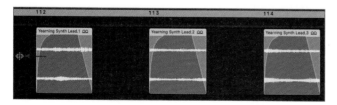

Feel free to continue adjusting all your fade lengths and curves, listening to your edits each time until you get them to sound the way you want. The beginning of all the regions has a smoother attack and no longer produces a click sound.

9   Click the **Tool** menu and choose the **Pointer** tool (or press T twice).

You can convert a volume fade into a speed fade to emulate the sound of a tape or turntable starting or stopping at a region boundary. In each 2-bar pattern, let's add a speed-up fade at the beginning of the first region and a slow-down fade at the end of the last region. You'll use the Select > Same Subposition key command that you used earlier in the Piano Roll.

10   Click an empty area in the workspace (or press Shift-D) to deselect all regions.

11   On the Yearning Synth Lead track, click the first region to select it and then press **Shift-P**.

You may need to zoom out if you want to see the selected regions. On the Yearning Synth Lead track, all four regions positioned on a downbeat are selected (at bars 1, 3, 5, and 7). However, the regions on the other four tracks are also selected because they start at bar 1. Let's deselect them.

12   One by one, **Shift**-click the four Tough Kit and Free Fall Piano regions on the first four tracks to deselect them.

Only four regions on the Yearning Synth Lead track remain selected.

13   On the first selected region, **Control**-click the fade-in and choose **Speed Up**.

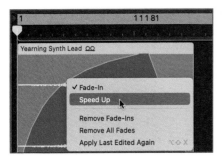

The fade-in turns orange, indicating that it is now a speed fade. Listen to it; the speed-up fade sounds just like a tape or turntable starting. Feel free to adjust the length and curve of the speed fade just as you would a volume fade.

14 Click the last region in bar 1 to select it and then press **Shift-P**.

All four regions at the same sub position are selected.

15 On one of the selected regions, **Control**-click the fade-out and choose **Slow Down**.

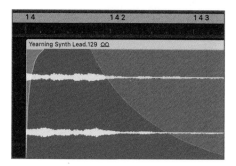

Adjust your speed fades lengths and curves until it sounds good.

16 On the Yearning Synth Lead track header, turn off the **Solo** button.

17 Choose **File** > **Save** (or press Command-S) to save your project.

Create Apple Loops

To save a beat, bass line, or riff that you may want to reuse in future projects, you can convert Audio, MIDI, Pattern, or Session Player regions into Apple Loops. Your Apple Loops will automatically match the tempo (and when appropriate, the key) of the project into which you import them. In this exercise, you'll save your sliced Yearning Synth Lead region into a new Apple Loop. First, you'll consolidate all the slices into a new 8-bar audio file.

1 **Command**-drag from *1 1 1 1* to *9 1 1 1*.

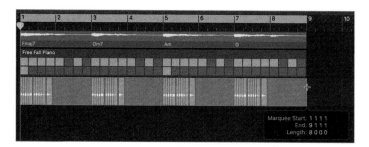

2 Choose **Edit** > **Bounce and Join** > **Join** (or press Command-J).

Logic Pro bounces the marquee selection, and a new 8-bar-long Yearning Synth Lead audio region is created on the track.

3 Drag the Yearning Synth Lead merged region to the Loop Browser.

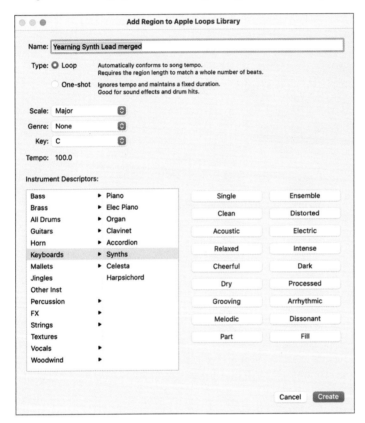

The Add Region to Apple Loops Library dialog opens.

NOTE ▸ When dragging a region to the Loop Browser, you can select the *Loop* type only when the number of beats in the region is an integer. This function uses the project tempo to tag the transient positions and works best for audio files that match the project tempo. If the selected region's number of beats is not an integer, the Type parameter will be set to One-shot and dimmed, and the resulting Apple Loop will not automatically match a project's tempo and key.

4 In the dialog, choose the desired descriptors and click **Create** (or press Return).

Logic Pro bounces the section as a new Apple Loop and indexes it in the Loop Browser. This new loop is now part of the Apple Loop library on your Mac, and you can use it in any project. Creating your own Apple Loops is a good way to catalog your production elements. The next time you stumble upon a great idea for a beat, a riff, a bass line, or a chord progression that may not be a good fit for the current project, don't throw it away—consider adding it to your Apple Loops library to save it for later.

If you want to hear the result of the completed exercises in this lesson, you can open an example project and compare it with your work.

5 Save your project and close it.

6 Open Logic Book Projects > **09 Future Nostalgia**.

Take a moment to explore the project and listen to the individual tracks to verify that the project you've created sounds the same as this example.

7 Choose **File** > **Close Project** (or press Option-Command-W) and don't save.

In this lesson, you've edited pattern regions in Step Sequencer to create a drum beat and step automation for a plug-in, programmed a bass line's MIDI notes and pitch bend automation in the Piano Roll, and edited a synthesizer Apple Loop in the Tracks view, slicing and joining Audio regions and applying volume fades and speed fades. With a growing number of tools and techniques to make your musical ideas come to life, you're really sharpening your music producer skills!

Key Commands

Keyboard Shortcuts	Description
General	
Control-B	Opens the Bounce in Place dialog
Control-Option-Command-M	Converts Pattern or Drummer region to MIDI
Control-Shift-Return	Creates a new track assigned to the same channel strip
Left arrow	Selects the previous region or note
Right arrow	Selects the next region or note
Command-J	Joins the selection into one region
Option-	Trims a region to fill the space within the locators
Shift-F	Selects all following
Shift-P	Selects notes (Piano Roll) or regions (Tracks view) on the same sub position
T	Opens the Tool menu or reverts to the Pointer tool (when the Tool menu is open)
Tracks View	
Piano Roll	
A	Toggles the automation area
Option-O	Toggles the MIDI Out button
Option-Up/Down Arrow	Transposes Selected Notes Up/Down 1 semitone

Keyboard Shortcuts	Description
Step Sequencer	
' (apostrophe)	Turns the selected step on or off
Option-Command-L	Toggles the Learn mode
Command-Delete	Deletes the selected row
Option-Shift-B	Opens or closes the Pattern Browser
Control-Shift-Command-Delete	Clears the current pattern

10

Lesson Files

Time

This lesson takes approximately 60 minutes to complete.

Goals

Create instrument tracks quickly with drag-and-drop workflows

Separate vocal and instrument stems from a fully mixed audio file

Turn a sustained vocal note into a synth-pad sound

Slice and reshuffle audio in real time with Beat Breaker

Sample a kick drum in One Shot mode

Sample a drum beat and slice it into individual drum hits

Create vocal chops

Import a vocal sample into Sample Alchemy to resynthesize it

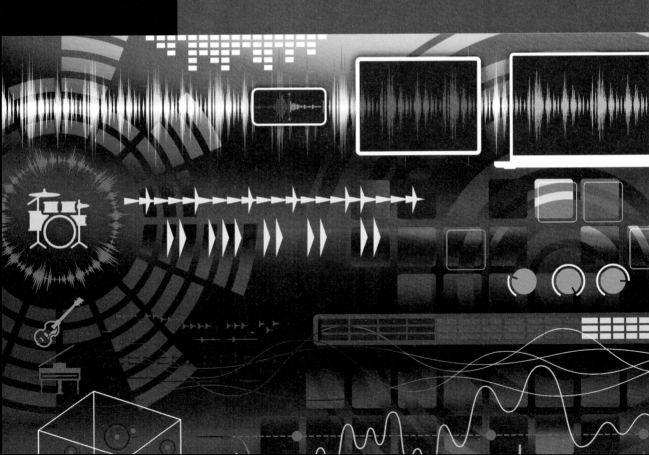

Sample Audio

Shortly after the first analog tape recorders appeared, around 1935, composers started using the recording medium as a compositional tool. They sliced the tape with razor blades, reattached the pieces in a different order using adhesive tape, and changed the tape speed to alter the playback speed and pitch.

Today, computers let you sample and manipulate audio in endless ways. In this lesson, you'll get a glimpse of Logic Pro's sampling tools. You'll extract vocals, drums, and bass stems from a full mix, and sample the stems to create a variety of sampler instruments.

> **NOTE** ▶ A *stem* is a submix of all tracks from the same instrument family. For example, a vocal stem contains all the lead and backup vocal tracks.

Always consider the source of your sampling, and if any of that material is copyrighted, make sure you thoroughly research sample clearance. Two easy ways to avoid worrying about potential legal issues are to sample your own instruments or sounds, or to sample the royalty-free Apple Sound Library content (such as software instruments or Apple Loops) that you downloaded along with Logic Pro.

Extract Vocal and Instrument Stems

Whether you want to sample a song to create a remix or to reuse a piece of audio in a new musical production, separating stems allows you to access submixes of the individual instruments that compose a mix. In this exercise, you'll import an audio file of a fully mixed song and split it into four stems: vocals, drums, bass, and a fourth stem containing all other instruments.

1   Choose **File** > **New** (or press Command-Shift-N).

2   In the Create New Track dialog, click the **Audio** button, make sure **Mic or Line** is selected, and click **Create** (or press Return).

Let's use a key command to import an audio file on the selected track.

3   Press **Command-Shift-I**.

4   In the Open File dialog, choose **Logic Book Projects** > 10 Moments.m4a and click **Open** (or press Return).

The audio file is added to the Audio 1 track. The project is not at the right tempo, which means you can't use the ruler to select specific bars on the timeline. Let's fix that.

5   Choose **Edit** > **Tempo** > **Apply Region Tempo to Project Tempo**.

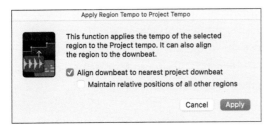

An alert asks you if you want to also align the detected downbeat in the audio file to the nearest downbeat in your ruler. It's already aligned here, so it doesn't matter either way.

6   Click **Apply**.

Logic Pro analyzes the file, and then in the LCD display, the project tempo is set to *128 bpm*. The ruler now matches the bars in the song.

7   Listen to the project.

Moments (by Darude) is an energetic dance track that blends rock and electronic drums, with uplifting vocal performances, arpeggiated guitars, and classic analog synth sounds. Let's separate the mix into individual stems.

8   Make sure the audio region is selected and in the Tracks area menu bar, choose **Functions > Stem Splitter**.

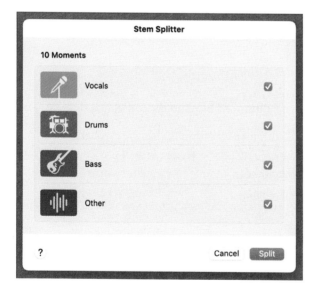

NOTE ▸ Stem Splitter is available only on Macs with Apple Silicon chips (M1, M2, M3, M4, and so on). If Stem Splitter isn't available on your Mac, close this project, open Logic Book Projects > 10 Moments (Stems) and jump to the next exercise.

The Stem Splitter dialog opens and lets you choose up to four stems: Vocals, Drums, Bass, and Other (a single stem that contains all the other instruments in the mix).

9 Keep all four checkboxes selected and click **Split** (or press Return).

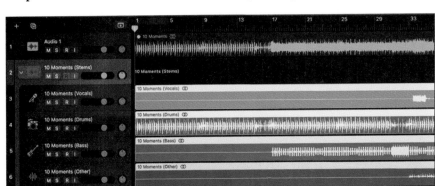

After the process is completed, a new summing track stack named *10 Moments (Stems)* is created with four subtracks—one for each stem.

On the Audio 1 track, the original audio region is muted. If you listen to the project now, you hear the four stems together, and it sounds just like the full mix.

TIP ▶ To unmute a region, select it and press Control-M.

10 Click the **S** (Solo) button on each subtrack to listen to the individual stems.

The stem separation is good. The full mix incorporates heavy reverberation effects, so you can hear residual reverb or other artifacts in some parts of the stems, but you'll still be able to isolate sections that you can sample to create new instruments.

11 Save the Logic Pro project under the name and location of your choice and keep it open for the rest of this lesson.

Now that you've extracted stems from the song, you'll select specific samples of the different stems to create new drum and vocal sampler instruments.

Create Quick Sampler Instrument Tracks

Quick Sampler allows you to quickly turn a single audio file into a sampler instrument. Depending on the type of material you're working with (such as a drum hit, a sustained vocal note, or a drum beat), you can choose to slice the sample, loop it, add modulation, apply filters, and use envelopes to further manipulate the sound.

Sample One Shot Drums

The easiest way to use samples in your productions is to import or record a single note from an instrument in Quick Sampler that you can then play using keys or drum pads on your MIDI keyboard. In this exercise, you'll import a kick drum from the drum stem, carefully adjust the sample end point, and apply a fade-out to avoid clicks.

1   On the 10 Moments (Drums) track (track 4), **Command**-drag to select the first drum hit.

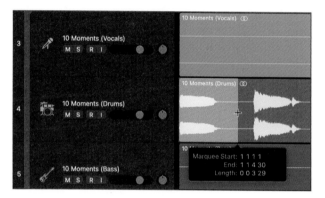

2   Drag the selection to the empty area below the track headers and in the menu that opens, choose **Quick Sampler (Original)**.

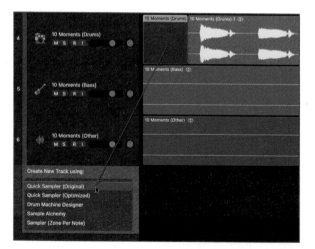

A new software instrument track is created with Quick Sampler in the instrument slot. Quick Sampler opens, and the audio file you dragged is imported into Quick Sampler. Quick Sampler recognized a single note in the audio file and determined it was appropriate to use Classic mode. Below the waveform, the Root Key is set to C3, which is the default when choosing Original when importing an audio file.

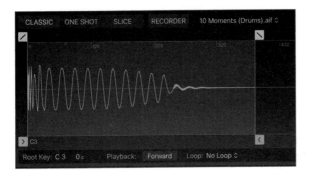

3   Play a C3 note on your MIDI keyboard.

Your kick sample is triggered; however, in Classic mode the sample stops playing back when you release the note. Let's make sure the entire sample is played no matter how long you hold down the key or pad used to trigger it.

4   In Quick Sampler, click the **One Shot** button.

In One Shot mode, the sample plays back from the start marker to the end marker, even if you release the key earlier. This mode is adapted for drum sounds—you can trigger drum hits with pads or drum controllers that send short notes and still play the full duration of the drum sample.

Let's remove the hi-hat note that you hear at the end of the kick sample. On the waveform, the kick drum looks like a clean sine wave, whereas at the end, the noisier hi-hat note looks like a thicker waveform.

5   Drag the end marker to the beginning of the hi-hat note.

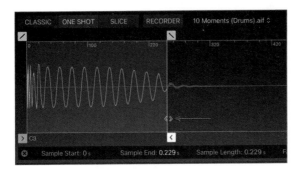

You no longer hear the hi-hat; however, you still hear a click noise at the end of the sample. Let's add a fade-out to get rid of the click.

6   Drag the gray fade-out marker to the left to adjust the length of the fade-out.

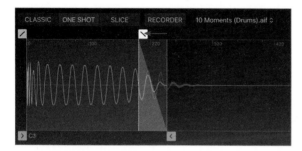

Don't hesitate to readjust the position of the end marker and the fade-out marker to make the click disappear.

7   Close the Quick Sampler window.

8   On track 7, double-click the track name and enter *Kick*.

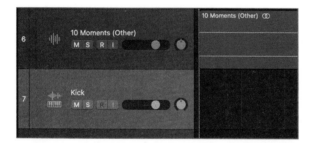

You've turned a single kick note from the drum stem into a Quick Sampler instrument that you can now sequence or play with a MIDI controller. You've selected One Shot mode to make sure that notes of any length always trigger the entire sample and adjusted the end and fade-out markers to clean up the kick drum sample.

Slice a Drum Beat

When you import an audio file that contains multiple drum hits, Slice mode is automatically selected, and slice markers are positioned where transients are detected. Each slice is mapped to a MIDI pitch so that it can be triggered by a specific key or pad.

1   On the 10 Moments (Drums) track header (track 4), click the **S** (Solo) button.

2   Listen to the breakdown section that starts at bar 106.

In that section, the drums play half-time, and a heavy compressed reverb gives them a unique larger-than-life character.

3   Unsolo the drums.

4   **Command**-drag the audio region to select from bar 106 to bar 108.

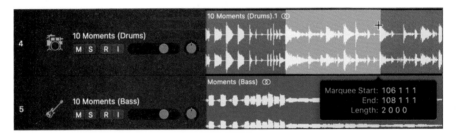

5   Drag the selection to the empty area below the track headers and in the menu that opens, choose **Quick Sampler (Original)**.

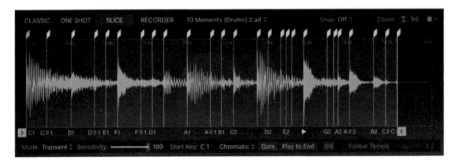

A Quick Sampler track is created, and Quick Sampler opens in Slice mode. On the waveform, slice markers are positioned where transients were detected. Below the waveform display, MIDI note pitches are assigned to each slice, starting on C1 and ascending chromatically.

6   On your keyboard, play some of the notes assigned to the sample slices.

For each note you play, the corresponding slice is triggered. Too many transients were detected, resulting in too many short slices, so let's lower the sensitivity.

7 Drag the **Sensitivity** slider to *44*.

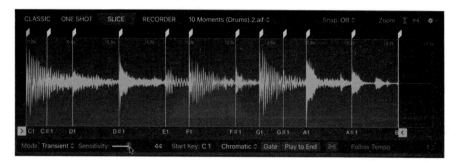

There are fewer slice markers, resulting in fewer samples. The first kick sample is still too short, so let's remove the second slice marker.

NOTE ▸ In some cases, slice markers may show up in different positions when you perform this exercise. If this happens, manually adjust the markers as necessary.

8 Double-click the 2nd slice marker (assigned to C#1).

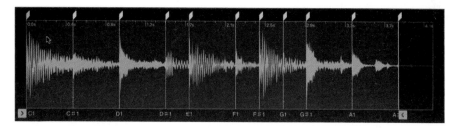

The marker is removed, and your first kick sample (C1) is longer.

9 Double-click the 8th slice marker (assigned to G1).

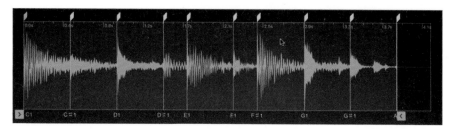

Notice that the last drum hit on the waveform is missing a slice marker. You'll add one now.

10 Click the waveform at the beginning of the last drum hit.

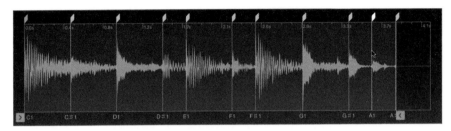

A new slice marker is added, and you can play an A#1 to trigger the last drum hit. Now that all your drum hits are mapped to individual notes, you'll manipulate the sound of the samples to give your drum kit a low-fi quality.

11 Turn on the **Filter**.

12 Drag the **Drive** knob up to around *33%*.

The filter is distorted, and the drum sound starts to break up, making the samples sound powerful.

13 Drag the **Cutoff** knob down to around *83%*.

The high frequencies are attenuated, and the drums are muffled.

14 Click the **Type** pop-up menu and choose **LP 24dB Lush (Fat)**.

The high frequencies are cut off sharply, and the drums are sounding heavy, gritty, and deep. You can toggle the Filter On/Off button to compare the filtered sound with the original one. Let's adjust the envelope to shorten the samples.

15 At the bottom of the Amp section, drag the **Sustain** handle (the horizontal line after the second point) down and to the right.

16 Adjust the envelope so that **S** (Sustain) = *0%* and **D** (Decay) = *645 ms*.

> **TIP** ▶ To adjust the numerical values directly, drag them vertically or double-click them and enter a new value.

17 Close the Quick Sampler window.

18 On track 8, double-click the track name and enter *Big Drums*.

You've imported a drum beat with multiple drum hits, sliced it in Quick Sampler, and fine-tuned the slice markers to assign each slice its own MIDI note. You then dialed a distorting low-pass filter and shortened the amp envelope of each slice to give your new drum sound a unique character.

Loop Samples in Classic Mode

To create your own synthesizer pad with a vocal quality, let's sample a sustained note from the vocal stem, import it into Quick Sampler, and loop it seamlessly, allowing you to sustain the sound for as long as needed.

1   Solo the 10 Moments (Vocals) track (track 3).

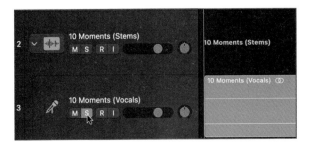

2   Listen to the phrase that starts at bar 65.

The singer sustains a note at the end of the word *tonight*.

3   Unsolo track 3.

4   **Command**-drag the audio region from bar *66 4 1 1* to bar *67 2 1 1*. If needed, **Command-Shift**-drag the start or end of the marquee selection to fine-tune the selection.

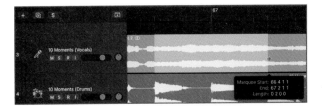

To create a Quick Sampler instrument from the vocal note, you'll choose Optimized. In that mode, Quick Sampler analyzes the sample's pitch to tune it and sets the Root Key accordingly.

5 Drag the selection to the empty area below the track headers, and in the menu that opens, choose **Quick Sampler (Optimized)**.

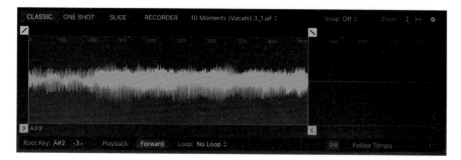

Quick Sampler opens in Classic mode. The A#2 pitch is detected and assigned to the Root Key with a slight tuning adjustment of –3c (cents).

6 Play a few keys on your MIDI keyboard.

The A#2 key triggers the original sample, and other keys transpose the sample so it plays the correct pitch.

7 Adjust the start and end markers until you hear only the beginning of the word "night" (without the "t" at the end).

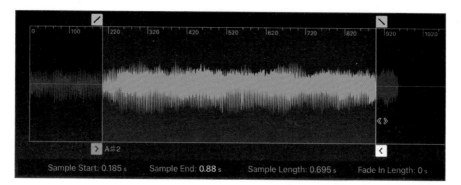

Continue playing an A#2 note while you adjust the parameters in Quick Sampler.

8   Below the waveform display, click the **X** to the left of the parameter display bar.

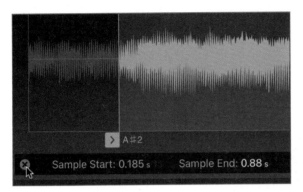

The parameters revert to the default view, and you can see the Loop parameter.

9   Click the **Loop** mode pop-up menu and choose **Forward**.

In the waveform display, yellow loop start and end markers let you set the loop boundaries. The loop section between the loop markers is yellow.

10   At the upper left of the waveform display, click the **Zoom Horizontal** button.

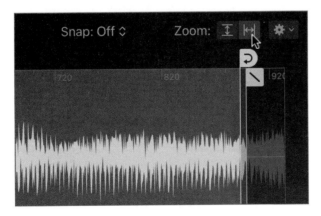

11 Drag the loop start and end markers to adjust them.

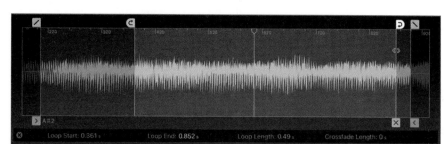

The goal is to have the loop sound as seamless as possible. Unless you're lucky, you're hearing a popping sound as the playhead skips from the loop end marker to the loop start marker. There are a few tools in Quick Sampler that can help that situation.

12 Click the **X** to the left of the parameter display bar to see the default parameters.

13 Click the **Loop** mode pop-up menu and then choose **Alternate**.

The sample alternates between forward and backward playback, making the loop more even. You can probably still hear clicks or pops at the loop start and end markers, but for now, try to focus on having the pitch and amplitude of the note sound fairly continuous. Once you're happy with your loop section, you can further polish the loop using a crossfade at the loop start and end markers.

14 Drag the crossfade marker to the left to create a crossfade at the loop start and end points.

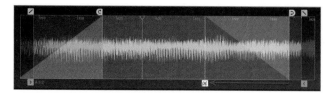

Adjust the length of the crossfade so that the popping sound disappears and the loop sounds smooth. You may need to readjust your loop start and end marker positions.

15 Play simple chords on your MIDI keyboard.

Since each pitch plays the sample at a different speed, the loop points for each note in the chord occur at different times, making them less noticeable.

16 In the envelope display at the bottom of the Amp section, move the pointer over the **Attack** handle (the first point).

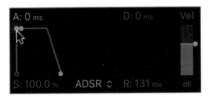

The Attack field (A) is highlighted.

17 Drag the point to the right to set the attack around *600 ms*.

18 At the lower right of the envelope shape, drag the **Release** handle to set the release to around *600 ms*.

The gradual attack and release produce a smooth and gentle pad sound.

19 Close the Quick Sampler window.

20 On track 9, double-click the track name and enter *Vocal Pad*.

You've repurposed a vocal recording into a synth pad. Feel free to try the same process with a sustained note from any instrument and further sculpt the sound using the filter as well as audio effect plug-ins.

Create Vocal Chops

Vocal chops—a vocal editing technique pervasive in today's pop songs—are sliced-up vocal samples sequenced together in a new way. The cuts are often small, unrecognizable pieces of words, sometimes just individual vowels, and the goal is to create a fun, creative sound effect that may sound like the singer's voice but doesn't necessarily have comprehensible lyrics. Tiny samples are rapidly repeated to create stuttering effects, and the use of pads to trigger the samples in a rhythmic fashion often results in syncopated grooves.

To get started building your vocal chops, you'll select the vocal phrase that you'll use for your new Quick Sampler instrument. Using Slice mode, you'll separate the phrase into three slices that can be triggered with three MIDI notes.

1   On the 10 Moments (Vocals) track, listen to the phrase that starts at bar 113.

    You'll select the part where the singer says, "just like this."

2   **Command**-drag the audio region from *113 2 2 1* to *115 1 1 1*. If needed, **Command-Shift**-drag the start or end of the marquee selection to fine-tune the selection.

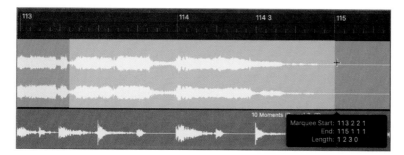

3   Drag the selection to the empty area below the track headers and in the menu that opens, choose **Quick Sampler (Optimized)**.

    A new Quick Sampler track is created, and Quick Sampler opens in Classic mode.

4   Click the **Slice** button.

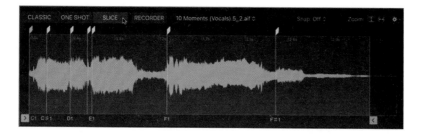

Slice markers appear on the waveform display where transients were detected. Too many transients were detected, so let's reduce the number of slices.

5   Below the waveform display, drag the **Sensitivity** slider to *33*.

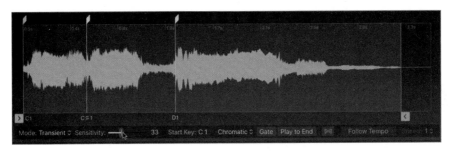

Only three slice markers remain, with three notes assigned to one word each:

▶   C1 = just

▶   C#1 = like

▶   D1 = this

6   Play C1, C#1, and D1 notes on your keyboard.

Each time a sample is triggered, the entire sample plays, as in One Shot mode. To better control the length of the vocal notes you perform, you'll use Gate mode. In Gate mode, the sample plays only for as long as you hold down the key (or for the duration of the MIDI note on the track).

7   Below the waveform display, click the **Gate** button.

8   Play a short C1 note on your keyboard.

Now only the beginning of the slice plays, and playback stops when you release the key. For greater control, let's make the envelope release more abruptly.

9   In the Amp section on the envelope display, drag the **R** (Release) value all the way down to *0 ms*.

10 Play short C1, C#1, and D1 notes in rapid succession.

If you play fast, syncopated beats by hitting keys or drum pads on your controller, you may notice that some of the samples don't trigger fast enough. For such percussive performances, results are sometimes better when the slice markers are a little bit farther into the word, cutting off some of the slow attack.

11 Move your slice markers a little farther past the attack of each word.

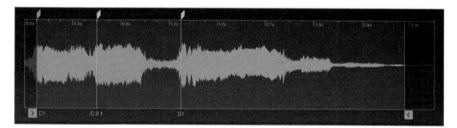

Now the attacks of the notes are more abrupt, and you can play percussive stuttering riffs.

12 Close the Quick Sampler window.

13 On track 10, double-click the track name and enter *Vocal Chop*.

You've imported your vocal sample in Quick Sampler, chosen the Slice mode, adjusted the sensitivity slider to get the right number of slices, and turned on Gate mode to make sure the samples you trigger stop playing back when you release the key. All that's left is to play or sequence notes to create your vocal chop!

Use Beat Breaker

Beat Breaker is an audio effect plug-in that allows you to manipulate the incoming audio signal. It buffers a specific length of audio (by default, four beats) and divides it into slices. For each slice, you can choose which part of the buffer plays and control the playback speed, volume, and number of repetitions (to create stuttering effects). While drums are an obvious application for Beat Breaker, you can produce intriguing rhythmic effects with any kind of audio material.

Reorder Slices and Change Playback Speed

First, let's insert Beat Breaker on the Other stem to process a guitar arpeggio. You'll resequence the notes from the arpeggio and change some of the notes' playback speed and direction.

1 Click the 10 Moments (Other) track header to select it.

2 Solo the 10 Moments (Other) track (track 6).

3 Drag the upper half of the ruler to create a cycle area from bar 33 to bar 37.

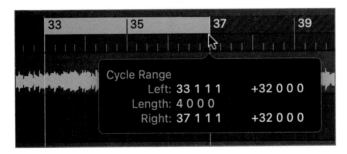

4 On the 10 Moments (Other) channel strip in the inspector, click an Audio FX slot and choose **Multi Effects > Beat Breaker**.

5 Press the **Space** bar to start playback.

Slice marker   Playhead

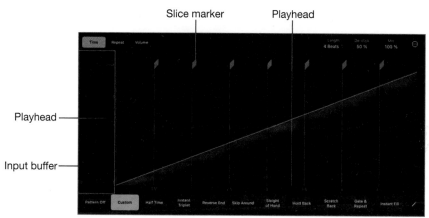

Playhead ——

Input buffer ——

At the top left, three edit mode buttons (Time, Repeat, and Volume) let you manipulate the slices in different ways. In the center, the lines over the slices are orange to
indicate that Time mode is currently selected.

On the far left, a playhead indicates which section of the input buffer is currently
playing. In the center, slice markers determine the position and length of slices in the
output pattern produced by Beat Breaker, and a playhead indicates which slice is currently playing.

By default, all slices are 0.5 beat (half a beat, which is an eighth note) long, and the slice
markers are numbered after their position in the output pattern. You'll make the second
slice (to the right of the 1.5 slice marker) play a different section of the input buffer.

6 Drag the second slice up to a different position.

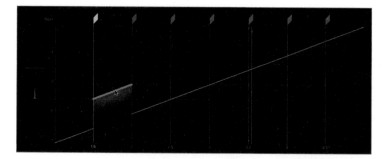

You hear a different piece of audio during the second half of beat 1. A light gray horizontal mapping line indicates which section of the input buffer will play for this slice.

7 Drag the second slice all the way down.

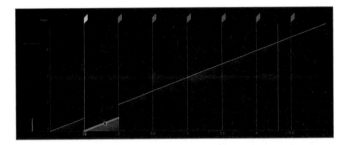

The first two slices play the first eighth note of the input buffer. Let's make the second slice play twice as fast. Three parameters are listed at the top (Input Beat, Speed, and Curve), which is helpful if you want to set a specific value.

TIP ▶ Drag a parameter value to adjust it, or double-click it and enter a new value. Option-click a value to reset that parameter to its default value.

8 Drag the second slice to the right so the **Speed** parameter is *200%*.

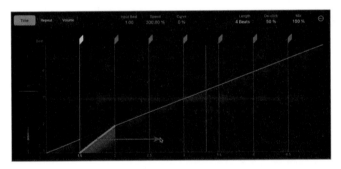

Let's make the third slice play in reverse.

9 Drag the third slice to the left so the **Speed** parameter is *−100%*.

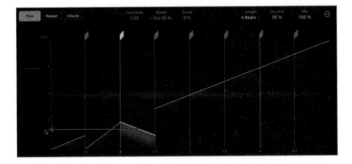

Now, let's create a speed-fade effect where the last slice speeds up then slows down abruptly.

10 Double-click the handle at the top of the 4.5 slice marker to delete it.

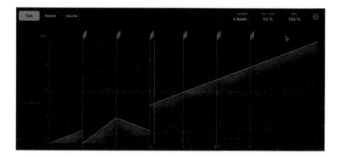

The last slice is now one beat (a quarter note).

11 Drag that slice all the way down.

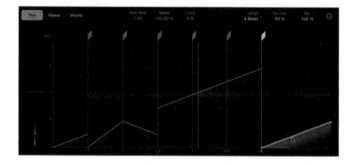

To create a speed-fade effect, let's bend that slice's orange line.

12 **Command**-drag the line to the right so the **Curve** parameter is *35%*.

Curve value

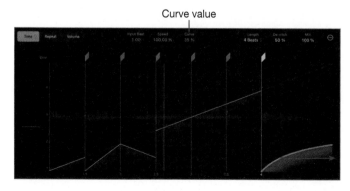

Now the last slice starts playing fast and slows down quickly, which sounds like a DJ stopping a turntable.

You've dragged slices up and down to choose which part of the input buffer they play, dragged them left and right to adjust their playback speed and reverse their playback direction, and Command-dragged them to create a speed fade.

Repeat Slices and Create Volume Curves

Let's explore the two remaining edit modes in Beat Breaker. Repeat mode lets you adjust the number of repetitions of each slice to create stuttering effects, and you can set the volume of each slice or create volume curves in Volume mode.

1   Click the **Repeat** button.

The lines on the slices are magenta to indicate you're in Repeat mode.

2   Drag the slice 2.5 up until the **Repeats** value is *3*.

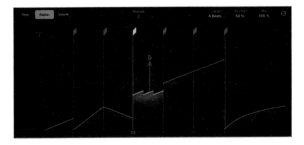

The slice produces a stuttering effect with a triplet feel. Let's adjust the volume of the slices.

3   Click the **Volume** button.

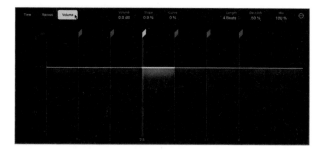

The lines on the slices are yellow to indicate you're in Volume mode.

4   Drag slices up or down to adjust their volume as desired.

5   Drag the last slice to the right to create a volume ramp up.

The volume ramping up on that slice accentuates the end of the speed-fade.

6   On the slice to the right of the 2.5 slice marker, drag the line to the right to create a ramp up and then **Command**-drag to the left to bend the volume curve.

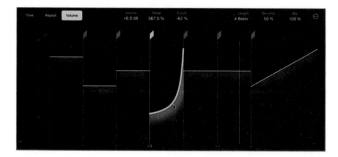

TIP ▶ Click a slice to select it and Option-click one of the parameter values at the top to reset it, or Option-click the line to reset all three values.

The rapid crescendo effect works nicely with the triplet stuttering you created earlier in Repeat mode.

7 Close the Beat Breaker window.

8 Unsolo the 10 Moments (Other) track.

You've used Beat Breaker to reshuffle the notes from a guitar arpeggio, adding various effects to each individual note. Working in real time lets you be creative and fine-tune the playback parameters as the track is playing.

Use Sample Alchemy

Sample Alchemy allows you to resynthesize an audio sample by applying various synthesis techniques like additive, granular, or spectral synthesis. Various play modes let you loop, scrub, or arpeggiate the sample, offering numerous creative possibilities.

Let's import a vocal sample into a Sample Alchemy instrument and explore some of the various play modes and synthesis techniques available.

1 Solo the 10 Moments (Vocals) track (track 3).

2 Listen to the part that starts at the end of bar 119.

   The word "this" moves between several different notes in succession. Let's turn a sample of that single word into a Sample Alchemy instrument.

3 On the audio region, **Command**-drag from *121 1 1 1* to *122 2 1 1*.

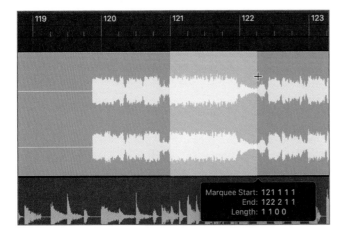

4 Drag the marquee selection below the track headers and choose **Sample Alchemy**.

A Sample Alchemy instrument track is created, and Sample Alchemy opens with the sample Moments (Vocals) loaded. The pitch detection is based on the F note sustained at the end of the sample, so the sample plays at its original pitch when playing an F3 note.

5 On your MIDI keyboard, play an F3 note.

With the default settings of the Granular synthesis technique, the resynthesized sample sounds close to the original.

6 Play other notes and some chords.

The sample follows the pitch of the notes you play. Unlike with classic samplers like Quick Sampler, the playback speed of the sample remains constant when playing different pitches.

The vertical position of the A source handle is mapped to the first parameter in the synthesis module (Size).

7 Move the **A** source handle all the way down.

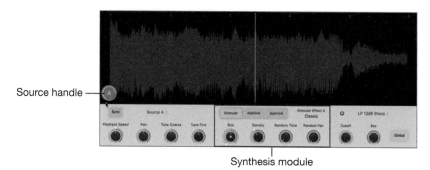

Around the Size knob at the bottom, a white dot indicates the current value of the parameter as adjusted by the vertical position of the source handle. Lower values produce a grainy, throaty sound.

8   Move the **A** source handle back to the center of the waveform and move it to the right.

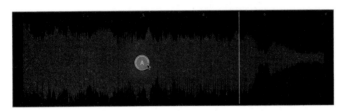

The horizontal position of the source handle determines the playback starting point.

At the top of the waveform are five play modes. Let's switch to Loop mode to loop the sample.

9   Click the **Loop** button.

Play modes

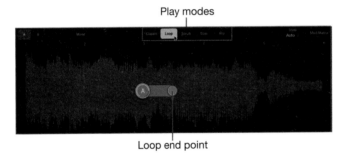

Loop end point

The part of the waveform between the A source handle and the loop end point plays forward repeatedly.

10 Adjust the position of the **A** source handle and the position of the loop end point.

TIP ▶ Move the loop end point before the source handle to play the sample in reverse.

Let's try the Scrub play mode.

11 At the top of the waveform, click the **Scrub** button.

In that mode, only the part of the sample at the source handle position plays, and you can move the source handle to scrub the sample.

12 Move the **A** source handle over the waveform.

You can record the movement of the source handle so that the scrubbing motion is retriggered every time you play a note.

13 At the top left of the plug-in, click the **Motion** button.

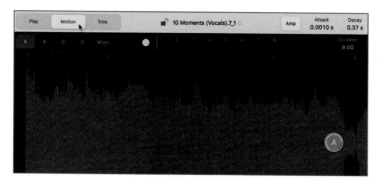

At the top of the waveform, the Record button is enabled, and Sample Alchemy is ready to record the motion of the source handle.

14 Move the source handle horizontally and vertically over the waveform, and when you're finished, release your mouse button to stop the recording.

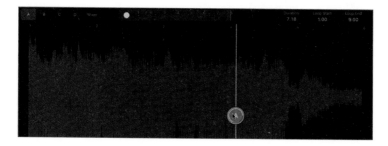

The motion of the source handle is recorded on a timeline next to the Record button.

15 Play a few notes and chords.

All the notes you play retrigger the scrubbing motion that you recorded. Let's clear the motion recording and try a different synthesis technique.

16 To the right of the timeline, click the **Clear** button.

The timeline is clear.

17 At the top left of the plug-in, click the **Play** button.

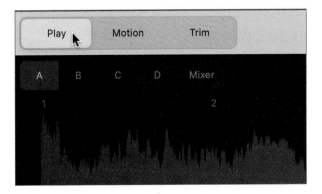

18 In the synthesis module below the waveform, click the **Additive** button.

The Additive effect used for source A is currently set to Partial Lock, which produces an artificial sound where the pitch remains constant throughout the entire sample playback.

19 At the top of the waveform, click the **Arp** button.

In Arp mode, holding a single note simply repeats the note, while holding a chord arpeggiates the chord. You can turn on more than one source and place their source handles in different positions on the waveform.

20 At the top left of the waveform, click the **B**, **C**, and **D** source buttons.

Three new source handles appear for sources B, C, and D.

21 Play a four-note chord.

The chord is arpeggiated, and the four notes trigger the four sources in sequence.

22 Reposition the four source handles horizontally to trigger different sections of the sample, and vertically for different timbres.

TIP To tweak the timbre of a source, click its handle to select it and adjust its parameters in the Source, Synthesis, and Filter modules in the lower section of the plug-in.

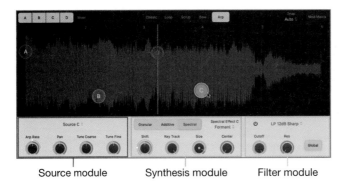

You've loaded a vocal sample in Sample Alchemy and surveyed the different play modes and synthesis techniques, adjusting the source handles over the waveform to adjust playback starting positions. Sample Alchemy is a one-of-a-kind, powerful instrument, and you've barely scratched the surface. So if you enjoy these kinds of sounds, take the time to explore the parameters in the lower section.

Key Commands

Keyboard Shortcuts	Description
Tracks area	
Command-Shift-I	Imports an audio file

11

Lesson Files

Time   This lesson takes approximately 60 minutes to complete.

Goals   Set the project tempo by detecting the tempo of a recording

Make an imported audio file follow the project tempo

Create tempo changes and progressive tempo curves

Make a track follow the groove of another

Use Flex Time to time-correct or time-stretch audio

Use Flex Pitch to tune vocals

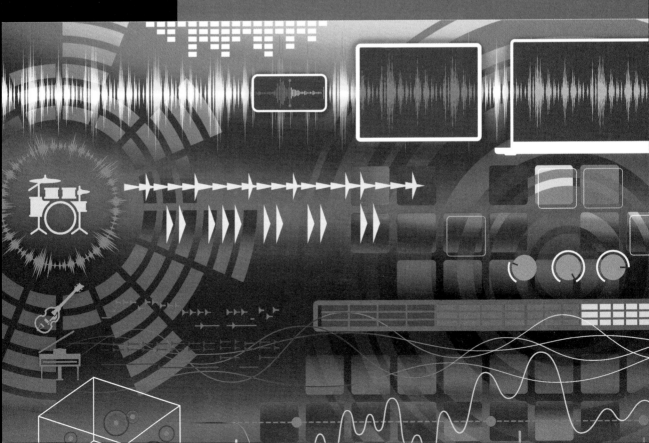

Edit the Timing and Pitch of Audio

The use of loops and samples has become omnipresent in modern music. New technologies encourage experimentation, and it is increasingly common to find a sample of a Middle Eastern instrument in a modern rock song, a sample of classical music in a pop song, or a sample of a pop song in a hip-hop track.

Mixing prerecorded material into a project can lead to exciting results, but the material must be carefully selected to ensure that it seamlessly blends into the project. The first challenge is to match the prerecorded musical material's tempo with the project's tempo.

Even when you record your own performances, precisely correcting the pitch and timing of an individual note can help you reach the perfection expected by a demanding audience. You can use note correction to fix imprecisions (or mistakes) in the recording, or you can use it creatively. Furthermore, special effects, such as Varispeed or time-stretching, can provide new inspiration.

In this lesson, you'll match the tempo and groove of audio files to make sure they combine into a musical whole. You'll manipulate the project tempo to add tempo changes and tempo curves, apply Varispeed, and use Flex editing to precisely adjust the position and length of individual notes and correct the pitch of a vocal recording.

Adapt the Project Tempo to the Tempo of an Audio File

Imagine that while listening to various recordings, you've found a recording of drums you like because of the way it grooves at its original tempo. To build a project around it, you need to adjust the project's tempo to match the recording. When the two tempos match, you can use the grid to edit and quantize regions, or add Apple Loops and keep everything synchronized.

Detect the Tempo of an Imported Recording

In this exercise, let's import a drum recording into a new project, let Logic Pro detect the tempo of the drums, and set it as the project tempo.

1   Choose **File** > **New** or press **Shift-Command-N** and create one audio track.

You'll now set up Smart Tempo so that Logic Pro detects the tempo of the audio file that you import and sets the project tempo accordingly.

2   In the LCD display, click **KEEP** and choose **ADAPT - Adapt Project Tempo**.

The global tempo track opens so you can easily spot any tempo changes that Logic Pro may create. The tempo curve is orange, and in the LCD display, the project tempo and time signature are also orange, indicating that those parameters are ready to adapt to the audio file you're about to import.

3   Press **Command-Shift-I**.

4   In the Open File dialog, choose **Logic Book Projects** > **11 Slow Drums.aif** and click **Open** (or press Return).

Logic Pro detects that the audio file you're importing has a sample rate of 44.1 kHz, whereas your new empty project has a default sample rate of 48 kHz. Let's change the project sample rate to 44.1 kHz.

5 Click **Change Project** (or press Return).

A progress bar appears while Logic Pro analyzes the file, and then an alert asks if you want to show the Smart Tempo Editor, which allows you to perform more advanced tasks like editing the beats detected by Logic Pro in the imported audio file. Let's open it.

NOTE ▶ If Logic Pro has previously analyzed this audio file (for example, if you've already completed this lesson), this alert won't appear. To remove the analysis information embedded in the audio file, select the audio region and choose Edit > Tempo > Remove Tempo Information from Audio File. Then restart this exercise in a new project.

6 Click **Show** (or press Return).

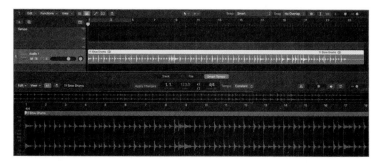

The Smart Tempo Editor opens at the bottom of the main window. In the LCD display, the tempo is set to *123 bpm*.

7   In the control bar, click the **Metronome** button (or press K).

8   Listen to the song.

The drums are in sync with the metronome; however, they play at half the speed. You can correct this in the Smart Tempo Editor.

9   In Smart Tempo Editor, click the **/2** button.

The Smart Tempo Editor displays a tempo value of *61.5*. In the LCD display, the tempo value does not show decimals, so its value is rounded to *62*.

NOTE ▸ To see the exact project tempo value, click the List Editors button (or press D) and then click the Tempo tab.

10   Listen to the song.

Now the drums are perfectly in sync with the metronome.

11   In the control bar, click the **Editors** button (or press E) to close the Smart Tempo Editor.

12   In the LCD display, click **ADAPT** and choose **KEEP - Keep Project Tempo**.

13   Click the **Metronome** button, or press **K**, to turn the metronome off.

14   Choose **File** > **Save** (or press Command-S).

15   In the Save dialog, enter a name and a location for your project, and then press **Return**.

Now that you've set the project tempo to match the drums tempo, you can add Apple Loops, and they will automatically match the tempo of your drums. You can also use the grid in the workspace to cut an exact number of bars in a region.

Import Apple Loops

You'll now use the Loop Browser to add an Apple Loop to your drums track.

1   In the control bar, click the **Apple Loops** button (or press O).

Let's find an audio bass loop. First, you can specify the type of Apple Loop you want to search for.

2   At the upper left of the results list, click the **Loop Type** button.

Let's limit the search to only audio Apple Loops.

3   Click **Audio Loops** to keep only that choice selected.

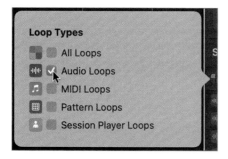

Only audio Apple Loops are shown in the results list.

4   At the top of the Loop Browser, click the **Instrument** button, and then click the **Elec Bass** keyword button.

5   At the top of the Loop Browser, click the **Genre** button, and then click the **Chillwave** keyword button.

Feel free to preview a few of the loops before moving on.

6   Drag **Brooklyn Nights Bass** to the workspace, below the Drums track at bar 1.

7   Move the pointer to the upper-right corner of the Brooklyn Nights Bass region and drag the Loop pointer to bar 13.

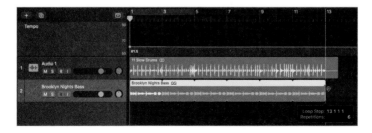

8 Listen to the song.

The bass loop plays in sync with the project tempo, which means it's in sync with the drums. The bass loop is playing in the key of the project (C), which sounds too low. Loops generally sound more natural when they're played in their original key. With no transposition to process, the timbre of the loop is closest to the original recording, and you hear fewer *artifacts* (distortion resulting from the time-stretching or pitch-shifting process). Let's change the key.

9 In the LCD display, click the key signature (C major) and in the pop-up menu, choose **E Minor**.

The key signature is now E minor, and the loop plays in the new project key.

10 Choose **File** > **Save** (or press Command-S).

Match an Audio File to the Project Key and Tempo

Many current music genres find inspiration in older music, and it's common for producers to use samples of older recordings, whether for a vocal part or an orchestra hit. Recycling existing material to use in a new song can present a challenge when the existing material has rhythmic and melodic or harmonic content. You must make sure that the sampled recording plays at the current project's key signature and tempo.

Smart Tempo allows you to automatically match the tempo of an imported audio file to the project tempo, and the Transpose parameter in the Region inspector makes it a breeze to change the pitch of that imported file.

1 Choose **File** > **Project Settings** > **Smart Tempo**.

You'll make this project turn on the Flex & Follow region parameter for imported audio files so they sync up to the project tempo.

2 Click the **Set Imported Files To** pop-up menu and choose **On**. Close the Settings window.

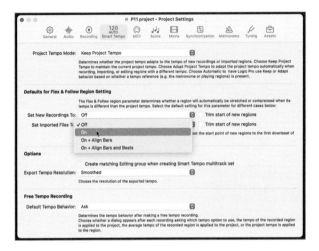

Logic Pro will analyze any audio file you import to detect its original tempo and time-stretch it, as necessary, to make it play back at the project tempo. Let's import a guitar part.

3 In the control bar, click the **Browsers** button (or press F) and in the Browser pane, click the **All Files** tab.

4 Navigate to **Logic Book Projects**.

Before importing **11 Groovy Guitar.wav**, let's try to play it along with the project.

5 Press the **Space** bar to play the project.

6 In the All Files Browser, click **11 Groovy Guitar.wav** (or press Option-Space bar) to preview it.

It's obvious that the guitar wasn't recorded in the same key or at the same tempo as the current project.

7   Drag **11 Groovy Guitar.wav** below the bass track at bar 1.

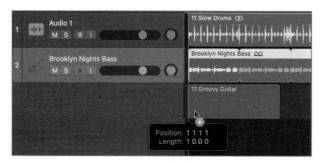

In the Region inspector, the Flex & Follow parameter of the 11 Groovy Guitar region is set to On.

8   Play the project from the beginning.

The guitar plays at the right tempo, but in the wrong key! You'll fix that later, but for now, let's focus on the timing of the guitar.

9   In the bass track header (track 2), click the **M** (Mute) button to mute the track.

10   Listen to the project.

The guitar and the drums play in time. Now, let's make the guitar play in the right key. The guitar was recorded in D minor, and the current project's key signature is E minor, so you need to transpose the guitar two semitones up.

11   Make sure the 11 Groovy Guitar region is selected and in the Region inspector, double-click to the right of the **Transpose** parameter.

12   Enter *2* and press **Return**.

The amount of transposition is indicated to the right of the region name (+2).

13   Unmute the bass track (track 2).

14   Listen to the project.

The guitar now plays at both the correct tempo and key signature. It still ends too early, and in the following exercise, you'll take care of copying the guitar a few times to make sure it fills up the 11 Groovy Guitar track.

15   Choose **File** > **Save** (or press Command-S) to save your project.

Create Tempo Changes and Tempo Curves

When you want to vary the tempo throughout a project, you can use the Tempo track to insert tempo changes and tempo curves. All MIDI regions and Apple Loops automatically follow the project tempo, even when tempo variations occur in the middle of a region. The **11 Groovy Guitar.wav** file is not an Apple Loop, but earlier you chose to turn on Flex & Follow Tempo for imported audio files, so that region will also follow the project's tempo curve.

Create and Name Tempo Sets

In this exercise, you'll create a new tempo set and name both the current and new tempo sets. You'll create a new tempo curve in the new tempo set, and later switch between the original tempo and the new tempo curve.

1   In the Tempo track header, from the **Tempo** pop-up menu, choose **Tempo Sets > Rename Set**.

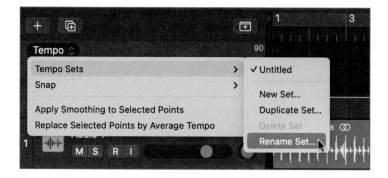

A text field appears on the Tempo track header.

2   Enter *Original* and press **Return**.

3   From the **Tempo** pop-up menu, choose **Tempo Sets > New Set**.

A new tempo set is created with a default value of *120 bpm*. A text entry field appears, ready for you to enter a name for the new set. In this set, you'll make the tempo go gradually faster, so let's name it Accelerando.

4   Rename the new tempo set *Accelerando* and listen to the song.

The bass and guitar tracks play at the new tempo (120 bpm); however, the drum track (which was imported into the project before you changed your Smart Tempo settings to turn on Flex & Follow Tempo for imported audio files) continues playing at its original recording tempo. To make sure the drum track's tempo is properly analyzed, you need to temporarily revert the project tempo to the original drums tempo before you turn Flex on.

5   In the Tempo track header, click the **Tempo** pop-up menu and choose **Tempo Sets** > **Original**.

In the Tempo track, you see the correct drums tempo of *61.5 bpm*.

6   On the Slow Drums track, click the **11 Slow Drums** region to select it.

7   In the Region inspector, set **Flex & Follow Tempo** to **On**.

8   In the Tempo track header, click the **Tempo** pop-up menu, choose **Tempo Sets** > **Accelerando**, and listen to the song.

Now all tracks in the project play at the new 120 bpm tempo. Let's edit the guitar track so that the guitar plays throughout the song.

9 **Option**-drag the 11 Groovy Guitar region to bar 5, and then **Option**-drag it again to bar 9.

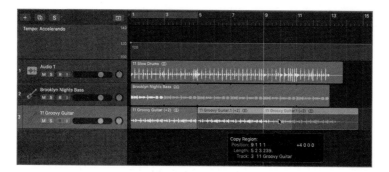

The guitar plays throughout the song, and when the drums stop at bar 13, you can hear the end of the Guitar region with the last two notes of the guitar riff echoing.

Create Tempo Changes and Tempo Curves

You now have two tempo sets. Let's edit the new one to create a tempo that starts at 60 bpm and progressively ramps up to about 90 bpm within the first couple of bars.

1 In the Tempo track, drag the tempo line down to *60 bpm*.

Although the line seems to stop at the bottom edge of the Tempo track, keep dragging down until you see the desired tempo value displayed in the Help Tag. When you release the mouse button, the scale in the Tempo track header updates, and you can see the new tempo.

Let's insert a tempo change at bar 3.

2   Click the tempo line at bar 3.

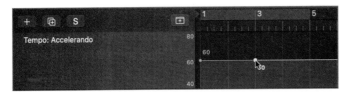

A new tempo point is inserted at bar 3 with the current *60 bpm* value.

3   Drag the line that is located to the right of the new tempo change up to a value of *90 bpm*.

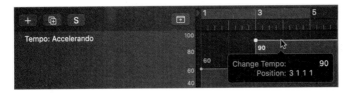

TIP ▶ To reposition a tempo point, drag the tempo point horizontally.

4   Listen to the song.

The tempo changes abruptly at bar 3. To smooth the tempo change, you're going to accelerate the tempo from 60 bpm at bar 1 to 90 bpm at bar 3.

5   At bar 3, position the mouse pointer on the corner below the 90 bpm tempo point.

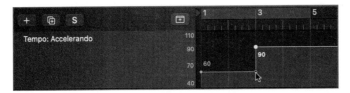

6   Drag the tempo point upward and to the left.

You can precisely adjust the tempo curve by dragging the tempo point farther to the left, up, or in both directions.

7 Listen to the song.

The tempo now ramps up progressively between bar 1 and bar 3.

8 Click the **Global Tracks** button (or press G) to close the global tracks.

9 Choose **File** > **Close Project** and save the project.

You can create complex tempo maps to add excitement to your arrangements. Sometimes, a chorus that's a bit faster than the rest of the song is all an arrangement needs to really take off. Or you can use tempo curves to create a *ritardando*, which is a gradual slowing down of the tempo, typically used at the end of a song. All your Apple Loops and MIDI regions will automatically follow the tempo map, and you can use a flex mode for each audio track that you want to follow the tempo map.

Make a Track Follow the Groove of Another Track

Playing all tracks at the same tempo is not always sufficient to achieve a tight rhythm. You also need to make sure they play with the same feeling. For example, a musician may play slightly late to create a laid-back feel, or they may add some swing to their performance by delaying only the upbeats.

To learn how to get your tracks to play with the same feel, let's open a new project with a drummer playing a swing groove, and then make a shaker on another track follow the groove of the drummer.

1 Open **Logic Book Projects** > **11 Swing Groove** and listen to the song.

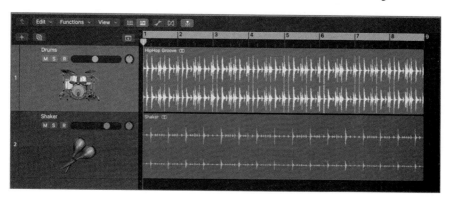

Even though both tracks play at the same tempo, the drums are playing a hip-hop shuffle groove, whereas the shaker is following a straight sixteenth-note grid. Feel free to solo the individual tracks to clearly hear each instrument's feel.

Let's zoom in so you can see the individual drum hits on the waveforms.

2   Press **Return** to go back to the beginning of the project.

3   Press **Command-Right Arrow** nine times to zoom in on the first two beats (so you can see 1 and 1.2 in the ruler).

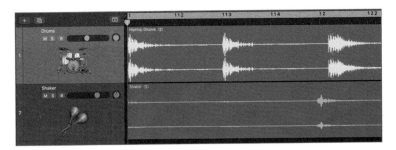

Below the 1.2 grid mark in the ruler, you can clearly see that the waveforms on the two tracks are out of sync.

To make the shaker follow the groove of the drums, you need to set the Drums track as the groove track.

4   Press **Option-T** and in the **Track Header Components** popover, select **Groove Track**.

At first glance, nothing seems to have changed in the track headers.

5   Position the pointer over track number (1) of the Drums track.

A gold star appears in place of the track number.

6 Click the gold star.

The gold star appears in a new column on the track header to indicate that the Drums track is now the groove track. On the Shaker track header, in the same column, you can select the checkbox to make that track follow the groove track.

7 On the **Shaker** track, select the **Match Groove Track** checkbox.

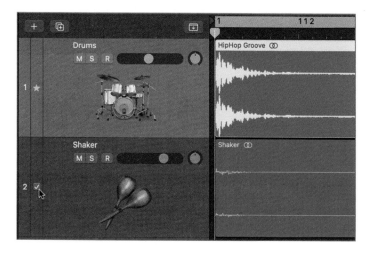

The waveform on the Shaker track updates so that the notes are in sync with the notes on the groove track.

8 Listen to the song.

The shaker now follows the groove of the drums, and they play in sync.

9 Solo the Shaker track.

10 While listening to the shaker, toggle the **Match Groove Track** checkbox to compare the original performance with the new groove.

When the checkbox is unselected, the shaker plays straight eighth notes and sixteenth notes.

When the checkbox is selected, the shaker plays the same hip-hop shuffle feel as the drums.

11   Unsolo the Shaker track.

12   Choose **File** > **Close Project** without saving the project.

Groove tracks work with multiple region types (Audio, MIDI, and Session Player regions). Experiment by applying the groove of a sample to your MIDI programming or by making a Drummer track follow the groove of a live bass recording.

Change the Project Playback Pitch and Speed with Varispeed

In the days of analog tape recording, engineers performed all sorts of tricks by changing the tape speed. Many major albums were sped up ever so slightly during the mixing process to add excitement to tracks by raising their tempos. This simultaneously raised the pitch, giving the impression of the vocalist reaching higher notes in the most emotional passages of the song. On the other hand, engineers would sometimes slow the tape during recording so that a musician could play a challenging passage at a more comfortable tempo. When played back at its regular speed during mixdown, the recording created the illusion of the musician playing faster. DJs are probably the biggest users of Varispeed techniques, which gives them control over the tempo and pitch of a track, allowing for seamless transitions from one track to the next.

Logic Pro takes this concept a step further, offering both the classic Varispeed—which, like a tape or record player, changes both the pitch and the speed—and a Speed Only mode, which allows you to change the speed without changing the pitch.

1   Open **Logic Book Projects** > **11 Moments** and listen to the song.

Most of the tracks in the song are packed inside track stacks. On the track headers, feel free to click the disclosure triangles to open the track stacks and peek inside. To explore deeper, you can solo different tracks or subtracks to hear them in isolation and become familiar with this song.

In the LCD display in the control bar, you can see that the song is in the key of G minor, and its tempo is 128 bpm. To use the Varispeed feature, you must add the Varispeed display to the control bar.

2   **Control**-click an empty space in the control bar and from the shortcut menu, choose **Customize Control Bar and Display**.

In the dialog's LCD column, the Varispeed option is dimmed. To turn it on, you first need to choose the custom LCD display.

3   In the **LCD** column, from the pop-up menu, choose **Custom**.

4   Below the pop-up menu, select **Varispeed** and click outside the pop-up window to close it.

A new Varispeed display appears in the custom LCD display.

01:00:00:17.38   0001 1 1 001   Speed Only   128.0000   4/4
     1 2 2 232   0009 1 1 001   ±0.00%   Keep Tempo   /16

5   In the Varispeed display, drag the *0.00%* value down to *−6.00%*.

The Varispeed display is shaded in orange. The tempo value turns orange, too, indicating that the song is no longer playing at its normal tempo due to the Varispeed feature. If your main window is wide enough to display all the buttons to the right of the LCD display, you'll see the Varispeed button turn orange to indicate that it's turned on.

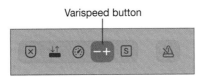

6   Listen to the song.

The song plays slower but retains its original pitch. Let's check the song's current playback tempo.

7   In the Varispeed display, click the **%** symbol and from the pop-up menu, choose **Resulting Tempo**.

The Varispeed display shows the resulting tempo of 120.320 bpm. You can now use the display to set the desired playback tempo.

8   Double-click the *120.320* tempo value and enter *118 bpm*.

The song plays slower but still at its original pitch. This would be perfect for practicing a part by playing along with your instrument. You could even record your part at this speed and then turn off Varispeed to play the whole song (including your newly recorded part) at the normal speed.

Now let's apply the classic Varispeed effect that changes both the playback speed and pitch.

9   In the Varispeed display, click **Speed Only** and from the pop-up menu, choose **Varispeed** (Speed and Pitch).

10 Listen to the song.

Now the song plays both slower and lower in pitch. This is the classic Varispeed effect available on tape machines and turntables.

11 In the Varispeed display, click the **bpm** symbol and from the pop-up menu, choose **Detune** (Semitones.Cents).

12 Double-click the −1.41 detune value and enter −2.00.

13 Listen to the song.

Now the song plays slower and pitched down by two semitones. If your singer isn't at the top of their game that day and can't reach their usual high notes, you could record at this slower speed and later turn off Varispeed to play the whole song at the higher pitch.

14 In the control bar, click the **Varispeed** button to turn it off.

In the LCD display, the Varispeed display is no longer orange, indicating it's been turned off, and the project plays at its original speed and pitch.

Edit the Timing of an Audio Region

In Logic Pro, Flex Time is a tool that allows you to edit the timing of individual notes, chords, drum hits, or even smaller portions of audio inside an Audio region. When using Flex Time, the audio is first analyzed to locate transients (the attacks of individual notes), and Logic Pro positions transient markers on top of the waveform. You can then create Flex markers, drag them to change the positions of the transients, and determine how the audio material around the markers is moved, time-stretched, or time-compressed.

Time-Stretch the Waveform Between Transient Markers

In this exercise, you'll use Flex Time editing to correct the timing of a guitar.

1   On the GTRs track (track 30), click the disclosure triangle to open the track stack containing all the guitar tracks.

   Let's correct the timing of a few guitar notes on the blue region at bar 31 on the Gtr New track.

2   On the Gtr New track (track 35), click the blue **gtr new** region to select it.

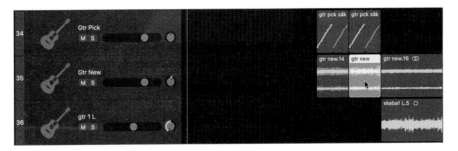

3   Choose **Navigate > Set Rounded Locators by Selection and Enable Cycle** (or press U).

   A cycle area is created that corresponds to the selected region. Both guitars on tracks 34 and 35 play the same rhythm. Let's listen to the two guitars together.

   TIP ▶ To solo multiple consecutive tracks in the Tracks view, click and hold a track's Solo button and drag down to slide across the other track headers.

4   In the track headers, solo both the Gtr Pick (34) and Gtr New (35) tracks.

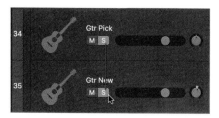

5   Listen to the two guitars at bar 41.

The two guitars are not playing the third note together (bar 41, beat 2).

6   Press the **Space** bar to stop playback.

When Cycle mode is on, the Go to Beginning button can go to the beginning of the cycle area or the beginning of the project.

7   In the control bar, click the **Go to Beginning** button.

The playhead moves to the beginning of the cycle area (bar 41). You'll now use Command-Down Arrow to zoom in vertically, use Command-Right Arrow to zoom in horizontally, and scroll as needed to see the first three notes at bar 41 on the Gtr New track.

8   Scroll and zoom in to see the first three notes at bar 41 on track 35.

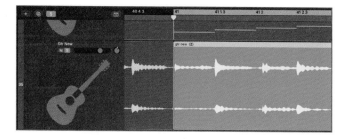

You'll be correcting the guitar note on the Gtr New track (track 35) at bar 41 beat 2.

9   In the Tracks area menu bar, click the **Show/Hide Flex** button (or press Command-F).

Show/Hide Flex button

Each track header shows a Track Flex button and a Flex Mode pop-up menu.

10 In the Gtr New track header (track 35), click the **Track Flex** button.

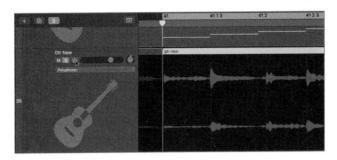

Flex editing is turned on. The region on the track is darker, and transient markers appear as dashed vertical lines where Logic Pro detects the attack of a new note. The Flex Mode is set to Polyphonic by default, which is appropriate for this track.

NOTE ▶ Polyphonic mode is intended for instruments that play chords (piano, guitar), Monophonic is used with instruments that produce only one note at a time (vocals, wind), and Slicing is for moving notes without time-stretching any audio (good for drums).

The third note (at *41 2 1 1*) in the region is late.

11 In the upper half of the waveform, place the pointer over the transient marker of the third note.

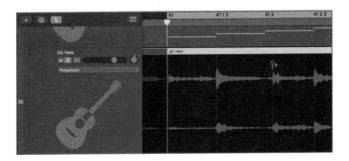

The pointer turns into a Flex tool and looks like a single flex marker with a + (plus sign) next to it. This symbol indicates that clicking or dragging will insert one flex marker on the transient marker. When you drag the flex marker, the waveform is stretched between the region beginning and the flex marker, and between the flex marker and the region end. Let's try it.

12 Drag the **Flex** tool to the left to *41 2 1 1*.

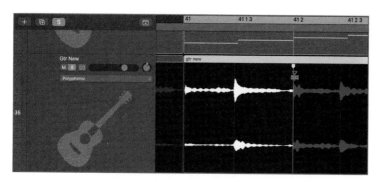

After you release the mouse button, the flex marker looks like a bright vertical line with a handle at the top.

When you click a flex marker, a flex drag indicator in the region header above the flex marker shows how the flex marker was moved from its original position. You can click the X symbol inside the flex drag indicator to delete that flex marker (and return the waveform to its original state).

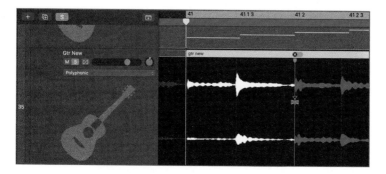

The waveform to the left of the flex marker is white, indicating that it was time compressed. The waveform to the right of the flex marker was time expanded. As a result, all the notes to the right of the flex marker have changed their positions, which is not what's wanted here.

13 Choose **Edit** > **Undo** (or press Command-Z).

The waveform returns to its original state.

14 In the lower half of the waveform, place the pointer over the transient marker of the third note.

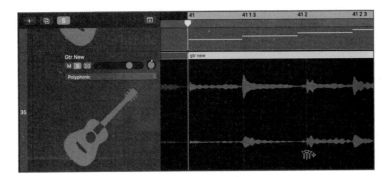

The Flex tool looks like three flex markers with a + (plus sign). Clicking it creates three flex markers, one at each of the following positions:

▶   On the transient marker you're about to drag

▶   On the transient marker before (which will not move)

▶   On the transient marker after (which will not move)

15 Drag the **Flex** tool to the left to snap the flex marker to *41 2.*

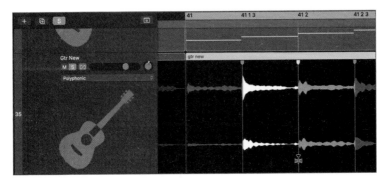

The second note is time-compressed, the third note is time-stretched, and the rest of the region remains unaffected.

16 Listen to the edit.

The timing is now tight. Let's zoom out.

17 In the workspace, click an empty area (or press Shift-D) to deselect all regions.

18 Press **Z**.

You can see all the regions in the workspace. To toggle the solo status of all tracks at once, you can click the Clear/Recall Solo button.

19 At the top of the track headers, click the **Clear/Recall Solo** button (or press Option-S).

All tracks are unsoloed.

20 On the GTRs track header (track 30), click the disclosure triangle to close the track stack.

Time-Stretch a Single Note

In the previous exercise, you used Flex editing to correct the timing of a note. This time, you'll use it for a creative purpose: to stretch a vocal note and make it sustain over a longer period of time than the singer was originally holding.

1 In the VOCALS track header (track 20), click the disclosure triangle to open the track stack.

You'll stretch a note at bar 114 in the red **V lead half tempo_1** region on track 21.

2 Scroll and zoom as necessary so you can see the note at bar 114.

3 Drag a cycle area from bar 113 to bar 116 and listen to the song.

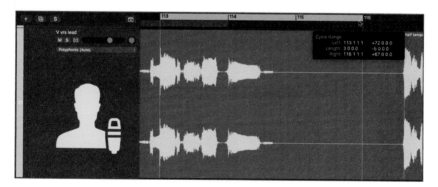

You are going to lengthen the last word ("this") to make it four beats longer.

4   In the V vrs lead track header (track 21), click the **Track Flex** button.

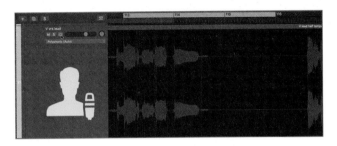

Transient markers appear over the waveform.

NOTE ▸ Make sure you have a sufficient vertical-zoom level to display the transient markers in Flex view.

5   Position your pointer in the lower half of the waveform, over the end of the note.

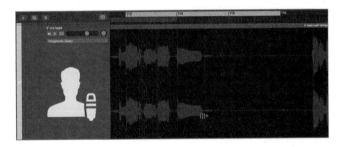

6   Drag the flex marker to *115 3 1 1*.

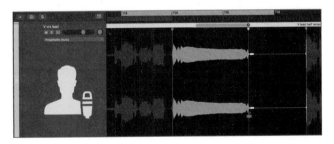

As you drag the flex marker, the LCD display shows its position (where it normally shows the playhead position). Three flex markers are created, and the note is lengthened.

7   Listen to the stretched vocal note.

The sustaining vowel of the word "this" sounds great! However, the last consonant ("s") was shortened and sounds a bit too short now. Let's undo the edit and use another technique to retain the entire length of the "s" consonant at the end of the word "this."

8   Choose **Edit > Undo** (or press Command-Z) to undo.

You'll create a marquee selection to select the "s" consonant portion of the waveform and drag it to move it. This creates four flex markers: one on the transient before the marquee selection (the beginning of the word "this"), one on each boundary of the marquee selection (which will not be stretched), and one on the transient after the marquee selection.

9   **Command**-drag to select the "s" consonant at *114 3 1 121*.

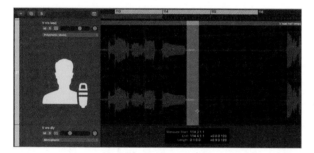

Positioning the pointer in the upper half of the marquee selection turns the pointer into the Hand tool, which lets you move the selection without stretching it.

10   Drag the upper half of the marquee selection to around *115 3 1 1*.

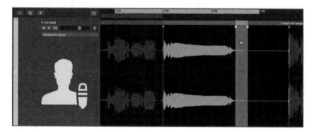

11   Click an empty area of the workspace to deselect the waveform and listen to your edit.

It sounds great! The word "this" is stretched, but the "s" consonant at the end has the same length as before.

12   Zoom out so you can see all your regions in the workspace.

13   Click the cycle area (or press C) to turn off Cycle mode.

Tune Vocal Recordings

Hitting pitches perfectly on every single note can be a challenge for singers. Tuning software allows you to correct pitches in a recording. It can be useful for saving an emotional take that contains a few off-pitch notes, or even to refine the pitch of a good performance.

In Logic Pro, Flex Pitch allows you to precisely edit the pitch curve of a single note, along with the amount of vibrato. In this exercise, you'll use Flex Pitch to tune the vocals in the pink regions on the Ad Lib track (track 27).

1   On the Ad Lib track (track 27), click the pink **Ad Lib 2** region in the CHORUS 2 section to select it.

2   Press **Z**.

The selected region fills the workspace.

3   Choose **Navigate > Set Locators by Selection and Enable Cycle** (or press Command-U).

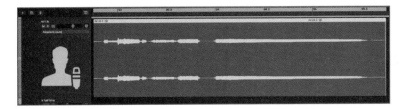

4   In the Ad Lib track header, click the **Solo** button (or select the track and press S).

From now on, you can press the Space bar to toggle playback on and off.

5   In the Ad Lib track header, click the **Track Flex** button.

Flex is turned on for that track, and transient markers appear over the waveform. Logic Pro automatically selects the Polyphonic (Auto) mode; however, to tune the pitch, you'll use the Flex Pitch mode.

6   In the track header, click the **Flex Mode** pop-up menu and choose **Flex Pitch**.

As in the Piano Roll Editor, the note pitches are represented as beams on a grid. (You may need to scroll up or down to see the note beams.) On the grid, light-gray lanes correspond to the white keys on the piano keyboard, and dark-gray lanes correspond to the black keys. The section of a note beam that intersects with the closest lane is colored, and the height of the hollowed-out section of the beam represents the amount of deviation from the perfect pitch. When a note plays at the perfect pitch, it sits exactly on a lane, and the beam doesn't have any hollowed-out section.

7   Click the second note to select it.

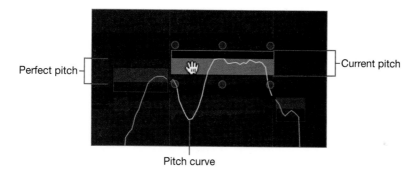

Perfect pitch

Current pitch

Pitch curve

On top of the frame, a light-gray line represents the pitch curve so that you can see pitch drifts and vibrato.

8   Listen to the vocals.

The singer sings "moments just like this," alternating between G and F notes. There are a few problems with the singer's pitch that you'll correct. The selected note is the beginning of the word "moments," and it sounds sharp.

9   **Control**-click the beam and from the shortcut menu, choose **Set to Perfect Pitch**.

The beam snaps to the closest lane, and the entire beam is colored, indicating that the note plays at the perfect pitch.

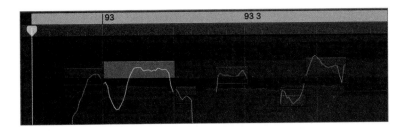

The next note is the end of the word "moments," and it also sounds sharp. However, it's so sharp that Logic Pro detected it as an F#. Let's try to correct it.

10 **Control**-click the beam of the following note and choose **Set to Perfect Pitch**.

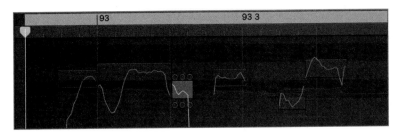

TIP ▶ To quickly tune an entire region, Control-click the background and choose "Set all to Perfect Pitch."

The beams snaps to an F#. The "ments" end part of the word "moments" now sounds exactly one semitone sharp: It should be an F. To transpose it, you can simply drag it vertically as you would drag a note in the Piano Roll.

11 Drag the **F#3** note to an **F3**.

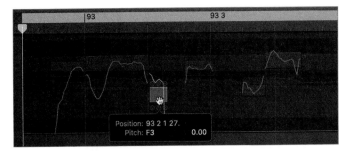

While you hold down the mouse button, you can hear the pitch of the audio signal at the exact horizontal position you clicked in the pitch curve.

The word "moments" now goes from a G to an F, and the pitch sounds perfect. The next note for the word "just" is a G, but the intonation is flat.

12 **Control**-click the next note and choose **Set to Perfect Pitch**.

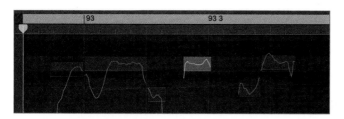

Now, the pitch of "just" sounds the same as the beginning of the word "moments"—perfect.

The next two beams represent the word "like." However, the first one is only there because the singer ramps up into the right pitch at the beginning of the word. So you'll leave it alone, tuning only the next beam, which represents the vowel part of the word "like."

13 **Control**-click the second beam of the word "like" and choose **Set to Perfect Pitch**.

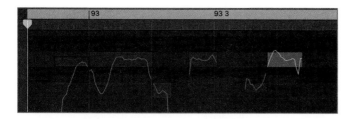

The beam snaps to a G, which is the correct pitch for that note; however, it still sounds a little sharp. Look at the pitch curve: The beginning of the "i" vowel in "like" goes up too high. Let's tame that.

As you position the pointer in the vicinity of the colored beam, hotspots appear around the beam that allow you to perform various adjustments.

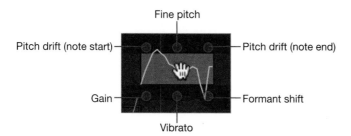

NOTE ▸ Sometimes, pitch correction can alter the timbre of a sound, especially when you play a note several semitones away from its original pitch. At some point, pitching up a vocal makes the singer sound like a chipmunk, whereas pitching it down makes the singer sound like a hulking monster. Dragging the Formant hotspot up or down helps you adjust the timbre to make it sound more realistic.

14 Drag the lower-mid hotspot to set **Vibrato** to *0%*.

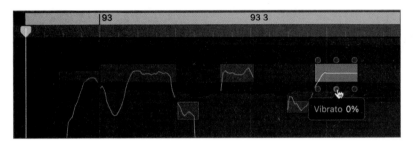

TIP ▸ To adjust a parameter on multiple notes, select the desired beams (or press Command-A to select them all) and adjust the parameters on one of the selected beams.

The pitch curve of that note is flatlined, and the pitch now sounds perfect. Let's try to flatten the pitch curve of the last sustained note on the word "this."

15 On the last note in the region, drag the lower-mid hotspot to set **Vibrato** to *0%*.

The pitch is perfect, but it sounds unnatural, almost synth-like. Even for this dance music production, that effect is a bit over the top.

16 Drag the lower-mid hotspot to set the **Vibrato** to *50%* to halve the pitch deviations around the perfect pitch.

Feel free to continue adjusting the pitch of the notes in other regions on the Ad Lib track. Don't be afraid to experiment with the other hotspots (pitch drift, fine pitch, gain, and formant pitch) and if you're not happy with a result, choose Edit > Undo (or press Command-Z).

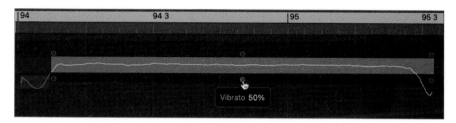

You now have a large repertoire of techniques that you can use to edit the tempo of a project and the timing of its regions, and you can make a track follow the groove of another track. Mastering these techniques will give you the freedom to use almost any prerecorded material in your projects, so keep your ears tuned to interesting material that you could sample and loop for your future songs.

Flex Time and Flex Pitch editing can help you correct imperfections in a performance, bringing your material to a new level of precision. Using Varispeed, tempo curves, groove tracks, and Flex Time and Flex Pitch editing techniques, you have a full palette of time and pitch manipulation techniques that you can use to correct imperfections or be creative.

Key Commands

Keyboard Shortcuts	Description
General	
Option-S	Clears or recalls all track solo buttons
Command-F	Show/Hide Flex
K	Toggle Metronome Click

12

Lesson File   Logic Book Projects > 12 Distortion

Logic Book Projects > 12 Lights On

Time   This lesson takes approximately 90 minutes to complete.

Goals   Add saturation to enhance the character of instruments

Adjust volume levels and pan positions

Filter frequencies with an equalizer plug-in

Add depth with delay and reverberation plug-ins

Use a compressor to make a vocal level consistent

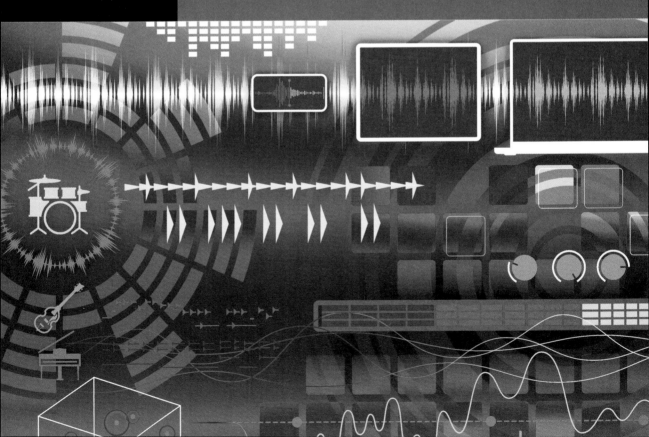

Lesson **12**

Mix a Song

Mixing is the art of positioning and blending the individual instruments and sounds within an audio landscape—the stereo sound field. A good mix can make the difference between an amateur demo track and a professional production. Mixing should carefully balance two goals: combining all the elements into a cohesive whole and, at the same time, keeping them sufficiently defined so listeners can distinguish among them. In other words, make the musicians sound as if they are playing in the same room, while ensuring they don't mask one another and muddy the mix. A good mix is like a completed puzzle in which all the pieces (all the instruments) fill their proper places in the sound field without overlapping.

When mixing, you should be faithful to the genre of the song. In Lesson 10, you worked with a song, "Moments," that had a larger-than-life polished sound because its music genre, dance, is often mixed with large public address (PA) systems and nightclubs in mind.

In this lesson, you'll add saturation to instruments in the Project One song that you used in Lessons 1 and 2. You'll then mix vocal tracks in an indie-folk song in the context of a modern pop production that combines many layered instruments and vocal tracks to achieve a more realistic and intimate sound while still being big and full of energy.

Use Saturation to Add Character

Saturation has long been a secret weapon of professional sound engineers. Originally produced by overdriving analog gear like consoles, mic preamps, or compressors, saturation enhances the harmonic richness of your instruments. The intensity of this effect can produce different results: Subtle amounts can result in a warm, punchy sound that helps an instrument find its place in the mix, while pushing the equipment harder can create gritty, fuzzy tones that add a unique character to the instrument.

First, you'll explore ChromaGlow, a saturation plug-in that uses machine learning to emulate a range of vintage analog equipment—such as tape machines, compressors, and mic preamps—then you'll use parallel processing to blend the unprocessed sound of a bass guitar with the distorted sound of a bass amp.

> **NOTE** ▸ ChromaGlow is a new machine-learning plug-in that supports only Apple Silicon. It won't open in machines running Intel chips.

Use ChromaGlow on Drums

In ChromaGlow, you can choose among five saturation models—each one has two styles to choose from. Let's use ChromaGlow to process a drum track, giving it a warmer sound and a strong character.

1 Open Logic Book Projects > **12 Distortion**.

This project is a version of Project One, which you worked with in Lessons 1 and 2 and that is ready for you to add distortion effects to.

2 Solo the Drums track (track 1).

3 In the upper half of the ruler, drag from bar 1 to bar 3 to create a cycle area.

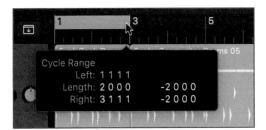

4 Listen to the drums.

Without distortion, the drums sound dry, clean, and punchy.

5 On the Drums channel strip in the inspector, click the empty slot below the Channel EQ plug-in and choose **Distortion** > **ChromaGlow**.

6 Turn the **Drive** knob up to *56%*.

The drums sound distorted. They also sound compressed and warm. As you dial various parameters, use the plug-in's On/Off button to compare the sound of the original drums with the sound processed through ChromaGlow.

Let's focus on the intro.

7 Toggle ChromaGlow on and off while listening to the drums in the intro (bar 1 to bar 3).

On the Drums channel strip, look at the Peak Level display above the meters.

TIP ▶ Click the Peak Level display (or stop and restart playback) to reset it.

The original drums peak at *−0.4 dBFS*, and when processed through ChromaGlow, they peak at *−8.6 dBFS*. The gentle compression added by ChromaGlow smooths out the transients and boosts the release tails, producing a richer, livelier sound that peaks lower.

8 Click the **Style** pop-up menu and choose **Colorful**.

Now, the drums have a strong character; however, the kick is quite muddy, and the toms at the end of the intro are too distorted. Let's clean it up.

9   Click the **Bypass Below** button.

The original sound of the kick and toms is restored.

10   Drag the **Bypass Below** field down to *90 Hz*.

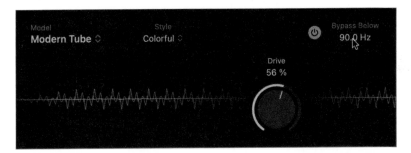

The sound is clean and dry but a little lifeless and sterile. ChromaGlow compresses and thickens the sound, the side stick is thicker, and the hi-hats are compressed and more present.

Note that the peak level on the channel strip is lower when the volume sounds louder.

11   Unsolo the Drums track.

12   Click the cycle area (or press C) to turn off Cycle mode.

13   Close the ChromaGlow window.

Processing the drums through ChromaGlow gives them a vibrant, lifelike quality. The resulting compression boosts the live room ambiance, making the drums seem louder despite their lower peak level.

Use ChromaGlow on Strings

Let's use ChromaGlow to give the strings a thicker, textured sound.

1 Click the Strings track header (track 4) to select it.

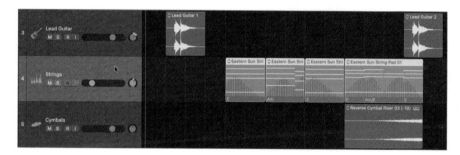

All the MIDI regions on the track are selected.

2 Solo the Strings track.

3 Press **U**.

Cycle mode is on, and the cycle area matches the selected regions.

4 Listen to the strings.

The strings sound clean and reverberated.

5 In the inspector on the Strings channel strip, insert ChromaGlow below the Channel EQ plug-in.

6 In ChromaGlow, turn the **Drive** knob up to *97%*.

The strings sound heavily distorted, with sizzling, abrasive high frequencies.

7   Click the **Model** pop-up menu and choose **Retro Tube**.

The high frequencies are tamed. The distortion is softer, and the strings sound warmer. Let's use the High Cut parameters to filter the sound and give it a low-fi character.

8   Click the **High Cut** button.

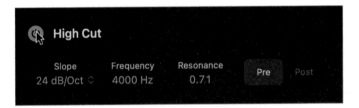

The filter gives the strings a synth-like quality. You still hear some high-frequency rattling, for example, around the middle of bar 5. You'll filter those out by positioning the High Cut filter after the distortion in the *signal chain* (the chain of audio processing stages that the signal goes through).

Note that even though the strings are perceived as louder with ChromaGlow on, the peak level on the channel strip is lower.

9   Click the **Post** button.

The high-frequency rattling sound disappears.

10 Drag the **Resonance** value up to *32.0.*

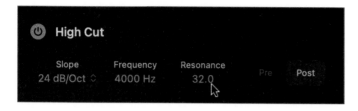

The sound is whistling, like a synth with a resonant filter.

11 Drag the **Resonance** value all the way down to *0.10.*

The filter is softer, and the strings retrieve some of their natural character.

At bar 13, when the strings play lower notes, the low frequencies become boomy. This excess low end can make an instrument muddy and mask other elements in the mix. To keep this under control, let's use the Bypass Below parameters at the top right of ChromaGlow.

12 Click the **Bypass Below** button.

13 Drag the **Bypass Below** field up to *500 Hz.*

ChromaGlow adds texture and character to the strings without denaturing them too much. The narrower frequency spectrum makes them sound like strings from an old movie soundtrack.

14 Unsolo the Strings track.

Now that the strings sound is richer and more focused, you can turn them down.

15 Drag the **Strings** volume fader down to *−20.0.*

16 Close the ChromaGlow window.

17 Turn off Cycle mode.

As with any tool, do not hesitate to exaggerate the settings to better hear the difference between models while experimenting and learning. Once you've achieved the desired sound, you can dial down the amount of saturation to use only what's necessary for the mix.

Add Distortion Using Parallel Processing

In Lesson 3, you used parallel processing to add reverb to a synth, sending the synth signal to a bus to apply the reverb on an Aux channel strip. Let's use the same technique to add distortion to the bass and blend the dry sound with the distorted sound.

1 Click the Bass track header (track 2) to select it.

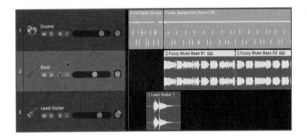

All the regions on the Bass track are selected.

2 Press **U**.

3 Solo the Bass track.

First, let's insert a bass amp plug-in directly on the Bass channel strip to hear what the bass sounds like when 100% of its signal is distorted.

4 In the inspector on the Bass channel strip, click the Audio FX slot and choose **Amps & Pedals > Bass Amp Designer**.

5   In the plug-in header, click the **Settings** pop-up menu and choose **Growler**.

That setting produces a lot of distortion. The bass loses its original character, and the notes no longer have a percussive attack.

6   On the Bass channel strip, click the Sends slot, and choose **Bus** > **Bus 3**.

An Aux 3 channel strip is created and displayed on the right in the inspector.

7   Drag the **Bass Amp** plug-in from the Bass channel strip to the Aux 3 channel strip.

8   On the Bass channel strip, slowly raise the **Bus 3 Send Level** knob up to *−9.0 dB*.

You hear a blend of the original dry bass sound mixed with the gritty sound of the bass processed through the Bass Amp Designer plug-in, and you can dial the dry/wet balance with the Send Level knob.

9   Save the project if you want to and close it.

Parallel processing allows you to finely control the blend between the distorted and unprocessed signals. It's an effective technique for applying strong distortion while preserving the original character of the sound.

Organize Windows and Tracks

A little organization can go a long way toward making your mixing session more productive. It can save time by minimizing the need to constantly open and close panes, or zoom and scroll the workspace to locate tracks or navigate the song. The more you streamline your workflow, the easier it will be for you to focus on finding a place in the mix for each specific sound or instrument.

Use Track Stacks to Create Submixes

As you build an arrangement, you may find yourself layering multiple instruments and vocal tracks to get a fuller sound. Modern pop productions often use short sound effects in strategic positions in the arrangement to keep renewing the excitement throughout the song. All those elements add up and increase the track count. Without organization, the Tracks area can quickly become bloated and make finding the tracks you want to adjust frustrating.

In Logic Pro, *track stacks* allow you to display a group of tracks as a single track in the Tracks area. You can open the stack when you need to access individual tracks. In this lesson, you'll be working with a song that has many tracks that are submixed in groups of related tracks—such as all the microphones used to record a drum kit, all the guitar tracks, or all the sound effects peppering the mix with ear candy. Let's explore the song and then create a new summing track stack to submix an ensemble of backup vocal tracks that you'll later process as a group.

1   Open Logic Book Projects > **12 Lights On**.

Look at the track number on the last track at the bottom of the Tracks area (Ami falsetto). This project contains 86 tracks! Some of the tracks are grouped in track stacks, recognizable by the disclosure triangle next to the track icons: Live Drums (track 1), Program Drums (track 13), Guitars (track 33), Keys (track 48), and FX (track 58).

NOTE ▸ Originally, this Logic Pro project contained over 150 tracks. To work with a manageable number of tracks, some of the original tracks were bounced into stems, such as the Backup Vocals stem on track 79.

2   On the Live Drums track (track 1), click the disclosure triangle next to the icon (or press Control-Command-Right Arrow).

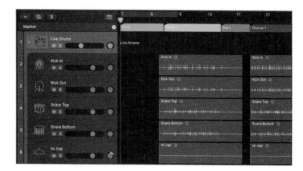

The track stack opens. You see 11 subtracks for all the microphones used to record this drum kit.

3   Click the triangle again (or press Control-Command-Left Arrow) to close the track stack.

Let's open all the track stacks to see all 86 tracks.

4   On any track stack, **Option**-click the disclosure triangle next to the icon.

All five track stacks open.

5   In the Tracks area menu bar to the right, click the **Vertical Auto Zoom** button.

Even at this low, vertical zoom level, you may not see all 86 tracks at once. Feel free to scroll down to see all the tracks. Let's close the track stacks.

6   On any track stack, **Option**-click the triangle to close all the track stacks.

7   In the Tracks area menu bar, click the **Vertical Auto Zoom** button to turn it off.

356 Mix a Song

Listen to the song. The mix sounds good, but a few instruments need work. Feel free to open track stacks and use Solo mode to focus on individual tracks or groups of tracks. The Lead Vocal (track 78) is raw, and you'll process it with EQ, compression, delay, and reverb plug-ins. In the Pre 2 section, you'll automate a track in the FX stack to make it ramp up in volume throughout the pre-chorus. In the Break section, you'll automate the pan of the vocal chops inside the FX stack to make them move on either side of the stereo field. Later, you'll give your entire mix a quick mastering treatment to add excitement and optimize the loudness.

Let's create a track stack for the green and blue backup vocal tracks at the bottom of the workspace.

8 Click the **Duvid disto** track header (track 80).

9 **Shift**-click the **Ami falsetto** track header (track 86).

10 Choose **Track** > **Create Track Stack** (or press Shift-Command-D).

11 In the track stack dialog, make sure **Summing stack** is selected and click **Create** (or press Return).

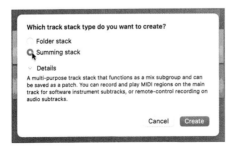

All the selected backup vocal tracks are packed into a track stack. You'll later use this summing track stack to process all the backup vocals together. Let's name the track stack and choose an icon.

12 Rename the track *Heys*.

13 On the Heys track header, **Control**-click the icon and choose an icon appropriate for backup vocals.

14 Click the triangle to close the Heys track stack.

The Tracks area is streamlined, which will make it easier for you to find your way around the tracks. Now that you have fewer visible tracks, you can zoom in a bit vertically.

15 Click an empty area in the workspace (or press Shift-D) to deselect all regions.

16 Press **Z**.

The tracks are zoomed in vertically to fill the workspace.

When working with high track counts, consider creating summing track stacks for groups of instruments (such as drums, guitars, keyboards, and vocals) to streamline your work-space and to make it easy to process and mix ensembles of related tracks.

Use Screensets to Switch Between the Tracks Area and the Mixer

When mixing projects with many tracks, navigating the Tracks area can be a challenge when the Mixer pane is open at the bottom of the workspace. Screensets allow you to store and recall various window layouts (including the window sizes, their positions on the screen, their zoom levels, the tools selected in the tool menus, and so on) for differ-ent tasks. In this lesson, you'll use two screensets to save different window layouts. One screenset will display your main window, and the other will include your Mixer. As you work on the mix, you can switch between these screensets using key commands.

Let's create the two screensets and study their behaviors.

1 At the top of your screen, look at the main menu bar.

The Screenset menu displays the number of the current screenset (1).

2 Click the **Screenset** menu to open it.

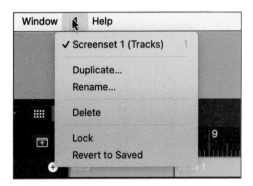

The menu lists only one screenset, with a default name in parentheses, Screenset 1 (Tracks). To create a new screenset, you only need to press a number key.

3 Close the **Screenset** menu.

4 Press **2**.

NOTE ▶ If you use an extended keyboard with a numeric keypad, make sure that you press the 2 key on the alphanumeric keypad. Pressing the numerical keypad lets you jump to the markers in the Marker track.

A new screenset is created with a main window of a different size and zoom level from screenset 1.

5 Choose **Window** > **Open Mixer** (or press Command-2).

A Mixer window opens on top of the main window. You won't need the main window in screenset 2, so let's close it.

6 Click the main window beneath the Mixer window to bring it to the front, and press **Command-W** to close it.

Let's make the Mixer window bigger.

7   In the Mixer title bar at the left, **Option**-click the green window zoom button.

The Mixer window occupies the full width of the screen.

8   Click the **Screenset** menu.

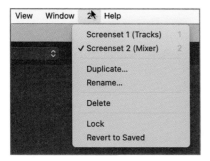

The menu lists the two screensets with an appropriate default name for each.

9   From the **Screenset** menu, choose **Screenset 1** (Tracks) or press **1**.

Screenset 1 is recalled, and you can see the main window.

By default, screensets are unlocked. You can open multiple windows, adjust their sizes and positions, open the desired panes, choose different tools, and so on, and the screenset will memorize your layout.

10   **Control-Option**-drag around any region to zoom in on it.

11 Press **2** to recall screenset 2 and press **1** to recall screenset 1.

Screenset 1 is recalled with the zoom adjustments you made in step 10.

When you're happy with the arrangement of a screenset, you can lock it to make sure that it always returns in that state. First, let's zoom out.

12 Make sure no regions are selected and press **Z**.

In the workspace, you can see all your regions again.

13 From the **Screenset** menu, choose **Lock**.

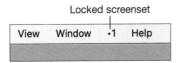

A dot appears next to the Screenset menu to indicate that the current screenset is locked. Let's observe the behavior of a locked screenset.

14 Zoom in on a region, change the tools in your tool menus, open some panes, such as a browser and an editor, and open some windows from the **Window** menu.

15 Press **1** to recall screenset 1.

The screenset is recalled in the state it was when you locked it, and all the changes you made in step 14 are lost.

16 Press **2** to recall screenset 2.

17 From the **Screenset** menu, choose **Lock** to lock screenset 2.

You have adjusted the layout of two screensets to easily switch between the Main window and the Mixer using the number keys. To accomplish a task in your project, you'll often zoom in, open panes and windows, or change tools. When you're finished with the task, recalling a locked screenset with only the Tracks area open at a zoom level where you can see all the project's regions and with your default tools selected saves a lot of time.

Customize a Locked Screenset

In the previous exercise, you learned that locked screensets are always recalled in the state in which you locked them. When you want to customize a screenset that was previously locked, you can unlock it, apply the desired changes, and lock it again.

Now, let's customize the Mixer window in screenset 2 to display only the tools you need in this lesson.

1 Make sure you are in screenset 2 (the Mixer window) and from the **Screenset** menu, choose **Unlock**.

After making a decision during a mixing session, you'll want to quickly locate the components you need on the correct channel strip in the Mixer. However, by default, the channel strips in the Mixer window show you nearly all the available channel strip components. Because you won't need to access some of them, you can hide them.

2 In the Mixer window, choose **View** > **Configure Channel Strip Components** (or press Option-X).

3 In the shortcut menu, deselect **Audio Device Controls**, **Setting Menu**, **MIDI Effects**, **Group**, and **Automation**; and select **Track Number**.

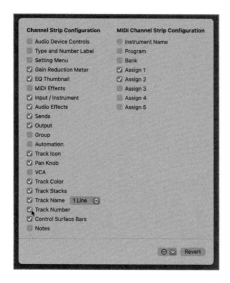

The features you don't need are now hidden, and track numbers are displayed at the bottom of channel strips, which makes them easier to identify.

4 Click outside the shortcut menu to close it.

Some of the track, plug-in, and output names are abbreviated to fit the narrow channel strips. For example, track 79's channel strip is displayed as "Back…ocals." You can choose to view wide channel strips, which are easier on the eyes and avoid name abbreviations.

5   In the Mixer, click the **Wide Channel Strips** button.

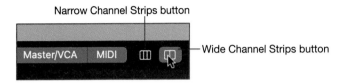

Narrow Channel Strips button

Wide Channel Strips button

The channel strips grow wider. The name on track 79's channel strip is now "Backup Vocals."

To avoid any further changes to this screenset, let's lock it again.

6   From the **Screenset** menu, choose **Lock** to lock screenset 2.

7   Press **1** to recall screenset 1.

You took the time to get rid of the clutter in the Mixer, which will reward you later when you must quickly identify channel strips, see where they are routed, and adjust their settings.

Adjust Volume, Pan, EQ, and Reverb

To give an instrument its place in the sound field, you can adjust four parameters: the instrument's volume, its lateral position in the sound field, its depth or distance, and its frequency spectrum. Those parameters are interrelated, and changing one often means that you'll need to readjust the others.

Let's now mix the ensemble of backup vocals that you packed into a summing stack in a previous exercise. You'll first adjust their volume balance, spread them out in different positions in the stereo field, EQ their submix, and send them to a bus to apply reverb.

Balance Volume Levels

When you start producing, adjusting the volume of instruments seems like an obvious task that can easily be overlooked to spend time on more advanced challenges like EQ or compression. However, to achieve a professional mix, finding the right levels for each individual track is of paramount importance. A vocal mixed even slightly too low will make the listener strain to decipher the lyrics, and a snare that's just a tad too loud can quickly become jarring and make the listener lose interest. To avoid those costly mistakes, make sure you take time to focus on the volume of each instrument.

You'll first create a cycle area, recall screenset 2 to see the Mixer, and balance the volume faders of the backup vocals channel strips.

1   Make sure the Heys track (track 80) is selected.

2   Click the first Heys region (at bar 58) to select it.

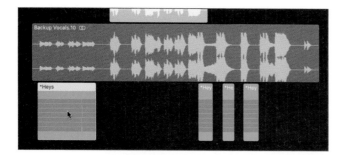

3   Choose **Navigate > Set Locators by Selection and Enable Cycle** (or press Command-U).

Cycle mode is turned on for the cycle area that corresponds to the selected Heys region.

4   Press **2** to recall screenset 2 and see the Mixer.

The Heys track stack's channel strip is selected in screenset 2, making it easy to find it.

5   At the bottom of the Heys channel strip, click the disclosure triangle.

The Heys track stack opens, and you can see the subtrack channel strips. Look at the channel strip names. There are two tracks for Duvid, two for Dov, and three for Ami.

6   Click the **S** button on the Heys channel strip (or press S) to solo it.

Listen to the ensemble of backup vocals singing "hey, hey, hey…." Let's start balancing Duvid's two tracks so they're about the same level.

7   Click the **S** button on the Duvid disto and the Duvid clean channel strips.

You hear mostly Duvid disto, but Duvid clean is too soft.

8   Drag the volume fader on Duvid clean all the way up, and then all the way down.

Turning a track's volume all the way up and then down allows you to clearly identify what that track sounds like within an ensemble of tracks, and it helps you find a good level to balance it with other tracks. You can also drag the volume fader of Duvid clean all the way down, listen to only Duvid disto for a few seconds, and then slowly raise the volume of Duvid clean until it sounds like both tracks have the same loudness.

9   Drag the **Duvid clean** volume fader to −9.0 dB.

To double-check that the two tracks are equally loud, you'll make sure you don't hear a jump in level when soloing one or the other during playback.

10 **Option**-click a **Solo** button on any of the soloed channel strips (or press Option-S) to clear all Solo buttons.

11 Click the **Solo** button on the Duvid disto channel strip.

12 Start playback and **Option**-click the **Solo** button on the Duvid disto and the Duvid clean channel strips.

The Duvid disto track still sounds louder than the Duvid clean track.

13 Drag the Duvid clean volume fader up to *−7.0 dB*.

The two tracks now have roughly the same perceived loudness.

Continue balancing the levels of the backup vocals in the Heys track stack, Option-clicking their Solo buttons one at a time, comparing their perceived loudness against the two Duvid tracks (and against each other). Different singers have different timbres, were recorded at different levels, and are processed with different audio-effect plug-ins, so vastly different amounts of gain may need to be applied to them to be perceived at the same loudness.

14 **Option**-click the **Solo** button on the Heys channel strip (track 80).

You can now hear a balanced submix of the seven voices. Every individual backup vocal can be heard clearly, which makes for a richer- and thicker-sounding vocal ensemble.

Pan Instruments in the Stereo Field

In real life, your brain determines the position of a sound source in space by comparing the sounds arriving in your left and right ears. You compare different parameters such as time, frequency spectrum, and level. In a mixer, you localize sounds in the horizontal plane by adjusting the relative levels sent to the left and right speakers.

When a mono channel strip's Pan knob is centered, the mono signal is sent to both the left and the right speakers at equal levels, making you perceive that sound as coming from the center of the stereo field, right in the middle of the left and right speakers. As you turn the Pan knob, for example to the left, the level sent to the right speaker is decreased, and you perceive the sound coming from the left side of the stereo field. When the pan is all the way to the left (which is known as panning "hard left"), no signal is sent to the right speaker. All the signal comes from the left speaker, and you perceive the signal coming from that direction.

In the Heys track stack, the three singers sharing the backup vocal duties each have a couple of tracks. To spread them out, you'll work with one singer at a time, panning their tracks on either side of the stereo field.

1 Solo the Duvid disto and the Duvid clean tracks.

Duvid disto is heavily processed by a guitar amp plug-in and has a unique character, whereas Duvid clean sounds natural. To blend the two timbres together, you'll keep them fairly centered but separate them slightly so they're on either side of the stereo field.

2 On the Duvid disto channel strip, drag the **Pan** knob down to −*11*.

3 On the Duvid clean channel strip, drag the **Pan** knob up to +*13*.

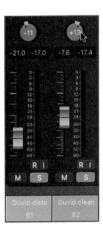

The two vocals are separated, and it's already easier to tell them apart, which makes their mix wider and richer sounding.

TIP ▶ When panning tracks, monitoring your mix with headphones helps clearly localize sounds even when using subtle amounts of panning. At the same time, headphones tend to exaggerate the width of your mix, whereas speaker monitors give you a more realistic image. For best results, alternate between monitoring with speakers and headphones.

You'll pan the two Dov backup vocals hard left and hard right to give a lot of width to the ensemble.

4 Solo the Dov and Dov double tracks.

5 Pan Dov all the way to the left (−*64*) and pan Dov double all the way to the right (+*63*).

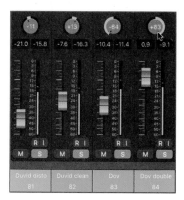

You'll pan the Ami and Ami double tracks to fill the rest of the stereo field.

6 Solo the Ami and Ami double tracks.

7 Pan Ami to −*31* and Ami double to +*34*.

Let's listen to the ensemble.

8 **Option**-click one of the yellow **Solo** buttons (or press Option-S) to clear all Solo buttons.

9 Solo the Heys track stack.

On the Ami falsetto track, Ami sings one octave higher, which gives that track a unique character, and you'll keep that track in the center of the mix. All the backup vocals are now nicely separated, and it sounds like a group of singers placed in different positions in front of you.

10 Click the **Solo** button on the Heys track stack to unsolo it.

11 At the bottom of the Heys channel strip, click the disclosure triangle to close the stack.

12 Press **1** to recall screenset 1.

Panning the vocal tracks in different positions across the stereo field gives width to the ensemble. Separating the singers in the horizontal plane allows the listener to better distinguish each individual performance, producing a richer, livelier mix.

Use EQ to Shape Frequencies

The sound of an instrument consists of several frequencies mixed in varying amounts. By applying an EQ plug-in to attenuate or boost certain ranges of frequency, you alter the timbre of the sound, like how you would change the sound of your music player by tweaking the bass or treble EQ settings.

EQ plug-ins help shape the frequency spectrum of your instruments, focusing them in a specific frequency range and helping each instrument cut through the mix. Equalizing (EQ'ing) an instrument can also decrease undesirable frequencies in its recording to make it sound better and keep it from masking other instruments in the same frequency range.

In the Heys section, the mix contains deep, low-frequency elements on nearly every track in the song. If you solo the tracks, you'll hear a subkick on track 13, the bass plays low notes on track 30, the guitars play heavily distorted chords on track 33, and the keyboards play ultra-deep dubstep wobbly sounds on track 48. To allow the backup vocals to soar above this massive mix of low-frequency elements, let's cut off all low-frequency content from their submix. Make sure the Heys track (track 80) is selected and solo it.

1 In the inspector on the Heys channel strip, click the thumbnail **EQ** display.

A Channel EQ plug-in is inserted in the first slot of the Audio FX area, and the plug-in window opens.

EQ band   Band On/Off button

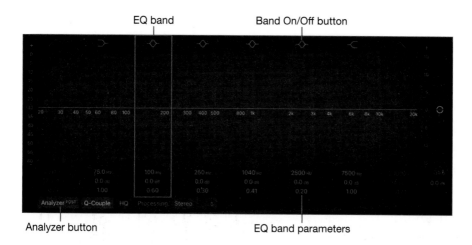

Analyzer button   EQ band parameters

The Channel EQ plug-in allows you to adjust eight bands of EQ. You can toggle a band on and off by clicking the button at the top of that band. By default, the first and last bands are turned off, and all the other bands are turned on. Each band's settings are shown below the graphic display in the EQ band fields. All the bands that are turned on by default have their Gain parameters set to *0.0 dB*; and in the graphic display, the EQ curve is flat, which means that the Channel EQ is not currently affecting the audio signal on the channel strip.

The Analyzer button toggles the frequency analyzer, which displays the post-EQ frequency spectrum curve of the sound on the graphic display when the track is playing.

2   Click the **Band 1 On/Off** button to turn it on.

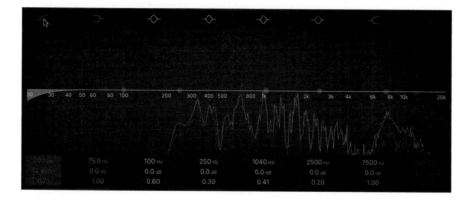

The first EQ band's shape (a low-cut filter) appears on the graphic display. You can see that the low frequencies are slightly attenuated around *20 Hz*.

You can use the Space bar to start playback so that you can hear the results of your adjustments in the Channel EQ plug-in.

3   In the **EQ band** field, drag the frequency up to around *1000 Hz*.

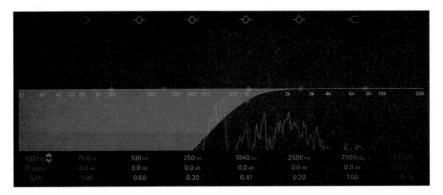

A lot of low-frequency content is cut off, and the backup vocals sound tiny. Let's back up and cut off a more reasonable number of low frequencies.

4   Drag the frequency to around *500 Hz*.

The backup vocals sound fuller again but without the muddy, low frequencies. To make the low cut a little stronger while keeping the frequencies above 500 Hz, you can make the EQ curve's slope steeper.

5   Below the frequency, drag the slope up to *24 dB/Octave*.

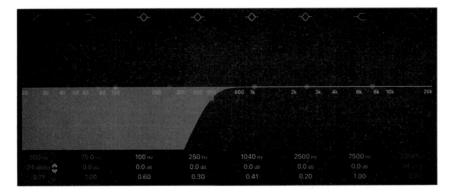

Listen while toggling the Channel EQ off and on. You can also try toggling the Solo button on the Heys track stack to compare the backup vocals with the Channel EQ off and on within the context of the rest of the mix.

You've used the Channel EQ plug-in to change the frequency spectrum of the backup vocal track stack. Cutting off the low frequencies helps give this vocal ensemble its place in the frequency spectrum of the mix, leaving ample room for the low-frequency elements on the other tracks.

Add Depth and Distance with Delay and Reverb

Now, let's use a couple of different delay plug-ins to position two of the vocals in different spaces: You'll place one of Duvid's vocals in an intimate space at a short perceived distance and one of Ami's vocals farther away in a larger space to give depth to the mix. Then you'll add reverb to the sum of the backup vocals to give dimension to the ensemble and make the group of vocals more coherent.

1   Press **2** to recall screenset 2.

2   At the bottom of the Heys channel strip, click the disclosure triangle to open the track stack.

3   Solo Duvid disto (track 81).

4   In the Audio FX area, click a slot below the Guitar Amp Pro plug-in and choose **Delay > Tape Delay**.

    By default, the plug-in creates a 1/4 note echo. Let's dial in a shorter slapback echo effect and make it more subtle.

5   Click the **Note** pop-up menu and choose **1/16**.

The singer sounds like he's in a more intimate space. Let's make the effect a little more subtle.

6 In the Tape Delay Output section, drag the **Wet** slider down to *13%*.

On the Ami track, let's add a longer delay effect.

7 Close the Tape Delay plug-in window (or press 2 to recall screenset 2).

8 On the Ami channel strip (track 85), **Option**-click the **Solo** button.

9 In the Audio FX area, click the slot below the Compressor plug-in and choose **Delay** > **Echo**.

10 Click the **Note** pop-up menu and choose **1/8 Dotted**.

11 Drag the **Feedback** knob down to *33%*.

12 Drag the **Wet** slider down to *6%*.

Ami sounds like he's in a larger room.

13 Close the Echo plug-in window (or press 2 to recall screenset 2).

If you scroll to the right of the Mixer, you'll see an Aux named Vocal Verb that has its input set to Bus 12. The Aux was set up to process vocal tracks in the song through a Space Designer reverb plug-in and a Channel EQ to cut off low frequency on the reverberated signal. To add reverb to the ensemble, you'll send the main track of the Heys track stack to that Aux.

14 On the Heys channel strip, **Option**-click the **Solo** button.

15 In the Sends section, click the first Send slot and choose **Bus 12** > **Vocal Verb**.

16 Drag the **Send Level** knob up all the way up and then all the way down.

You can clearly hear the reverb effect added by dialing in the Bus 12 Send Level knob.

17 Drag the **Send Level** knob to around −25 dB.

18 Unsolo the Heys channel strip and close the track stack.

19 Press **1** to recall screenset 1.

20 Click the cycle area (or press C) to turn off Cycle mode.

Listen to the song starting in the Break section, a little before the Heys section (at around bar 53). The backup vocals need to come down in level within the mix.

21 In the inspector on the Heys channel strip, drag the volume fader down to around −3.1 dB.

You've created different delay effects to place individual singers in virtual rooms of different sizes. The perception of having the backup singers in different spaces gives depth to the ensemble, and processing them all through the same reverb brings them together into a cohesive whole.

Build a Lead Vocal Chain

In mainstream pop music, as in many other genres where the song is the generic format, the lead vocals are the single most important element of the mix. A great deal of care must be taken to get the best possible sound for the singer. To achieve that goal, two fundamental plug-ins in your toolbox are an EQ and a compressor. An EQ helps carve the frequency spectrum to help the vocal cut through a mix that is already populated with many layered instruments and sound effects. The compressor gives the singer a consistent level to make sure that they don't pop out of the mix (which can almost sound like they're singing on top of an instrumental record played on another reproduction system) or that they don't fall below the other instruments (which would make the listener strain to hear the lyrics).

Use EQ to Shape the Frequency Spectrum

To shape the frequency spectrum of a vocal track, let's use the Channel EQ plug-in to attenuate some of its low rumbling, cut a metallic ringing frequency, and tame some of the higher frequencies.

1   Select and solo the Lead Vocals track (track 78).

2   Choose **Navigate > Set Locators by Selection and Enable Cycle** (or press Command-U).

3   On the Lead Vocals channel strip in the inspector, click the **EQ** thumbnail display to insert and open a Channel EQ plug-in, and start playback.

Very low-frequency content

A curve appears in the graphic display, showing the sound's frequency spectrum in real time. Listen closely to the vocals as you watch the occasional movement in the very low range of frequencies (to the left). In certain places, you can hear some low-frequency content in the recording, especially at the beginning of verse 2 where Duvid sings, "You got to shatter the silence with your beautiful noise." The very beginning of the word "you" has content just above 100 Hz that makes the attack of that word too boomy. The consonants "b" and "f" in the word "beautiful" create some very low-frequency content (down to the 40 Hz area), which results in popping sounds that may be challenging to detect on smaller speaker monitors or for an untrained ear, but they are clearly visible on the frequency curve.

You'll filter out those undesirable low frequencies.

4 At the upper left, click the **Band 1 On/Off** button to turn on the low-cut filter.

The first EQ band's shape appears on the graphic display. You can see that the low frequencies are slightly attenuated to around 20 Hz.

5 In the **EQ** band field, drag the **Frequency** parameter of the first band up to around *400 Hz*.

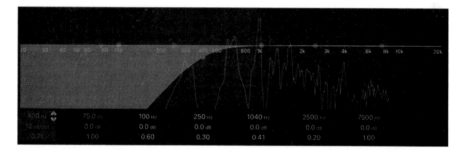

The EQ band shape updates in the graphic display. In the frequency curve displayed by the Analyzer, you can watch the low-frequency content disappear from the vocal signal. You can hear the undesired low-frequency content disappear, and the vocal sound is focused in the mid-range.

TIP ▸ To undo a plug-in parameter change, from the plug-in window's Settings pop-up menu, choose Undo. If you want to use Command-Z to undo plug-in parameter changes, from the plug-in window's Settings pop-up menu, choose Include Plug-In Undo Steps in Project Undo History.

Now you'll attenuate the nasal, metallic-twang frequency that makes the vocal sound a bit too much like the vocalist is singing in a tin can. Instead of adjusting the numerical settings in the parameter section, you'll drag the pointer in the graphic display to adjust the shape of individual bands.

6   Position the pointer over the upper half of the graphic display, and without pressing the mouse button, move the pointer from left to right.

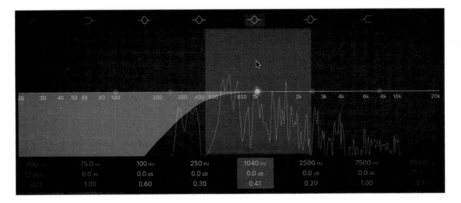

As you move the pointer horizontally, an EQ band, its On/Off button, and its parameters are shaded in different colors to show you which EQ band is selected. You can shape the curve of the selected band by dragging in the graphic display:

▶   To adjust the gain, drag vertically.

▶   To adjust the frequency, drag horizontally.

▶   To adjust the Q (or width, or resonance), vertically Option-Command-drag the pivot point (which appears at that band's frequency).

You first need to adjust the band's gain to see its shape on the graphic display.

7   Position the pointer to select the fifth band, which is currently set to a frequency of *1040 Hz*.

You'll use the classic seek-and-destroy EQ-ing approach: First, boost a narrow range of frequency, sweep the boost across the frequency spectrum to find the offending frequency, and then reduce the gain of the EQ band to attenuate that frequency.

8   Drag up so that the **Gain** parameter below reads around *+15.0 dB*.

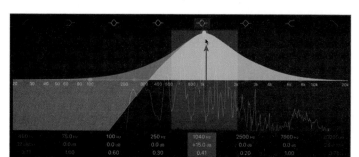

The shape of the selected EQ band appears on the graphic display, and the settings below it are adjusted accordingly. Let's narrow down the frequency boost.

9   In the EQ band field, drag the **Q** parameter to around *0.80*.

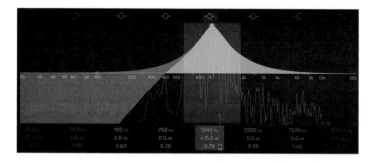

Now, while listening to the vocal, you'll sweep the frequency of the EQ band you are boosting. When dragging a band on the display, you can hold down Command to limit the dragging motion to a single direction, either horizontal (to adjust only the frequency) or vertical (to adjust only the gain).

10   Command-drag the band to the left and to the right and settle on a frequency of *3260 Hz*.

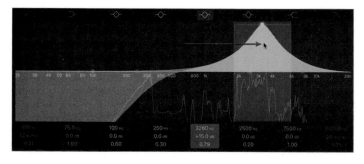

The metallic tin can-sounding frequencies are highly exaggerated, and you know you've found the right frequency to cut.

11 **Command**-drag the band down so that the **Gain** parameter reads *−13 dB.*

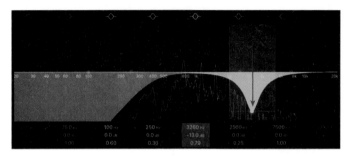

The vocal sounds less twangy. Remember to click that EQ band's On/Off button to compare the vocal sound with and without that EQ band applied.

Now you can remove some of the high frequencies to help focus the lead vocal in the mid-range of the spectrum.

12 Click the **On/Off** button of the last frequency band to turn on the high-cut filter.

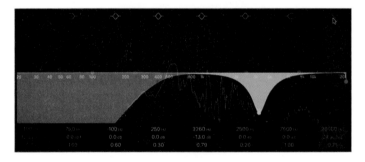

13 Turn the frequency down to *8350 Hz.*

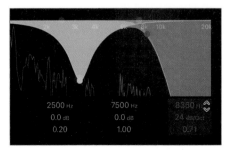

Now, the vocal sounds tighter, focused in the mid-range, which helps make the lead singer cut through this busy, layered mix. Let's compare the sound of the vocal with and without the Channel EQ. To make up for the loss of volume after cutting the three bands of frequency, you can turn the gain up in the Channel EQ.

14 To the right of the EQ curve, drag the **Gain** slider up to *+3.0 dB*.

15 In the plug-in header, toggle the **On/Off** button a few times.

The level discrepancy between the dry and EQ'ed vocal is minimal, so you can focus on the difference in the frequency spectrum between the two. The EQ'ed vocal is more focused in the mid-range, which makes it tighter and punchier and will help it cut through the mix.

16 Close the Channel EQ plug-in window (or press 1 to recall screenset 1).

17 Unsolo the Lead Vocal track.

Feel free to compare the dry and EQ'ed vocal in the context of the mix. However, because the Lead Vocal track's level is inconsistent throughout the song, you may have to raise its volume fader a bit. You'll level those volume inconsistencies with a compressor in the next exercise.

By applying an EQ plug-in to the vocal, you shaped its frequency spectrum to eliminate unwanted low-frequency noises and clarify the vocal, establishing its appropriate place in the frequency spectrum of the mix.

Use Compression to Control Dynamics

When recording instruments, musicians rarely play all the notes at the exact same volume. Singers need more energy to reach higher pitches, and they relax to sing low pitches, resulting in uneven loudness throughout a melody line. This variation can become a challenge when mixing, because some of the notes stick out and others are buried in the mix.

A compressor attenuates a signal when its level goes above a specific threshold. You can use it to lower the volume of loud notes and then raise the overall level of the instrument to increase the volume of softer notes.

In this exercise, you'll apply a compressor plug-in to even out the dynamic range of a vocal track, making sure that you can hear all the words at the same level. To focus on the balance of lead vocals against the rest of the mix, you'll mute the backup vocal track.

1   On the Backup Vocals track (track 79), click the **M** (Mute) button.

     If you've adjusted the level of the Lead Vocal track at the end of the previous exercise, you need to return it to its previous level for this exercise.

2   On the Lead Vocals channel strip (track 78), make sure the volume fader is set to *−12.1 dB*.

     Listen to the mix (minus the backup vocals). The Lead Vocals start at a decent volume, but at some point in Chorus 1, they start getting completely drowned in the rest of the instruments in the mix. In the middle of verse 2 (at bars 30 and 31), they become inconsistent, mostly weak, with some consonants shooting up in level. Let's work on that section.

3   Click the cycle area (or press C) to turn off Cycle mode.

4   In the upper half of the ruler, drag a cycle area from bar 29 to bar 32.

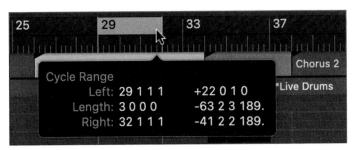

Feel free to toggle playback on and off as needed throughout this exercise. A quick way to insert a compressor on a channel strip is to click the Gain Reduction meter above the EQ thumbnail display.

5   On the Lead Vocals channel strip, click the **Gain Reduction** meter.

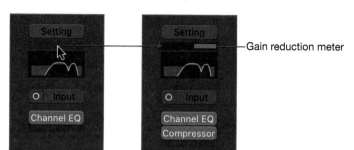

Gain reduction meter

A compressor plug-in is inserted below the Channel EQ, and the Compressor plug-in window opens. In this window, the Gain Reduction meter shows how many decibels the compressor is attenuating the audio signal. The movements of the needle on the meter indicates that different parts of the track are attenuated by *0* to *8 dB*.

Above the Gain Reduction meter, you can choose from different models based on vintage hardware compressors. Excluding Platinum, which is a transparent compressor, each circuit type adds its own color to the signal.

6   Click the **Classic VCA** button.

The compressor adopts the look of the dbx 160, an early voltage-controlled amplifier type compressor/limiter known for its simplicity and its punchy, aggressive vintage sound. On the Gain Reduction meter, note how some of the softest notes barely trigger the compressor (the needle stays close to *0*), whereas the loudest words ("girls" and "boys") get *5* or *6 dB* of attenuation.

7   On the Lead Vocals track header, click the **Solo** button.

Although the Compressor plug-in has many parameters, you'll adjust only the most important parameters, located below the Gain Reduction meter: the Threshold, Ratio, and Make Up knobs, and the Auto Gain buttons. The Make Up and Auto Gain parameters help compensate for the gain reduction by applying a constant gain at the output of the compressor. To focus on the gain reduction applied by the compressor, let's make sure no positive gain is applied at the output.

8   Click the **Auto Gain Off** button.

The Lead Vocal level drops a little bit. Now the compressor can only turn the volume down when the vocals reach levels higher than the Threshold parameter. Remember to turn the compressor on and off as you adjust it to compare the sound of the vocal with and without the compression effect.

Lowering the threshold will make sure that the compressor is working a little more even on the weakest parts of the audio signal, imparting more of its character to the vocal sound

9   Drag the **Threshold** knob down to −30 dB.

The compressor works even harder on the loudest sound (the "g" of "girl"), reducing the dynamic further and making the level more consistent.

You can adjust the amount of compression with the Ratio knob, which affects how much the signal that exceeds the threshold is reduced.

10 Drag the **Ratio** knob up to *3.1:1*.

Look at the meter; the compressor is attenuating the level by up to around *10* to *13 dB*. Let's compensate for that loss of gain.

11 Drag the **Make Up** knob up to *12 dB*.

Now, let's compare the difference in perceived loudness between the dry and the compressed vocals, while looking at the peak level display on the channel strip.

12 Turn the compressor off and look at the peak level display.

The level of the vocals isn't consistent. Remember to click the peak level display to reset it. On the Lead Vocals channel strip, some consonants like the "g" of "girls" make the level meter shoot up, and the peak level display goes up to *−13.4 dB*.

13 Turn the compressor on.

The level is consistent throughout the performance, and the vocals sound louder and more present. On the channel strip, the level peaks at *−12.7 dB*, which is close to the peak level of the uncompressed vocal. Let's hear the work of the compressor in the context of the full mix.

14 Unsolo the Lead Vocal track and toggle the compressor off and on.

When the compressor is off, the vocals are soft and their level inconsistent. With the compressor on, it sounds like the vocals float effortlessly right on top of the rest of the mix, making it comfortable to listen to them. Mission accomplished!

15   Close the Compressor plug-in window (or press 1 to recall screenset 1).

16   Unmute the Backup Vocal track (track 79).

17   Click the cycle area (or press C) to turn off Cycle mode.

You've used a compressor plug-in to make the lead vocals in your song sound consistent in level, which allows you to make them perceive louder while keeping a similar peak level. Having your tracks consistent in level throughout the song makes it easier to dial in their volume fader and have them stick to that level throughout the whole song.

Use Reverb to Add Depth

Now that you've carved the frequency spectrum of the vocals to give them a tight focus in the mid-range and compressed them to make them punchy and consistent, you can use reverb effects to add ambiance and place them in a virtual room. To not lose the presence of the lead vocal, you'll try to keep it up front and intimate, and you don't want to place the singer in a huge reverberated room. To give the lead vocal ambiance its own unique character, you'll first add a short reverb directly on its channel strip. Then you'll send both the lead vocal and the backup vocals to the Vocal Verb Aux that you used earlier for the Heys backup vocal ensemble.

1   On the Lead Vocals channel strip, click below the Compressor plug-in and choose **Reverb > Space Designer**.

2   In the Space Designer plug-in header, click the **Setting** pop-up menu and choose
Medium Spaces > Indoor Spaces > 1.2s Small Staircase.

That short reverb places the singer in a space without making the singer sound huge,
which wouldn't be appropriate for this mix. Still, there's too much reverb, and you
need to bring the singer back closer.

3   In the lower right in the Space Designer window, drag the **Wet** slider down to −24 dB.

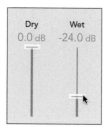

4   Close the Space Designer window.

To make it sound like the lead singer is in the same room as all the backup singers,
you can send some of its signal to the same reverb bus.

5   Click the **Send** slot and choose **Bus** > **Bus 12** > **Vocal Verb**.

To keep the lead singer up front, you'll dial only a subtle amount of reverb.

6   Drag the **Send** Level knob up to around *−25 dB*.

You're finished processing the Lead Vocals channel strip. To compare the original, dry vocals with the processed vocals, you can toggle all plug-ins and the send to Bus 12 on and off.

7   On the Lead Vocals channel strip, move the pointer to the **On/Off** button to the left in the first plug-in slot (Channel EQ).

8   Solo the Lead Vocals channel strip.

9   Drag down to turn off all plug-ins and the send to Bus 12.

You hear the original raw-vocal recording. It sounds just like what they are: a singer singing in a dead-sounding recording studio.

10   Move the pointer to the **On/Off** button on the Channel EQ and drag down to turn all plug-ins and the send back on.

The vocals have more punch and dimension, and they generally sound more commanding! Great work. Now that you're happy with the lead vocal, let's mix in a little more backup vocals.

11 Unsolo the Lead Vocals channel strip.

12 Select the Backup Vocals track (track 79).

13 On the Backup Vocals channel strip, drag the volume fader up to −7.8 dB.

You'll dial in a little more reverb for the backup vocals to give them a larger dimension.

14 Click the Sends section and choose **Bus 12 > Vocal Verb**.

15 Drag the **Send** Level knob up to −16.4 dB.

16 Save the project and keep it open for the next lesson.

You've set up a vocal chain using EQ, compressor, and reverb plug-ins to sculpt the lead vocal frequency spectrum and place them in a virtual space. The Compressor plug-in allowed you to give consistency to the level of the vocals, making it easier for them to find their place in a busy mix.

You finished your mix using effect plug-ins and adjusting the four main parameters of the instrument sounds (volume levels, pan position, frequency, and distance) to give each sound its own place in the stereo sound field.

Use a Few Tips and Tricks

As with any other art, mixing requires a combination of skill, experience, and talent. It takes practice to learn how to apply mixing techniques efficiently, and even more practice to learn to listen. Here are a few tips and tricks that will help you perfect your craft and become better at mixing your projects.

Take a Break

After you mix for a while and listen to the same song for the hundredth time, you can lose your objectivity and experience ear fatigue. Take frequent short breaks while mixing and return to the mix with rested ears. You'll be able to better judge your results.

Listen to Your Mix Outside the Studio

When you feel that your mix is pretty advanced and you are happy with the way it sounds in your studio, copy it to a portable music player and listen to it in another room or, even better, in your car while driving. You'll probably hear things you didn't notice in your studio and miss things you could hear clearly in your studio. You can take notes and return to your studio to rework the mix. Obviously, the mix will never sound the same in the studio and in the car, but it's the mixing engineer's job to make sure that all the instruments can be heard in most situations.

Compare Your Mix with Commercial Mixes

Compare your mix with commercial mixes you like. Build a small library of good-sounding mixes in the same genre of music as the songs you are mixing. You can open a new Logic Pro project, and place your mix on one track and a professional mix on another track so that you can solo and compare them.

Key Commands

Keyboard Shortcuts	Description
General	
Control-Command-Left Arrow	Collapses a track stack
Control-Command-Right Arrow	Expands a track stack
Number key on alphanumeric keypad	Recalls that numbered screenset
Mixer	
Command-2	Opens the Mixer window
Option-X	Opens a shortcut menu to configure the Mixer

13

Lesson File	Continue working from the file you saved at the end of Lesson 12
Time	This lesson takes approximately 45 minutes to complete.
Goals	Draw automation curves offline
	Record live automation in real time
	Use Mastering Assistant to get your project ready for distribution
	Export the mix as a stereo audio file

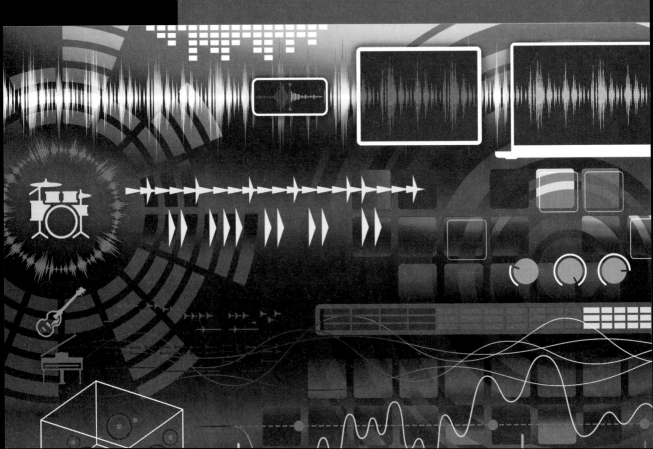

Lesson **13**

Automate, Master, and Export the Mix

You've reached the final phases of the music production process: mix automation, mastering, and bouncing the final mix to a stereo audio file that's ready for distribution.

Automation allows you to vary mix parameters over time to fine-tune each track's level and effects, or to add motion to a static mix. Mastering puts the final polish on your mix and optimizes its loudness for online streaming platforms.

Automate Mixer Parameters

When multitrack recorders first appeared in recording studios, they forever changed the way artists produce music. The ability to have separate recordings of individual instruments opened the door for experimentation, and artists and producers played with the mixing board's faders and knobs during the final mixdown—panning an instrument from left to right or riding a volume fader to change the level of a track throughout a song. Soon enough, two or three pairs of hands weren't enough to perform all the changes needed throughout a mix, and a solution was needed.

Eventually, mixing consoles were designed with faders that also generated a data stream. By recording those data streams onto a separate track of the multitrack tape, the console could automatically re-create those fader movements during playback. This started the era of automated consoles. Today, professional, computerized mixing boards and digital audio workstations are fully automated.

In Logic Pro, you can automate almost all the controls on a channel strip, including volume, pan, and plug-in parameters. In this lesson, you'll draw and edit offline automation to make a sound effect rise in volume during a pre-chorus, and record live automation to pan a sound effect left and right during a break.

Draw Automation Curves

In Logic Pro, the techniques used to create and edit track-based automation closely resemble those you used to create Pitch Bend automation in the Piano Roll in Lesson 9. Track automation lets you automate almost any channel strip controls independent of the regions on the track.

Drawing automation graphically is also known as *offline automation*, because you do not need to draw in real time.

1   To start this first exercise, continue working in the file you saved at the end of Lesson 12.

2   Click the disclosure triangle to open the FX track stack (track 58).

3   Select and solo the Guitar Scratch FX track (track 70).

The Guitar Scratch FX region (at bar 34) is selected.

4   Press **Command-U** to make the cycle area match the selection.

Listen to the Guitar Scratch FX. The region contains a reverberated and distorted rhythmic guitar scratch that has a constant level and is panned in the center. You'll apply volume automation to make the sound effect slowly ramp up in volume throughout the Pre 2 section and rapidly fade out at the beginning of Chorus 2.

5   In the Tracks area menu bar, click the **Show Automation** button (or press A).

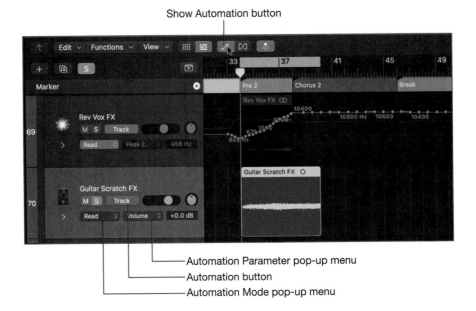

Show Automation button

Automation Parameter pop-up menu
Automation button
Automation Mode pop-up menu

In the Tracks area, tracks must be tall enough to display their automation curves, so the Tracks area is automatically zoomed in vertically. On the track headers, the Automation button, Automation Mode pop-up menu, and Automation Parameter pop-up menu appear. Some of the tracks already have existing automation curves.

TIP ▶ When an automation track is shown, you can edit regions (move, copy, resize, and so on) in the thin lane containing the region names.

6 On the Guitar Scratch FX track header, position the pointer over the **Automation** button and click the **On/Off** button that appears.

The automation is turned on for that track, and you can see an empty volume automation curve on the track.

7 Click anywhere on the automation curve.

A control point is created at the beginning of the project (bar 1) at the current volume fader value, *0.0 dB*, and the automation curve is yellow to indicate that some automation data is now present. In the track header, the Automation Mode pop-up menu displays the Read mode in solid green to indicate that the automation curve will be read upon playback.

8 Drag the automation point at bar 1 all the way down to −∞.

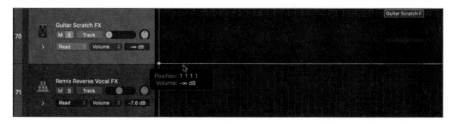

To make it easier to create the volume automation curve, feel free to zoom in on the Guitar Scratch FX region.

To create automation points, you can click the automation curve or double-click an empty area on the automation track. Don't worry about creating the points in precise positions for now; you can always drag them to move them later.

9   Click the automation curve at the beginning of the Guitar Scratch FX region.

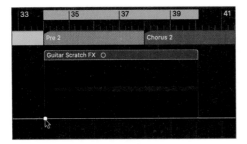

10   Double-click toward the top of the automation track, a little before the end of the Pre 2 section.

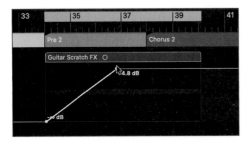

11   Click the automation curve at the end of the Pre 2 section.

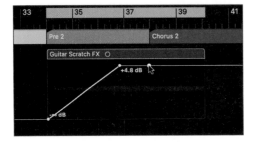

TIP ▶ To raise or lower a portion of an automation curve, select the portion with the Marquee tool, and then drag the selection up or down with the Pointer tool.

12 Double-click the automation track toward the bottom, a little after the beginning of Chorus 2 (around bar 39).

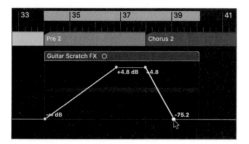

To change the way the volume ramps down at the end, let's bend the automation curve.

13 **Control-Shift**-drag the slanted line at the end of the Pre 2 section to the right.

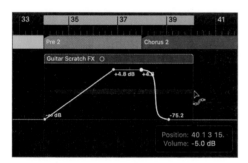

The pointer turns into an automation curve tool, and the line gets an S shape.

NOTE ▶ You can bend only slanted lines between two automation points of different values; you cannot bend horizontal lines between two automation points of the same values.

Dragging the line left or right lets you adjust the shape of the S curve.

TIP ▶ To revert a bent line to a straight line, Control-Shift-click the line.

14 Click the **Solo** button on the Guitar Scratch FX track header to turn it off.

Continue adjusting the automation curve while listening to the Pre 2 section until you get the desired volume automation curve for the Guitar Scratch FX region.

15 In the Tracks area menu bar, click the **Show Automation** button (or press A) to hide the automation tracks.

The automation tracks are hidden, but the Guitar Scratch FX is still in Read mode. Listen to the section in the cycle area. In the Guitar Scratch FX track header (and in the channel strip in the inspector), you see the volume fader ramp up slowly, and then rapidly fade out at the beginning of the chorus.

16 Click the cycle area (or press C) to turn off Cycle mode.

You've created an automation curve for a sound effect by creating automation points and bending the lines in between points. The volume automation curve makes the sound effect ramp up at the beginning of the pre-chorus, and then rapidly fade out when the chorus starts, producing a mysterious vibe that is sure to perk up the listener's ears in this calm section before the storm.

Record Automation in Real Time

Drawing automation curves offline as you did in the previous exercise is a good option when you know in advance the automation movements that you want to achieve, but sometimes you want to hear the song playing as you adjust channel strip or plug-in controls in real time.

To record live automation, you choose a live automation mode for the track(s) that you want to automate, start playback, and then tweak the desired plug-in or channel strip controls.

In this exercise, you'll record live Pan knob automation to make a sound effect move to various positions in the stereo field to add a surprise element to the break section.

1   Select and solo the Bollywood Vocal Chop track (track 66).

2   Press **Command-U** to make the cycle area match the selection.

Listen to the Bollywood Vocal Chop track. You can hear the stuttering gated vocal samples, not unlike the type of vocal chops you produced with Quick Sampler in Lesson 10. The sound comes from the center of the stereo field.

To record automation, there's no need to show the automation tracks or to go into Record mode. You choose an automation mode for the track; start playback; and move a knob, button, or slider—and the movements are recorded on the automation track. You'll later display the automation track to see the automation curve you're going to record now.

3   In the inspector on the Bollywood Vocal Chop track channel strip, click the **Automation Mode** pop-up menu and choose **Touch**.

4   Press the **Space** bar to start playback.

5   On the Bollywood Vocal Chop channel strip, drag the **Pan** knob up or down only during the first pass of the cycle area.

When the playhead jumps back to play the cycle area a second time, the Pan knob movements you performed during the first pass are re-created. Let's have a look under the hood.

6   In the Tracks area menu bar, click the **Show Automation** button (or press A).

7   On the Bollywood Vocal Chop track header, click the **Automation Parameter** pop-up menu and choose **Main > Pan**.

You can see the Pan automation curve you just recorded.

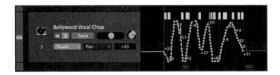

Let's delete the automation and try again, this time looking at the automation curve being created as you record it.

8   Stop playback.

9   Choose **Mix** > **Delete Automation** > **Delete Visible Automation on Selected Track** (or press Control-Command-Delete).

On the automation track, the Pan automation curve is deleted.

10   Start playback and drag the **Pan** knob up or down.

On the automation track, you see the Pan knob movements recorded as a Pan automation curve. You can continue adjusting the automation curve during subsequent passes of the cycle area. While you're in Touch mode, any existing automation on the track is read, as if Logic Pro were in Read mode. As soon as you hold down the mouse button on a knob or slider, Logic Pro starts recording the new values. When you release the mouse button, Touch mode behaves like Read mode again, and the automation curve returns to its original value or reproduces any existing automation on the track.

NOTE ▶ Latch mode works similarly to Touch mode, except that when you release the mouse button, the automation continues to record and the parameter stays at the current value. If automation is already present for that parameter on that track, the automation is overwritten until you stop playback.

You're finished automating the Bollywood Vocal Chop. To avoid recording more automation by mistake later, make sure you revert the automation to Read mode.

11   On the Bollywood Vocal Chop track header, click the **Automation Mode** pop-up menu and choose **Read**.

12 Unsolo the Bollywood Vocal Chop track.

13 Press **1** to recall screenset 1.

14 Close the FX track stack (track 58).

15 Click the cycle area (or press C) to turn Cycle mode off.

Using automation, you have added motion to your mix. You made a distorted guitar noise effect creep in during a pre-chorus to increase tension just before a chorus, and you panned vocal chops in various positions of the stereo field to create a surprise during a break. You drew offline automation on the track and recorded live automation while adjusting a knob. Let your imagination run wild and think of other applications to automate your own projects. For some truly creative effects, try automating instrument or audio effect plug-in parameters.

Master Your Project with the Mastering Assistant

On a professional project, you would usually send your final mix to a mastering engineer, who would put a final polish on the audio file using subtle amounts of EQ, compression, reverb, or any other processing needed to make the mix reveal its true potential.

When you don't have the budget to hire a mastering engineer, you can use Mastering Assistant to quickly get your mix ready for distribution.

1 Click the Live Drums (track 1) track header to select it.

2 In the inspector on the Stereo Out channel strip (on the right), click the **Mastering** slot (or choose Mix > Mastering Assistant).

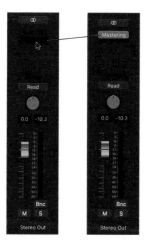

The Mastering Assistant plug-in opens and analyzes your project.

TIP ▶ To interrupt an analysis in progress, press Command-. (period).

TIP ▶ To analyze only a specific section of your project, turn on Cycle mode and position the cycle area over that section.

When the analysis is complete, the Mastering Assistant interface appears, and its parameters are automatically adjusted to optimize your final mix and make it ready for distribution.

3   Listen to the Verse 1 section and toggle the plug-in on and off to compare the unprocessed and mastered mix.

The mastered mix is punchier, and the vocals are more present. The Mastering Assistant has determined that the mix was too wide, so it's dialed down the Spread knob. The resulting mix is narrower, and the guitar on the left is closer to the center, which makes the mix more cohesive—it sounds like the instruments are playing together in the same room. However, the heavy panning in the unprocessed mix was an artistic decision, so let's bring back a little more width.

4   Drag the **Spread** knob up to *-0.07*.

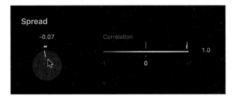

Now you have a slightly wider mix that retains its cohesiveness. When dialing the Spread knob, keep an eye on the Correlation meter and try to keep it close to +1 to avoid a phase issue and get a strong, focused stereo image.

The Loudness knob is in the center position, which means that the target is −14 LUFS-I (*Loudness Units Full Scale – Integrated*, a measurement of the perceived loudness over the duration of the entire song). That target loudness is suitable for most streaming platforms. You can use the Loudness knob if you need a louder mix like for EDM (Electronic Dance Music) played in a club.

NOTE ▶ At the top left of the plug-in, the Character menu allows you to select the sonic quality applied by Mastering Assistant. The character presets Transparent, Punch, and Valve are available only on Mac computers with Apple Silicon.

To make broad adjustments to the frequency distribution, you can drag three blue control points that are underneath the EQ curve.

5 Drag the mid-frequency control point up and to the right.

The upper mid frequencies are boosted. Let's go back to the optimal frequency distribution that was analyzed by the Mastering Assistant.

6 At the bottom left of the EQ curve, click the **Custom EQ** button to turn it off.

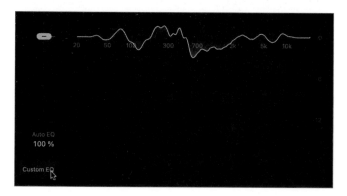

Your custom EQ is turned off, and the EQ curve returns to its original shape.

7 Close the Mastering Assistant window.

You've used the Mastering Assistant to perform a quick mastering of your song, making the mix punchier and more cohesive. You're now ready to export your song to share or distribute it.

Export the Master to a Stereo Audio File

In this final lesson, you'll bounce (render) your mix at the highest quality available: a raw uncompressed PCM (pulse-code modulation) wave file.

In the workspace, the last regions end at bar 84. When you are not sure of the exact end of a song, play the final few bars. Sometimes effect plug-ins, such as reverberation and delay, still produce sound after the end of the song. You'll give yourself an extra bar and end the bounce at bar 85.

1   Choose **File** > **Bounce** (or press Command-B) to open the Bounce dialog.

2   In the **Destination** column, ensure that **PCM** is selected and type *85* in the **End** field.

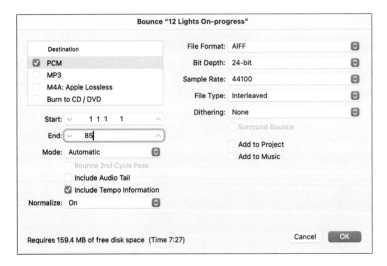

The Mode pop-up menu is set to Automatic. The bounce will be done offline (the mix is rendered as quickly as your Mac's processor allows it) unless real-time processing is required (for example, when using external instruments or effects).

3   Leave **Mode** set to **Automatic**.

The Normalize function automatically adjusts the level of the file so that it peaks at or below *0 dBFS*. If you have used mastering plug-ins to ensure that the Output peak meter peaks at *0 dBFS*, you do not need Normalize.

4   Set **Normalize** to **Off**.

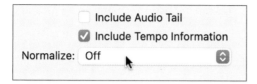

The File Format choices—AIFF, Wave, and CAF—all produce the same sound quality. The file format you choose depends mostly on which format is needed for further processing, such as mastering.

5   Click the **File Format** pop-up menu and choose **Wave**.

A bit-depth resolution of 24 bits gives you a larger file but yields the best audio quality.

6   Make sure the **Resolution** pop-up menu is set to **24 Bit**.

Sample Rate is set by default to the project sample rate. You should change this only if you want to convert the bounced file to a new sample rate.

The file type is Interleaved, which is the most common file type used.

Dithering can make a subtle difference in quiet sections of a song, or when a song is fading in or out.

7   Leave **Sample Rate** set to *44100 Hz*, **File Type** set to *Interleaved*, and **Dithering** set to *None*.

8   Click **OK** (or press Return).

A Bounce Output 1-2 dialog opens, and you can choose a filename and a location for the bounced file.

9   Name the file *Lights On* (the name of the song), press **Command-D** to save it to the desktop, and click **Bounce**.

A progress window appears, and in the Tracks area, you can see the playhead move faster than real time as the bounced file is created.

TIP ▸ To interrupt a bounce in progress, press Command-. (period).

When the progress window disappears, your bounced file is ready.

10 Press **Command-Tab** to go to the Finder.

11 In the Finder, choose **Finder** > **Hide Others** (or press Command-Option-H).

12 On your desktop, click **Lights On.wav** and press the **Space** bar to play the final version of the song.

You automated Mixer parameters offline and in real time to create some motion in your mix, and then you polished the sound of your mix and prepared it for distribution on streaming platforms with the help of Mastering Assistant. Finally, you bounced your project to export an uncompressed stereo PCM WAV file of your mix that you can share with your record label or upload to music distribution service websites.

Key Commands

Keyboard Shortcuts	Description
General	
Command-B	Opens the Bounce window
Command-Tab	Switches between open apps
Control-Command-Delete	Deletes the visible automation on the selected track

Index